Ordinary Resurrections

"What a gift! A magnificent testimony to the communion of grace through the human touch."

— Fred Rogers,
creator and host, *Mr. Rogers' Neighborhood*

"There is so much here that is so rich that I am nearly overwhelmed. . . . I found Jonathan Kozol's attentiveness to, respect for, and trust in the children constitute a kind of transformative enchantment. . . . *Ordinary Resurrections* is deeply religious but exactly in the best way without being excessively insistent. . . . I am glad about its publication, but I am more glad for the rest of us who will be summoned by it."

— Walter Brueggemann,
Columbia Theological Seminary

"Kozol's authenticity has not diminished with time, nor has his power to put a human face on Northern urban segregation."

— *Library Journal*

"The best agitators illuminate their passionate protests with visions of hope and rebirth, and Jonathan Kozol's new book is a loving portrait of schoolchildren who are sustaining themselves in spite of society's neglect. By demonstrating the resilience of children in a meditative and measured voice, Kozol quietly intensifies the indictment he has made in previous books of the inequalities that jeopardize the growth of children in our poorest neighborhoods. *Ordinary Resurrections* is a humane work of the spirit that holds up a candle in a dark time."

— Henry Mayer,
author of *All on Fire*

Ordinary
Resurrections

Also by Jonathan Kozol

DEATH AT AN EARLY AGE

FREE SCHOOLS

THE NIGHT IS DARK AND I AM FAR FROM HOME

CHILDREN OF THE REVOLUTION

ON BEING A TEACHER

ILLITERATE AMERICA

RACHEL AND HER CHILDREN

SAVAGE INEQUALITIES

AMAZING GRACE

Ordinary Resurrections

CHILDREN IN THE

YEARS OF HOPE

Jonathan Kozol

Perennial

An Imprint of HarperCollins*Publishers*

A hardcover edition of this book was published in 2000 by Crown Publishers, Inc. It is here reprinted by arrangement with Crown Publishers.

HarperCollins books may be purchased for educational, business, or sales promotional use. For information please write: Special Markets Department, HarperCollins Publishers Inc., 10 East 53rd Street, New York, NY 10022.

First Perennial edition published 2001.

Designed by Barbara Sturman

The Library of Congress has catalogued the hardcover edition as follows:
Kozol, Jonathan.
 Ordinary resurrections : children in the years of hope / Jonathan Kozol.
  1st ed.
   p. cm. ISBN 0-517-70000-X
   1. Children – New York (State) – New York – Social conditions.
 2. Mott Haven (New York, N.Y.) – Social conditions. I. Title.
   HQ792.U5 K69 2000
   305.23'0974'1 – dc21   99-059808

ISBN 0-06-095645-3 (pbk.)

01 02 03 04 05 ❖/RRD 10 9 8 7 6 5 4 3 2 1

for my father, Harry Leo Kozol,
and my mother, Ruth Massel Kozol,

and for Martha Overall

To the Reader

Events in this book take place for the most part during 1997 and 1998. A few events slightly precede this period and a final chapter updates certain narratives into the spring of 1999.

The names of children and most grown-ups are disguised. Their ages, the precise locations of their homes, and other details of their lives have sometimes been disguised as well. Grown-ups, however, who fill public roles, including teachers in the public schools, are in most cases introduced by their real names.

The stories in this book are drawn from notes, informal journals, children's recollections, and my own, and now and then, although not often, tape recordings of our conversations. Time sequences are sometimes changed, and conversations on related topics are at times combined. Other discussion of the way this book was written and the ways these conversations have been edited, as well as some discussion of constraints imposed by privacy considerations, are provided in the narrative, endnotes, and acknowledgments. Documentation for all matters that rely upon the public record is also included in the endnotes, which begin on page 343.

Ordinary
Resurrections

Introduction

Birds in the morning, Thomas Merton writes, ask God if it is time yet to begin the day. He speaks of the first chirps of the waking birds at dawn outside the windows of his hermitage. "They begin to speak," he says, not with a "fluent song" but "with an awakening question" that is their state at dawn. They ask God "if it is time for them to 'be.'" God, says Merton, answers "yes." Then, "one by one," they "wake up" to be birds.

Tabitha Brown is six years old in the first grade. Her teacher says that she's "a dreamer." She sits there sometimes in her class in vague ambiguous delight as if her thoughts are in a sweeter land than ours.

She nearly dies of shyness when I come into her class and sit down at the table next to her. But after I've been sitting with her for a while she gets up and brings a small container to the table and unclasps the top to show me that it holds two mealworms and a beetle, all of which have names. "This one's Ashley. This one's Mary-Kate. And *this* one," she says, pointing to the beetle, "is a boy and he's named Michael."

Her reading skills are just beginning to emerge, although it isn't clear how well she understands the words she reads. When I ask her questions she gives dreamy answers. I look at her and think of sleepy cats on windowsills complaining slightly if you try to interrupt their dreams. In a foolish mood one day I asked her if she had a tabby cat in her genetic line. She actually smiled when I said this and did not reject the notion out of hand. "Maybe!" she said, then seemed to find this funny and went off into a little gale of laughter that just rippled on the surface of her smile.

"Sweetheart?" her teacher says.

Tabitha looks up. The teacher bends over her chair and looks into her eyes, then opens her textbook to the proper page and centers it before her on the desk. Tabitha sits up erect and tries to concentrate.

The teacher is gentle with her. It's still morning in New York, and very *early* morning in this child's life. Good teachers don't approach a child of this age with overzealousness or with destructive conscientiousness. They're not drill-masters in the military or floor managers in a production system. They are specialists in opening small packages. They give the string a tug but do it carefully. They don't yet know what's in the box. They don't know if it's breakable.

"Sweetheart?" the teacher says again.

"Hello?" says Tabitha.

"Hello!" the teacher says right back at her.

Eleven o'clock. The children line up at the door. Tabitha's the last in line. One of the other children puts her arm around her shoulder as they wait to leave the room. The teacher watches her, then looks at me and smiles, and shakes her head.

"Where are they going now?" I ask.

"Recess!" she says. "Then lunch."

It may be nearly lunchtime in the world but, for this pleasant little girl, it seems as though it's only a few minutes after dawn. Her mind is yawning still. Soon enough she'll brush the cobwebs from her eyes and take a clear look at the world of vowel sounds and subtrahends and partial products, and some bigger things that lie ahead, like state exams, but not just now.

The children file with their teacher to the stairwell. She asks one of the boys to hold the door, and then she starts to lead them down the stairs. Tabitha looks around and waves goodbye to me.

I follow after them.

This is a book about a group of children whom I've come to know during their early years of life, not in the infant years but in the ones just after, when they start to go to school and start to poke around into the world and figure out what possibilities for hope and happiness it holds. Most of these children live within a section of the South Bronx called Mott Haven which, for much of the past decade, was the nation's epicenter for the plague of pediatric and maternal AIDS and remains one of the centers of an epidemic of adult and pediatric asthma that has swept across the inner-city populations of our nation in these years.

Some of these stories take place at an elementary school called P.S. 30 and some other public schools nearby. Others take place at a church, St. Ann's of Morrisania, which is Episcopalian and runs an afterschool for children in the neighborhood, including Tabitha and many of her friends from P.S. 30. All of these children are black or Hispanic. All are very poor; statistics tell us that they are the poorest children in New York. Some know hunger several times a month. Many have respiratory problems. Most have lost a relative or grown-up friend to AIDS. Some have previously lived in homeless shelters. A large number see their fathers only when they visit them in prison.

It is honest to observe, as well, that the community in which they live is one of the most deeply segregated concentrations of black and Hispanic people in our nation, with less than two tenths of 1 percent of school enrollment in Mott Haven represented by Caucasian children, and that racial isolation here, as elsewhere in our nation, is accompanied by inequalities in education and high rates of joblessness. Economic progress in some sections of New York has been impressive in the past ten years, and some of the consequences have been seen in even the most destitute communities of the South Bronx, but only to a very limited degree in this immediate community. Unemployment in the South Bronx, over all, remains at over 45 percent, according to The New York Times. It rises in the neighborhood served by St. Ann's to over 75 percent, according to the pastor of the church and teachers in the local schools.

I hope, however, that this book is neither bitter nor despairing, because despair and bitterness are not the words that ordinarily come to your mind when you spend time with children here. They live, admittedly, in what is known as "a bad section" of a racially divided city, but they live as well within the miniature and often healing world that children of their age inhabit everywhere in the United States. Statistical curses—dangerous words like

"AIDS," "incarceration," "needle drugs," "deficient school performance"—stand around them like unfriendly social scientists with cold prophetic powers; but the actual kingdom that they live in for a good part of each day is not the land of bad statistics but the land of licorice sticks and long division, candy bars and pencil sets, and Elmo dolls and, in the period in which this book takes place, bewildering computer toys called Giga Pets that make a squeaking sound and are the bane of their schoolteachers.

Their minor adversaries in the course of any average day are frequently mechanical or school-related: problematic pencil sharpeners, for instance, that devour pencils but don't sharpen them, intimidating spelling tests, an over-used and gummy pink eraser that does not erase the pencil marks but leaves a big unsightly smudge, an irritable teacher, a stubbornly resistant half-pint milk container that will not cooperate with children's fingers and refuses to become unstuck.

They wave at you covertly when you're visiting their school and walk into their classroom. They write each other notes you're not supposed to see. They miss their fathers. They get sick. Things frighten them. They cry, and when you kneel to comfort them they tell you, "It's my birthday in two weeks!" They love their mothers. They pray for their grandmothers. They talk to animals. They make up stories. If you have a dog they want to know its name.

I've known this group of children for a long time and have written of their neighborhood and other South Bronx neighborhoods before, first in a book on urban schools called Savage Inequalities, then in a book about the medical and social problems of the South Bronx, called Amazing Grace. Both were painful books to write and, readers say, painful to read. I came away from working on these books with deep discouragement about the social policies that shape conditions of existence for these children but renewed respect for their tenacity and courage and a sense of fascination and delight in the particulars of their emerging personalities.

In the discipline of writing books, however, I had never had much opportunity to get to know the children in unhurried ways and never felt entirely free from the relentless pressures that a writer often feels when he's entrapped by the demands of an agenda that he's set himself. I met some of these kids when I was 56 years old. I'll soon be 64. I felt a longing to carve out some years in which I could enjoy their company while I still had the health and strength to climb the stairs of their apartment buildings and to wander with them through their neighborhoods and through the hallways of their schools and be with them when they're at church and do things with them for six hours at a stretch without needing a time-out to rest while they were still determined to keep on.

Some of us try, at 64 or even older, to keep doing things with kids we did when we were 25 or 30; but our bodies and sometimes the tests our doctors give us tell us when our time for keeping up with six- and eight-year-olds is running out. I think I was afraid that, if I didn't do this now, I'd never have the chance again. So, starting in 1996, I tried to set aside extended periods of time to make this possible.

During these years, I've come to know a number of the teachers and school principals and parents, and especially grandmothers, of the children here. Some of the older women in the neighborhood, most of whom have very heavy burdens to sustain, have nonetheless been sensitive and shrewd in helping me to deal with worries of my own. This has been especially the case during the past three years, as I have seen my mother and father, both of whom are in their nineties, stricken down with illnesses that are to be expected when your parents reach that age but for the disabling effects of which few children ever find themselves emotionally or spiritually prepared.

I live alone. I've lived alone for a long time; and things inevitably grew lonelier during this period of years. Perhaps this is one reason why the friendship of the children in the St. Ann's neighborhood became increasingly important in my life. Perhaps, too, it will help explain why I was in no hurry to impose much discipline or structure on the hours that we spent together or to steer our conversations in particular directions. I didn't truly know my own direction at the time. I only knew I liked to be with them and that the world felt safer in their company.

Now and then, at times of sadness in the neighborhood — the death of someone who had been important to the children, or when someone's mother had been very ill, or when a child's pet was lost, or had been injured, or had died — a child would look up and ask me, simply, "Can we pray?" I would say yes, but I felt strange about this at the start, because I'm not a Christian and I've never been especially religious, not in formal ways at least. So I'd be hesitant at first, but I'd agree; and so I've ended up saying a lot of prayers without the certainty that I had any right to do this. Perhaps the illness of my parents has enabled me to listen with less awkwardness to children's prayers, and given me a reason at some moments to pray with them.

This is a book about the children's games and stories, and their silliness and sorrows, and the many intricate and sometimes elegant theologies they manage to create in order to invite into their lives the little mysteries that make them brave. I'm grateful to the priest and congregation of St. Ann's for giving me the privilege to share the lives of children here. I'm grateful also to the good schoolteachers of the neighborhood who made me welcome in their class-rooms. But most of all I'm grateful to the children, who have been so kind and generous to me, as they have been to many people who do nothing to deserve their loyalty and love, which aren't for sale and never can be earned, and who, with bashful voices, tiny fingers, sometimes un-intended humor, and wise hearts, illuminate the lives of everyone who knows them.

To all of these people, but especially the children, I would like to offer my deep thanks.

PART ONE

CHAPTER 1

A Narrow Lens

Elio is seven and a half years old. A picture of him taken near the doorway of the kitchen on the first floor of St. Ann's shows a light-brown child with a head shaped like an olive and a small stuffed rabbit under his right arm.

He's almost smiling in the picture. It's a careful look and it conveys some of the tension that is present in his eyes on days when he's been struggling to keep his spirits up. It's not a gloomy look, however; I have other photographs in which he looks as if he's close to breaking out in tears, but this one's balanced about halfway between cheerfulness and something like the vaguest sense of fear. If you studied it a while and were in an optimistic mood you might finally decide it was the picture of a child who is somewhat timid, almost happy, and attempting to be brave.

Fred Rogers took the photograph. He was in New York to do something for PBS and told me he would like to meet the children at the afterschool. We went together on the subway to Brook Avenue, walked to a local school to talk with kindergarten children there, and found our way to St. Ann's Church at three o'clock. He and Elio became acquainted with each other very fast.

Elio is like that. He makes friends with grown-ups easily. He isn't a distrustful boy; nor is he prematurely worldly-wise, as many inner-city children are believed to be and frequently portrayed in press accounts. He has no father to take care of him—his father is a long way from the Bronx, in one of the state prisons—but he has a competent and energetic mother, blessed with a congenial temperament and an immense amount of patience. She looks weary sometimes and develops a wry smile when he goes on for a long time with his questions; but she's understanding with him and she always tries to give him a good answer.

Some of the older boys here pick on him because he's very small. They usually get the best of him in verbal repartee because he has no skill at using words sarcastically and doesn't seem to know how to defend himself when he's been teased. Often he reacts by growing sullen and morose, at other times by breaking into tears; but now and then, just as it seems that he's regaining his composure, he goes to the boy who has been teasing him and hits him hard—he clobbers him!—right in the mouth or nose. Small as he is, he fights ferociously.

The grandmothers at St. Ann's, who help to supervise the children when they come here after school, are forced to isolate him in the kitchen when this happens so that they can keep an eye on him until he has calmed down. Miss Katrice, who helps to run the kitchen on most weekday afternoons, has many conversations with him on important subjects like repentance.

He was in a fight this afternoon. When I arrived I found him in the kitchen, sitting on a blue upended milk box in the corner opposite the stove. Tears in his eyes, he had the overheated look of the unjustly persecuted. When I asked Katrice what happened, she just nodded at him as if that was all it took to make it clear that he'd been misbehaving.

"Fighting again . . . ," she grumbled, as she piled milk containers on the counter.

His moods change rapidly. He cries if he's been teased, or if he thinks that he's been left out of a joke, or game, or conversation, or if someone fails to keep a promise that was made to him. When, on the other hand, he's been surprised by being given something he did not expect, the look of satisfaction that can sweep across his face is like a burst of summer sunshine in the middle of the darkest winter afternoon and it immediately makes one feel ashamed to recognize how little it has cost in time or in attentiveness to make this moment possible.

On 42nd Street one afternoon, I see a man who's selling imitation baby chicks that make a realistic sound — "cheep cheep!" — when held within the warmth of someone's hand. A group of kids are looking at the chicks with fascination. They cost only five dollars. Their father buys them one. I buy one too and find a box to put it in. When Elio unwraps the box the next day in the kitchen of St. Ann's and rests the yellow creature in his hand and it begins to "cheep," his eyes grow wide. "Katrice!" he says, and strokes the chick repeatedly and brings it up to show the priest. The next afternoon, he says, "I put him in his box next to my bed." But, one week later, when Katrice refers to it again — she asks him if he's "taking good care" of his chick — he looks bemused by this and, though he says that he still has the chick, it doesn't seem of interest to him anymore.

One day in the end of March, while sitting with me in one of the reading rooms upstairs, he tells me of his aunt.

"I feel so sorry that my Titi died," he says.

Titi is a Spanish word for "auntie," a diminutive of *tía* (aunt), used by Hispanic children in the neighborhood, and Elio has several aunts. I ask which of his aunts he means.

"My best one," he replies.

I ask if he means his mother's sister, but he doesn't want to be precise about it in the way that I would like.

"She was my best Titi," he insists, and leaves the matter there.

Two days later, he comes up to me looking concerned and staring straight ahead of him, directly at my shirt.

"Uh-oh . . . ," he says.

I look down to see what's wrong.

"Oh, Jonathan! I fooled you! April Fool's!"

The lives of children in poor neighborhoods are studied, and their personalities examined and dissected, often with a good deal of self-confidence, by grown-ups far away who do not know them but rely on data generated by researchers to come up with various conclusions that are used to justify political decisions. This is inevitable, I guess. Societies and governments need to rely on generalities to organize their understandings and establish policies.

Sometimes, though, these generalities seem much too big, too confident, and too relentless. It feels at times as if the world of adult expertise is taking hundred-pound cement blocks, labeled "certitude" and "big significance," and lowering them down onto the shoulders of a six- or seven-year-old boy, then telling him, "Okay, you carry this for ten or fifteen years. Then, if we learn something new, we will come back and give you some new labels you can carry." Sometimes the size and weight of all of this signification make it hard to see if there is still a living body underneath.

It's easy to forget how much of the existence of a seven-year-old child has to do with things that are not big at all and do not lend themselves to generalities and are, indeed, so small and so specific they would seldom earn a mention in a government report or book of sociology. The life of a child, after all, is made up not of social "constructs" or developmental "trends," but of much smaller things like stomachaches or hurtful words or red Crayola crayons. A narrow lens, I think, is often better than a wide one in discerning what a child's life is really like and what distinguishes one child's personality and inner world from those of twenty other children who may live in the same neighborhood and go to the same church or school and, from the vantage point of someone at a university or institute who has to think in terms of categories, might appear to lead the same kind of existence.

I think of this inevitably when I'm with Elio because his character and tastes do not belong to any of those intellectual compartments in which inner-city children of his economic class and race are generally placed, and it would be a foolish and insulting waste of time and scholarship to try to label him or see him in these ways. But I think of this, as well, when I'm with certain of the older children at the church, because it is the differences between them, rather than their similarities, that always strike me as the most important, and most interesting, things about them.

Ariel is ten years old. She's sitting with her legs crossed on the floor beneath the altar in the smaller chapel of St. Ann's. I agreed this afternoon to help her with her homework, but she's cruising through the lesson on her own, her textbook open on her knees, her loose-leaf notebook slightly to the side.

A friend of mine who came to visit here not long ago told me that Ariel reminded her of "one of those aristocratic oval-faced madonnas by Murillo in the Prado." Dressed with her familiar neatness in her dark-blue skirt and light-blue blouse, her white socks folded over and a black-and-orange band made out of yarn on her left wrist, she sits there looking up at me from time to time, a pencil in one hand, an expression of serene and comfortable concentration in her eyes.

After she's been working on her math for maybe twelve or fifteen minutes, Elio's face appears between the two doors of the chapel. He enters the room without a word, approaches the chair in which I'm sitting, stuffs one hand into the tight front pocket of his blue jeans, and extracts a folded dollar bill. Then, coming close enough to whisper in my ear, he asks me, "Will you buy a piece of candy for me with my dollar?"

He whispers it so loud, however, that the older child can't help hearing what he says. As soon as he's gone, she imitates a groan and puts one of her hands against her chest, the way a grown-up woman might at hearing something that she finds outrageous.

"I can't *believe* he asked you to buy candy!"

But later in the day, after she's finished with her long division and her other homework lessons and is lying on her stomach on the chapel floor, leaning on her elbows, looking up in the lethargic yellow light at the plain wooden crucifix along the wall, she gets more thoughtful about Elio.

"You really ought to buy the candy for him, I suppose. He gets upset so easily. . . ."

Collecting all her books and pencils and returning them to different sections of her canvas bag, she says, "Believe me! You don't want to be with Elio when he's upset!"

Sometimes, when he does become upset, I've seen her do something, or say something to him, that isn't easy to re-capture — because things like these take place so quickly — but which has a subtlety and tenderness that seem to be quite natural to her. She has a modest way of understating her own decency and seems to know the way to bring a bit of comfort to another child without acting overly benevolent and without appearing to exact a price in too much gratitude. Some girls her age can be a trifle sanctimonious in showing kindness to a younger child. Ariel's not like that. She seems to have a sense of tact and taste that makes it possible for her to do nice things for other kids without pomposity.

The older boys at St. Ann's are attracted to her. To hide their awkwardness, they look for ways of teasing her. She never seems to let it rattle her composure.

One day, a number of the boys are watching her and doing what they can to interrupt her concentration while she tries to make a yo-yo climb the string attached to her forefinger and then make it fly out in a circle and return to her without losing momentum. As she methodically drops and lifts the yo-yo, which has a light that flickers on and off as it goes up and down, she tells me that they tease her in exactly the same way at school.

"It's to make me pay attention to them, but it doesn't work," she says, "because I know *exactly* why they do it."

Sitting with me later at a table near the bottom of the stairs that lead into the room in which the children play and do their homework before having supper at the church, she opens her mouth and sticks her finger in so I can see a tooth that she's about to lose. "If it falls out tonight," she says, she'll put it "in a velvet box I keep beside my bed."

"Do you think there's a Tooth Fairy?"

"I doubt it," she replies.

She opens a package of Life Savers, offers one to me, and takes one for herself. I crunch the Life Saver in my teeth. A moment later, she crunches her Life Saver too.

"I did the same as you. . . ."

She smiles slowly, secretly, as if there's something in this that may need to be explored.

A few minutes later, when I come downstairs from meeting with the priest, she's in a silly mood because she and another girl were tickling each other. "I'm drunk!" she says, collapsing on the table.

Playful at playful times, reserved at times that call for dignified restraint, she seems to find it effortless to move from one mood to another. "She seems to skip along through life," I once said to Katrice when we were watching her at play; but she notices when someone else is having a hard time and doesn't simply pass that person by. She notices when Elio is in one of those moods that he gets into on some days in which it seems he's trying hard to find his way into a zone of happiness but looks as if he's terrified that he's about to cry.

"I *ain't* goin' to cry," he told me one day when he had been speaking of his Titi once again.

Ariel was playing near us, but she stopped her play the moment that she heard his words.

"I feel like cryin' about it," he said bravely. "But I *ain't* goin' to do it."

She studied his face to see if he could keep up his resolve. He looked at her, and bit his lip, and she said something to him that I can't remember now but which was just enough, whatever it was, to calm the storm and send him back into the afterschool with a determined look of courage in his eyes.

Sometimes she says nothing at all but barely seems to graze his arm or shoulder with this little wand of friendliness she has, and then leans down to check that he's okay. Some children have this gift, a healing presence that is tender without being coyly philanthropic. Her characteristic acts of kindness to another child are small gestures. They seem natural to her. They're almost always just the right size for the person who receives them.

St. Ann's Church, on St. Ann's Avenue, was built during the 1840s by the son of Gouverneur Morris, who is known to us today because he wrote the eloquent preamble to the U.S. Constitution. Physically, it's a small church, but it's easy to forget this since so many people from the neighborhood are in the building on a given day. The largest numbers are the children who come to the afterschool. Other children come late in the day or in the early evening when the priest, who is a woman and whom children here call Mother Martha, can be found at quiet moments in the garden of the church, so they can have a chance to be alone with her.

Some of the children also wait here for her in the morning if there isn't food at home or if they want advice or just aren't feeling organized enough to get themselves into a state of mind to go to school. Often they're sitting on the church stairs waiting for her when her car pulls up. She takes them to the coffee shop two blocks away and gets them breakfast and then brings them to their teachers.

Eighty children come here to the afterschool. There's a large room on the ground floor where they gather as they come into the building. Upstairs, on the second and third floors, there are six or seven rooms in which they have their classes and receive instruction on computers. At the end of the afternoon they come downstairs again to say their prayers and have their dinner.

Miss Katrice, who lives a few blocks from St. Ann's, is almost always present in the kitchen when the kids are here. She helps to serve their meals and also runs the free food pantry, which is open several days a week. Her daughter, Nancy, runs the afterschool and keeps in contact with the children's parents and their teachers. She also helps the children plan their study schedules, sends them upstairs to their classes, settles them into their chairs at suppertime, and leads them in their prayers.

The small dimensions of the church have much to do with the unusual experience of physical and moral safety that attracts the children here, and also with the feeling of protectedness and intimate religion that is so important to the older women who come here to take care of the children. Several women from the congregation, one of them a great-grandmother, Mrs. Winkle, who is nearly 83 years old, come in the afternoon to congregate around a table at the far end of the afterschool, where they can keep a close eye on the kids and be available to them at times of need.

The church reminds me of the very modest Roman Catholic churches I have visited in Mexico and Haiti, and the mission churches of New Mexico and Arizona where I used to meet with organizers of the migrant workers, most of whom were Mexican-American and used to bring their children or grandchildren with them to political prayer meetings. The presence of the very young and very old, together, in the same place, at the same time, is a part of the protective feeling.

The sanctuary of the church is relatively plain. The walls are painted a pale green. Some of the lights on the ceiling do not work. It holds at most 250 people. Members of the congregation stand and speak and share the readings of the Sunday prayers. The pastor chooses children from the neighborhood to serve as acolytes. Wearing white robes with ropes around the waist, they enter in a dignified procession with the priest. One child swings the incense. Another holds the cross. At the end of the service they do it all again.

While the services take place, and for at least two hours afterwards, hungry people who arrive here often several hours earlier receive their Sunday dinner, which is served at the same tables where the children on the weekdays do their homework in the afterschool. Generations young and old succeed each other at these tables, as they also do before the altar of the sanctuary where the bread and wine are served.

Homeless people come on foot from underneath the bridge connecting the South Bronx to Queens and from some other similarly isolated places to which they were driven, in effect, when New York City more or less ejected homeless people from the midtown areas around Grand Central Station and Times Square by making their activities — panhandling, or talking loudly to themselves, or crying publicly, consuming alcohol, or sleeping in the streets — essentially illegal.

Some of them walk a long way for their dinner, and Katrice does not believe they come here only for the meal, because they linger afterwards and stand with her around the kitchen door and watch the other people and don't seem to want to leave. Elderly men who have no place to bathe, whose fingernails are long and curved, whose eyes are sometimes glistening from drugs or alcohol, come up to her and kiss her — "How you doin'? Lookin' fine this mornin', Miss Katrice!" — and sometimes hug her just a little longer than they really should and even make audacious comments to her that the children hear and comment upon later.

The room clears out on Sunday afternoons by two or three o'clock. Katrice and those who share the cooking obligations with her clean the kitchen while the pastor walks the dog who lives here at the church. Soon after three, Katrice turns out the lights and checks a few last details with the priest, then locks the door.

"Well, okay. . . . I guess that's it," she says.

Sometimes, once the church is locked, Katrice and Mother Martha stand together for a few last minutes, chatting there with one another on the street. The two women, different from each other in so many ways—their race, their background, and their education—give each other a lot of strength somehow. The children give the grown-ups strength as well. There's a reciprocity in this that isn't easy for a person who is not a member of the church to understand.

There are a number of things like this about the life of a community of faith that I don't understand and which religious people tell me I try too hard to explain. Sometimes the answers never come. Sometimes they come when you're not looking for an answer. The answers I remember longest are the ones that answer questions that I didn't think of asking.

CHAPTER 2

The World According to Pineapple

April 10. A sunny afternoon, but cool. Elio is upstairs with a group in the computer room. The rest of the kids are down here in the big room on the ground floor, finishing their homework.

Pineapple is struggling with the electric pencil sharpener next to the closet on the left side of the room. Eight years old, she huffs and puffs as she keeps putting the same pencil back into the sharpener, then looking at the point with obvious dissatisfaction, then putting it back in again, until it's down to almost nothing. She keeps staring at it with an irritated look, as if she knew that this was going to happen.

When she's done, she passes out the pencils to the children at her table, saving the one she's sharpened to a stump for last, then giving it to a boy she doesn't like because he teases her for being plump.

"This is s'posed to be a pencil?" asks the boy.

"Don't answer him," she tells the other children.

Grown-ups who spend time here with Pineapple comment on the confidence with which she uses her assertiveness to issue little orders like this to the other children. I can never tell why they obey her. Pineapple doesn't seem to understand the reason either, but she never seems reluctant to accept the power that the other children, girls especially, invest in her and she deploys it with comedic ease, as if she finds it funny that they let her exercise so much authority in coming to decisions.

"You sit here. You can sit over there," she says, arranging children at a reading table in one of the study rooms upstairs.

"Why is Raven way down at the end?" I ask.

"I don't know why. She *asked* me where to sit. So I said, 'Sit right there!'"

She doesn't seem to suffer any grave concern about the fact that she's so plump. She talks about it more with puzzlement, or petulance, as if she thinks that unknown forces in the world conspire to expand her waistline but that her healthy appetite has no connection with this.

"She has a nice compactly packaged personality," the pastor noted once as we were watching her among a group of other children. A pleasant kind of managerial assertiveness is very much a part of the completed package.

She can be assertive also when she talks to grown-ups and seems unaware that she is often going just a bit too far. She talks to me at times as if, between the two of us, she is the one in charge of things and simply asks me for a small degree of logical cooperation.

"Please tell me to do my work," she says to me one afternoon.

"Okay," I say.

She pats the seat beside her; I sit down. Next, she opens a spiral pad in which she's written her assignments for tonight and places it in front of me. Then, with her pencil in her hand, she waits for me to read her the assignments.

"Spelling book—pages 65 and 66."

She opens her spelling book and finds the page, looks up, and asks me, "Next?"

"Mathematics—pages 83 and 84."

She opens her mathematics workbook.

"Next?"

"Phonics lesson—'ess' sounds. Write them out."

She digs into her backpack, finds the phonics book, and spreads it open on the table. Finally, with all three books in front of her, she gives me her "approval" sign— thumb and finger in a circle—and begins to work.

She works for 25 or 30 minutes, asking me a question when she runs into an obstacle. She gets confused, for instance, in her mathematics homework, which is four-column subtraction, and she now and then reverses letters when she does her spelling lesson, studying a word she's copied out and telling me she thinks that "it looks funny," then erasing it and doing it correctly; but, for most of the half-hour, she works on her own and moves each book aside once she is done with it.

When she's finished, she places her notebook against her mathematics workbook and aligns them with each other, then aligns them with her spelling book and phonics book and slips them all into a certain section of her backpack, which she then zips shut. The neatness in the way she does this and the close fit of the three books and the notebook in the space she has assigned them seem to give her a good feeling of completion. When she zips her backpack shut, it feels definitive.

"Okay. That's it," she says. "I'm done."

She puts her pencil and eraser in a side-compartment of the backpack and gets up and, in this way, she brings the period of work to its conclusion.

She can speak sarcastically to other children and can, frankly, be a bit too blunt at times. "Your face is *shiny*, girl!" she said one afternoon to somebody whose mother had rubbed oil on her skin. "You could borrow the sun's job!" Usually, however, there's an element of foolishness that rescues her sarcasm and her jokes from real destructiveness. Like many of the children, she's alert to times when other children are too fragile to sustain the give-and-take of repartee; and when, as often happens at the after-school, one of the younger children suddenly begins to cry, or seems to be right at the precipice of tears, she switches gears almost immediately.

One afternoon, when she and Elio have finished all their homework, Nancy lets them go upstairs with me and with a girl named Piedad to play a spelling game before it's time to eat. Just as the three of them are getting settled in their chairs, however, Piedad begins to cry. There's a cubby-hole between some colored cardboard boxes that are piled up to function as bookcases. The seven-year-old child climbs right in somehow and curls up in a ball and doesn't answer when I ask what's wrong.

Pineapple stares at her a moment in the cubby-hole, then crawls right in beside her. Her feet stick out, but most of her is squeezed into the cubby-hole with Piedad. I was alarmed when Piedad refused to speak and was about to go downstairs to get Katrice or Mother Martha, but Pineapple makes her "okay" signal to me with her thumb and finger — and she winks at me! — so I get out the spelling game and sit with Elio. Within another minute or so, the two girls come out of the cubby-hole, and both of them are laughing.

ORDINARY RESURRECTIONS

"I wasn't really crying," says the younger girl.

Elio says, "You were pretending?"

"It was a game is all," Pineapple says.

I don't think that this was true; but Piedad's tears are gone and I don't want to bring them back, so I pass out the dice and spelling cards and we don't speak of this again.

Children do things like this for each other that an adult doesn't understand but knows he cannot do himself. Pineapple was eight years old that spring and I was nearing 61. But I felt powerless when Piedad began to cry, while Pineapple appeared to know exactly what to do.

I still don't think that Piedad had been pretending. She cries at times for reasons no one knows. When she cries, she sobs; her body trembles. Teachers who have spent their lives with children of this age know what to do when things like this occur. They'll sometimes get down on the floor and take the child in their arms and, if they need to, hold her like that for a while. I guess I didn't feel I had the right to do this; perhaps I didn't think that Piedad would have accepted it from me. She did accept it from Pineapple.

There's a great deal of this automatic and insightful kindness in the hearts of many of these children who have been acquainted with unusual degrees of loss and sorrow by the time they're eight or nine years old. They show it with their eyes and with their words, and rapid touches of their hands, and, when it's absolutely needed, with their arms wrapped tight around each other. They're good at being silly, but they're also good at being gentle.

Gentleness and generosity, however, will not help these children much in overcoming many of the problems they will face as they grow older and attempt to find their way around the academic obstacles that stand before poor

27

children of their color in our nation. Most of the children here, no matter how hard they may work and how well they may do in elementary school, will have no chance, or almost none, to win admission to the city's more selective high schools, which prepare their students for good universities and colleges. In a city in which four fifths of all the public high school students are black or Hispanic, only 8 or 9 percent of students at Stuyvesant High, the city's most selective high school, are black or Hispanic; and the children of the St. Ann's neighborhood have, statistically, the lowest chance of winning entrance to that school of all one million children in the city's schools.

Most of the children here end up at one of three or four large segregated high schools in the Bronx, the greatest numbers ending up at Morris High School, where 1,900 to 2,000 children are enrolled but only about 90 make it to twelfth grade and only about 65 can graduate. That's the way it is for many children in our northern cities now. Some of these children seem to cry for no good reason. They don't know much about the world at this point in their lives, but they may know more than we think.

In fighting off their times of gloominess and tears, the children here have loyal allies in the grown-ups at St. Ann's, especially the older women who preside over the kitchen in the afterschool but do much more than that, presiding also over all the minor squabbles, rivalries, and reconciliations that take place among the children on a normal afternoon. The children also know that they can turn to Mother Martha any time they choose, and interrupt her any time they want, no matter who is with her at the church. Some of the younger ones seem to keep track of where she is at every hour of the day. When she comes into the afterschool they watch her closely.

"That's Mother Martha," Pineapple announces.

"Don't you think I know who Mother Martha is?"

"I guess . . . ," she says.

"Do you know what she does?"

"Natch," she answers.

"What is it?"

"She's the priest."

"I know you know that she's the priest. What does she *do* here at the church?"

"What do you mean?"

"What is her job?"

"She says the prayers?"

"That's right. What else?"

"She takes care of the dog?"

"What else?"

"She bakes the bread."

"I don't think that's true."

"She sweeps?"

"Yes! I've seen her do that too."

"She buries people when they die?"

"Yes," I say.

"She stands in front of us and says . . . what's goin' on."

"What do you mean—'goin' on'?"

"With God."

"Okay. . . ."

"She signs a lot of papers?"

"Yes."

"Something else," she says, "but I can't think of it."

She watches Mother Martha, who is talking with a child's mother near the kitchen door.

"She's a teacher?"

"Sort of," I reply.

The conversation trails off with no ending. Many conversations that I have with children here have no real ending because there is almost always something else that's going on to serve as a distraction. Other children interrupt. A crash is heard when something gets tipped over in the kitchen. A group of boys and girls come down the stairs with a tremendous clatter from the gym and bring their voices, and their basketball, into the room. Only when the mothers come at six o'clock—or, in the winter months, as early as five-thirty—and the room begins to empty out and Miss Katrice stops work at last to make herself a cup of tea, and sometimes offers one to me, is there the kind of resting-point that you could call "an ending." It always has a slightly melancholy feeling.

"Okay. I'm goin' home," Katrice might say to Nancy or to Mrs. Winkle or Miss Elsie, who is one of her co-workers in the kitchen. "Are you goin' too?"

"I'm going to the store first."

"Well, okay . . . ," Katrice might say as she tucks in the cover of a carton of donated food that will be given out tomorrow at the pantry. "I guess that's all. . . ."

She told me once she never really likes to leave. Even when she's tired or is struggling against one of those winter colds that spread so quickly in a place where eighty kids and many grown-ups are in close and steady contact for so many hours every day, she says she feels a sense of let-down as she gets her coat and says goodbye to Mother Martha and goes out into the night and makes her way along the darkened streets.

It's easy to see why. There's so much life within this room during the hours when the kids are here—so many faces, voices, questions, fingers, elbows! Even when the children have gone home, reminders of their recent presence still remain here in the hats or coats or books or backpacks that a few of them routinely leave behind.

"Jonathan," Katrice once told me, "no one runs from good."

She puts away forgotten items before turning out the lights. Only then is there the feeling that the day has ended.

The church is empty only for about an hour once the children have gone home. Then the afterschool begins to fill again, but this time with a wholly different group of people: men and women in recovery from drugs who come here to participate in an addiction program to which some have been assigned by their probation officers as a condition of release from prison.

Some are the parents or the older siblings of the children in the afterschool. About one quarter of the fathers of the children in the afterschool are now in prison or have been in prison, some of them a long way from the Bronx in various state penitentiaries and some nearby at Rikers Island, which is New York City's largest prison and, with nearly 20,000 inmates, 92 percent of them black or Hispanic, is believed to be the largest and most racially consistent penal colony in the entire Western world.

The racial make-up of the prison population and that of the population of Mott Haven are essentially the same. The racial mix, such as it is, among the children of Mott Haven is represented by the presence of some 26 white children in a nonwhite population of 11,000 students in the elementary schools that serve the neighborhood. A segregation rate of 99.8 percent leaves two tenths of one percentage point as the distinction between legally enforced apartheid in the South of 50 years ago and socially and economically enforced apartheid in this New York City neighborhood today.

In the fall of 1993, when I first visited the public school that Pineapple attends, the principal told me there was only one white child in a student population of 800. Some months later when I visited again, that child was gone but there was now another white boy in the school. I asked his teacher, "How many white kids have you taught over the years?"

"I've been in this school for 18 years," she said. "This is the first white student I have *ever* taught."

In the spring of that year, which was four decades since the landmark court decision in *Brown* versus *Board of Education,* New York Newsday noted that the city's public schools were "the most segregated in the nation." For most black and Hispanic children in the city, said the paper, the idea of racial integration is "something to read about in history books," not something to be looked for in their daily lives or in the New York City schools.

People from outside New York who visit with me in the Bronx are sometimes startled, although more are simply saddened or bemused, to walk into the schools and see a demographic panorama reminiscent of those faded photographs from Tuscaloosa, Greensboro, or Jackson that are seen in documentary programs on TV and generally introduced as shameful and disturbing testimonies to benighted policies of unequivocal discrimination of which, we are told, the nation has since soberly repented.

In vast expanses of the South Bronx, in which residential segregation was encouraged and accelerated by the conscious policies of realtors, banks, and city planners starting in the 1950s, and where federal housing subsidies in recent decades have been used to underwrite a set of policies and practices that deepened pre-existing racial isolation, tens of thousands of black and Hispanic children never see white children in their schools or preschools, parks or playgrounds, churches, libraries, or stores. They don't *know* white children. White children don't know *them*. They're strangers to each other.

Unlike the children seen within those photographs of the old South, moreover, children in Mott Haven do not go to school with even a small number of the children of the middle class — the children of schoolteachers, ministers, or doctors, for example. Their separation from the nation's mainstream, for this reason, is more absolute; and, as writer and former Clinton administration official Peter Edelman has observed, this form of segregation, while it's not required by the law as in the old days in the South, "is even more pernicious."

Despite the isolation and betrayal that may be suggested by these governing realities, St. Ann's is not a place of sorrow but, at least during the hours when the children fill its corridors and classrooms with their voices and their questions and their paperpads and notebooks and their games, it is a place of irresistible vitality and energy and sometimes complicated hope, and now and then uncomplicated joy. For grown-ups in the neighborhood, it is an energizing place as well, although the burdens that they bring with them when they come here in times of crisis to seek out the priest can often seem at first quite overwhelming.

They bring drug problems to the priest, and warnings from the welfare system, and their medical concerns, which are more serious than those one would encounter on a routine basis in more affluent communities. Many women here suffer for months, or even years, not knowing that they have diseases like breast cancer, which would be detected sooner in most other sections of the nation — or, as is more commonly the case, they know what's wrong but can't obtain the surgical procedure that the diagnosis calls for. Many also suffer terrible depression: crushing episodes of virtual emotional paralysis for which, if they were middle class or upper middle class, they'd probably be given psychiatric care but in this neighborhood are likely to be given nothing more than "maintenance prescriptions" of strong medications, which can leave them feeling passive and depleted.

People come here when they're scared that they will die, and some when they would like to die. Some of those who get the most depressed are also diabetics. They run out of insulin. They come into the afterschool and ask for help. Katrice goes to the kitchen and brings orange juice. If they don't recover, they are taken to the hospital.

People come here also with court papers for arraignment of their teenage boys, or with eviction papers from their landlords. Mother Martha was a trial lawyer once. She went to Radcliffe College in the 1960s, then to law school, and then entered practice with a well-known lawyer by the name of Louis Nizer. She gave up the law during the 1980s when her younger brother died of AIDS, and entered seminary in New York; but the lessons that she learned during her years in court still turn out to be useful.

She can be a formidable adversary. Building managers and other representatives of absentee white landlords who imagine they can patronize her as they patronize their tenants learn a different lesson quickly. Tastelessly invasive journalists, local demagogues, and loan sharks and drug dealers in the neighborhood have also learned the risks of underestimating Mother Martha's strength of will. A man believed to have been selling drugs on St. Ann's Avenue who had a run-in with her told me, "I'll be honest with you, Jonathan. She frightens me more than the cops do when she knows I wasn't straight with her." The children, on the other hand, behave with likable irreverence in her company. They tease her when she seems disorganized or bangs her car into the curb or locks the door and leaves the keys in the ignition.

Mothers, whether they are members of the church or not, come here with children when they're ill; and children come here with their pets or with stray animals that they find sick or injured in the streets. They bring them in their arms, or in a box, which they deposit at the pastor's feet and then look up at her and wait, and watch, with worried eyes.

Cats and dogs lead shorter lives here in Mott Haven than most other places I have been. Some die from starvation, some from being beaten. Others freeze from being left outside in winter. The dog who lives here in the pastor's office came into the churchyard on a cold day seven years ago when he was close to death. The sexton found him near the back door of the church and wrapped him in a blanket and soon nursed him back to health. He's a beautiful and healthy dog today: a terrier who has a band of thick white fur around his neck and very big and pointed ears. He has a bed to sleep in underneath the pastor's desk. When various dignitaries come to visit at St. Ann's, the children sometimes bring them in to meet the dog who came to die but was reborn.

The priest makes many visits to the vet with children and their pets. They sit beside her in the car and hold their animals. When they cannot keep a pet and when no shelter will accept it, she may drive the children to a safe spot in Manhattan to release the animal. The children kiss their pet goodbye and say a prayer that somebody will soon come by and give it a good place to live.

The priest and children hate to let these animals go off alone into the streets of a big city; but there are priorities in neighborhoods where many children do not get enough to eat. Often it's the little playmate with four feet that has to pay the price for hunger in the child's home. The children, of course, don't always understand priorities like these. Sometimes grown-ups do not understand them either; but, too often in this neighborhood, there simply isn't any other choice.

CHAPTER 3

Kindness to Strangers

Gwendolyn Brooks has written with a special dignity about the spirits of young children. I used to read her poems to students when I was a fourth-grade teacher in the Boston schools. I'd never heard of Gwendolyn Brooks, or Langston Hughes, or any other black American writer when I was an undergraduate at Harvard College majoring in English literature. I learned of Gwendolyn Brooks for the first time from the parents of my students when I went to teach in a black neighborhood called Roxbury.

In one of her early poems, in which she speaks of children of about the same age as the St. Ann's children, she describes them as "my sweetest lepers" because, she says, too many are convinced somehow that they are "quasi," "contraband," "graven by a hand less than angelic." Some of their mothers, she writes, are forced to counsel them to be as inconspicuous as possible in order to escape potential dangers or attract too much attention. "Confine your lights," a mother tells her children. "Resemble graves." But some of them, the poet knows, reject this counsel and refuse to hide their lights. Sometimes, late into their teenage years, they stubbornly refuse to let the beautiful illumination of their spirits be subdued.

There are teenagers like this at St. Ann's. Erika, the beautiful child pictured on the cover of my former book, Amazing Grace, is one who hasn't let the light within her spirit be confined. Her intellect, morality, and loyalty to other children still burn brightly. Ariel, who will soon be a teenager, has that glowing quality as well. Strangers visiting the church are naturally drawn to students such as Erika and Ariel, and to the younger ones whose personalities and verbal styles, although still evolving, are already vivid and distinct.

The children, however, are not indiscriminate about the grown-ups they befriend. Elio, for instance, can be quick to show that he does not like certain visitors, especially the ones who speak to him in that peculiar singsong voice that grown-ups sometimes think they ought to use when speaking to young children.

I remember a man who came to visit in the fall of 1996 and who, while he was welcomed at the start, wore out his welcome soon. He was working on a documentary film and seemed to be sincere in his desire to do something helpful for the church and the community; but he had an over-earnest manner that the children did not like, and Elio avoided him and stiffened somewhat when he'd ask a question. Ariel and Pineapple weren't friendly to him either. I was surprised by this, because I liked him and I knew he liked the kids; but they appeared to sense something they didn't trust in him, some hint of altruistic condescension of which he was evidently unaware.

"They turn their backs on me," he said to Mother Martha after he'd been walking in the street for several hours and had tried in vain to get some of the kids he met to join in conversation with him.

"He found this inexplicable," she said. "I wanted to tell him, 'Listen! I did everything I could, but I can't make the children like you! They have the right, the same one that your own kids have, to choose the people they would like to spend their time with. You don't forfeit that because you're poor.'"

I told her Elio grew quiet in his presence.

"It doesn't surprise me in the least," she said. "I think our children have good taste. They may not know the way to say it, but I think they recognize when someone's friendliness is mixed with other motives that are partially concealed. Many good people who are utterly sincere have come to visit here, and a few who weren't sincere, and some who were sincere in that annoying way that is just humorless and boring. So our kids have had a lot of opportunities to learn how to make judgments."

Elio's opinions about strangers seem to be arrived at quickly. When he takes to someone, he does not waste time in making his good feelings known. He heads for that person like a World War Two attack plane on a mission, with his brown eyes smiling and his arms wide open. I've seen him do this with Katrice as well when, after she'd been sick for several days, he saw her come into the after-school. He headed straight across the room, arms wide, and then, right at the moment of collision, turned his cheek and pressed it up against her face, his eyes closed and his arms wrapped tight around her.

This is how he welcomed Mr. Rogers to St. Ann's, even though, according to his mother, he did not recall at first exactly who he was and had to be reminded by another child. "I think he just saw something that he liked about the man," Katrice observed when we were talking the next day. "Our kids can almost always tell when somebody's for real."

Some of the mothers and teenagers at St. Ann's were even more excited to meet Mr. Rogers than the children were. Several said they'd watched his program faithfully when they were children ten or twenty or even thirty years before. Earlier that day, when he and I were walking from the subway on Brook Avenue, a man driving a sanitation truck pulled over to the curb, climbed down from the truck, and gave a hug to Mr. Rogers. People are loyal to their own best memories. These things, thank God, cross all the lines of class and race and, in this case, of time.

"He did look tired," said Katrice. "He's not young but he paid good attention to the things the children told him. You could see that he was happy to be with them. . . .

"You know, Jonathan? They put our children here on the back burner for so long. It meant a lot to me that Mr. Rogers wanted to be with us and did not act hurried or important or superior. I think that he respected what we're doing with the children."

The weariness she saw in Mr. Rogers's eyes was noted by some of the children too while they were sitting with him at the piano in the sanctuary. Some of them remembered later that he had his bow-tie on but that he didn't have his sneakers or his sweater.

They studied his face so carefully that I was afraid they'd make him feel self-conscious, and they worried afterwards about his health because he grew a little weak while he was here and had to sit and have some juice and cookies.

One of the younger children asked me later if I'd noticed that he had grey hair, a question that occasioned a rebuttal from Pineapple.

"Don't be lyin', girl! His hair was black!"

But the first child said she knew that it was grey because, she said, "I touched it with my hand."

They do the same with me. Katrice's six-year-old granddaughter, Raven, for example, climbs up on the bench beside me in the afterschool to scrutinize my hair. She points to strands of grey and comes up close to study them and makes a lot of this, as if she were tremendously alarmed, then looks into my ears, then in my eyes and even at my nostrils, as if she were studying a horse. Elio, sitting on the other side of me, appears to be concerned as well. "Jonathan," he asks, "how old are you?" When I answer, "Almost sixty-one," he looks at me in disbelief, crosses himself, then runs across the room to share this information with Katrice.

Katrice explains to Elio and Raven that it's not polite to count the grey hairs on an older person's head. But Raven's curiosity is uncontainable. As soon as her grandmother goes back to the kitchen, she continues her examination. Each time she finds another grey hair, she says, "Uh-oh . . . ," until finally Katrice sweeps back out of the kitchen for a second time, lifts her off the bench, and, in her lilting but impatient Caribbean voice, instructs her, "Leave the man alone!"

They study grown-ups all the time. The girls look closely at the clothes that women wear, complimenting someone, for example, if she's wearing something pretty or remarking when one of the teachers comes into the afterschool with an attractive and elaborate braiding in her hair. The attention, however, that they pay to signs of age in older people seems to have an element of special curiosity. "Sixty-one" appears to strike them as inordinately old; and, when I once told Elio, in answer to a question he had asked about my mother, that she then was 93 years old, he seemed incredulous.

Mr. Rogers has been talking with young children for so many years, and in so many different settings, that I'm sure their curiosity about his age did not surprise him. When he wrote to me later, he enclosed an album of the pictures he had taken of the children at the church, with observations he had jotted down on yellow stick-on pages next to several of the photographs. "This one is my favorite," he had written just beneath the photograph of Elio with his stuffed rabbit.

"There was a real light in his eyes, not just a child's normal friendliness. I won't forget him," Mr. Rogers told me more than a year later. I thought of the comment that a teacher here in Massachusetts made about some of the children she had taught over the years. "There are some children who are like windows," she had written. "When you look into those windows you see something more than the kids themselves—more than innocence. . . . You see the deep, inextinguishable goodness at the core of creation."

When I'm with Elio, I feel persuaded that the light within his eyes will never be extinguished. But there are many men from the South Bronx in prison in New York today—Elio's father is just one of several thousand of these men—whose mothers and grandmothers can remember the same light of goodness in their eyes as well when they were six or eight years old. The light is darkened much too soon for many children in this neighborhood and others like it to be found in cities all over the nation; and the longing of so many to reveal their light and bring their gift of goodness to our nation's table is too often stifled and obliterated long before they are fifteen years old.

The natural gentility and spontaneity of many of the little ones like Elio are dirtied, tangled, twisted, and compressed too quickly. The grace and dignity of girls like Ariel are often coarsened and degraded by the time they enter junior high school, where, as teachers in the neighborhood observe repeatedly, a shell of hardness frequently is formed like a protective shield against the many injuries and disappointments that await them. Some of the children who are virtually bursting with poetic creativity when they are six years old evolve destructive substitutes for creativity and violent channels for their disrespected energies before they even get to junior high.

"I shall create!" wrote Gwendolyn Brooks in speaking of an angry adolescent in one of her most disturbing and widely admired poems: "If not a note, a hole. If not an overture, a desecration." Katrice looked over at Elio when we were speaking of those lines one afternoon after the children read the poem in which those words appear. She might have been thinking of her youngest son, who was apparently a bright and promising and joyful boy when he was growing up on Cypress Avenue but who has been incarcerated in a federal penitentiary in Illinois for nearly seven years. Before I left St. Ann's that day, I saw her sitting next to Elio at one of the long tables, turning the pages of a book, and talking quietly.

Mr. Rogers's sensitive reactions to the children at St. Ann's and the relaxed and easy way he got along with them are not surprising in the least to anyone who knows him or has seen his television program. Others who come to visit at the church may have far less intuitive connectedness with children of this age than Mr. Rogers does, but still appear to be affected deeply by the time they spend here. Some, like Mr. Rogers, are already well-informed about the inequalities in education, preschool opportunities, and healthcare that restrict the possibilities of life for children in the neighborhood. Those who aren't so well-informed and therefore tend to sentimentalize the situation here receive a bracing lesson in the economics of injustice if they take the time to sit and ask some questions to the priest.

Many find it hard to understand that families in this neighborhood subsist on far less money in a given year—typically about $10,000 in most of the family situations that I know firsthand—than many upper middle class Americans will spend on annual holidays or on the upkeep of a car. Many are surprised to learn how many children here do not get dental care, how many suffer from respiratory illnesses, how many have no medical insurance, and how many have—despite the rules that govern things like this in public school—not even had an eye examination and don't know, until a teacher questions them one day perhaps in first or second grade, that they need glasses.

Most disturbing to the teachers who come here to visit from the suburbs are the unabated inequalities in public allocations for the education of the children. It's become conventional in social policy debates in recent years to pose what often sound like neutral questions about whether money "really makes much difference" in the education of poor children: questions that are seldom posed when wealthy people contemplate the benefits of sending their own children to expensive private schools or when they move into exclusive suburbs in which public schools are spending more than twice what public schools in the South Bronx are spending on the children in this book. Despite the many ways in which this issue has been clouded, nonetheless, there are few areas in which the value we attribute to a child's life may be so clearly measured as in the decisions that we make about the money we believe it's worth investing in the education of one person's child as opposed to that of someone else's child.

New York City, at the time this book takes place in the late 1990s, spends about $8,000 yearly on each student overall, including special education (which is dispropor- tionately expensive), but considerably less than this — about $5,000 — on each boy or girl like Elio or Ariel in ordinary classrooms of the public elementary schools in the South Bronx. The press is inconsistent and gives sev- eral different numbers, but this is the figure that was given to me by the Chancellor of Schools in New York City when we met one night at dinner during the same year that I met Elio — "$5,200, to be accurate," he said.

If you had the power to lift up one of these children in your arms and plunk him down within one of the rela- tively wealthy districts of Westchester County, a subur- ban area that borders New York City to the north, he would suddenly be granted public education worth at least $12,000 every year and he would also have a teacher who is likely to be paid as much as $20,000 more than what a teacher can be paid in the South Bronx. If you could take a slightly longer ride and bring these children to an upper middle class school district such as Great Neck or Manhas- sett on Long Island, Elio and Pineapple and Ariel would be in schools where over $18,000 are invested, on the aver- age, in a child's public education every year.

These are extraordinary inequalities within a metro- politan community that still lays claim to certain vestiges of the humanitarian ideals associated with the age of civil rights and with the unforgotten dreams of Dr. Martin Luther King. No matter how these differences may be ob- scured or understated or complexified by civilized equivo- cation, they do tell us something about how we value Pineapple and Elio as human beings, both in their present status as small children who rely upon our decency and in their future destinies as adult citizens.

Many of the people who come up to visit at St. Ann's are prompted by religious motives when they come here the first time. Like most religious people, they believe that every child, of whatever race or economic situation, is of equal value in the eyes of God. In the eyes of God I'm sure we'd all like to believe that this is so; but, in the eyes of those who exercise real power in New York, it seemingly is not.

The differences are seen not only in the size of classes and the salaries of teachers but in dozens of associated matters such as the provision of attractive libraries, good exercise facilities, intensive counseling and guidance in selection of a course of study that will lead to university admissions, as well as all those other offerings, both pedagogic and aesthetic, that convey a sense of democratic amplitude and shape an ambiance of opportunity and graciousness in day-to-day existence.

The systematic nature of these inequalities is not discussed continually by teachers in the schools, although they cannot help but be aware of them. They have their work to do; and even those who live in New York suburbs, and perceive the differences firsthand, grow weary of sustaining oppositional positions and resolve to do what good they can from day to day, as teachers must, in incremental ways. Perhaps, at times, this is my state of mind as well.

It's also true that it is hard to think in terms so general, and oppositional, and large, when you are with specific children and have found yourself entangled in the details of their ordinary lives, which tend to be particular, and tiny, and diverting and disarming often in their pleasantness. The intimate setting in the church may also have a softening effect — at least it does for me — on ideology and anger. An illusion of equality is fostered in the presence of protected innocence. When Elio and Mr. Rogers sit together at the piano at St. Ann's and all the rest of us are joining them in singing songs that everybody knows, I'd be surprised if Mr. Rogers, at that moment, has his mind on anything as mighty and portentous as "unfairness in school finance." I would bet he's thinking more of piano keys and fingers.

Still, the facts are always there. Every teacher, every parent, every priest who serves this kind of neighborhood knows what these inequalities imply. So the sweetness of the moment loses something of its sweetness later on when you're reminded of the odds these children face and of the ways injustice slowly soils innocence. You wish you could eternalize these times of early glory. You wish that Elio and Ariel and Pineapple could stay here in this garden of their juvenile timidity forever. You know they can't. You have a sense of what's ahead. You do your best to shut it out. You want to know them as they are. You do not want to think too much of what may someday be.

CHAPTER 4

Three Generations

Tabitha Brown is sitting by herself at one of the long tables in the afterschool when I come down from the computer room one afternoon. On a piece of broad-lined yellow paper she's been working on a story for her teacher. "I have two fishes. One is pink and one is purple," it begins.

I was at P.S. 30 earlier today and spent an hour in her classroom. Elio's in her class, but he was sitting at a table in the back part of the room while Tabitha was sitting near the front, close to the blackboard and the teacher.

"You were in my class today," she says.

When I agree that I was there, she tells me that she sits as far away from Elio as possible because, she says, "he's bad" in class and tries to get her into trouble.

"What does he do?" I ask.

"He says bad things."

"What does he say?"

"He says, 'Fishy, fishy!'"

"That doesn't seem so bad."

"It's bad! It is! He comes right up behind me when the teacher isn't looking—and he *says* it!"

"Say it again?" I ask.

"Fishy, fishy!" she says, gulping like a minnow at air bubbles as she says the dreaded words a second time. Then she conceals her face in her two arms and leans down on the tabletop and shakes her head repeatedly.

"Does it have a secret meaning?" I ask Beverly, one of the tutors, who is standing at the far end of the table.

"Maybe!" she says. "They have this sweet world of their own. They make things up like this and then they get repeated and take on so much significance!"

"It seems innocent," I say.

"Innocence is her entire world," she answers as the child incrementally recovers from our conversation.

Late in the day, Tabitha approaches me while I'm with Elio next to the doorway of the bathroom at the bottom of the stairs. "He's bad!" she says, and shakes her head again. But fifteen minutes later, when the children settle in their chairs to say their prayers before they eat, I see her sitting next to him.

The afternoon ends, as many do here at St. Ann's, with several children waiting for their mothers in the afterschool while Miss Katrice, Miss Elsie, and Miss Margarita, who is yet another of the older women of the church, clean up the kitchen. Elio is gone, but Tabitha's still here, working on a drawing at a table next to Nancy, who is studying a list of children who have not yet brought permission slips for an upcoming visit to the country.

"I love XXXX," she's written on a drawing that includes a picture of a boy with giant shoes, a girl with long hair in an evening gown, a cat with spots, a house, maybe a church, because there's something like a cross on top. It's not too clear. She's scribbling really, more than drawing.

"Who is XXXX?" I ask.

She covers up the drawing when she sees me peering down and gives me an affronted look.

Katrice makes me a cup of tea. We leave together at six-thirty. I tell her of Elio's way of teasing Tabitha. She smiles at his words but makes no big deal out of this. She hears things every bit as silly almost every day and takes the sweetness and the humor of the children pretty much for granted.

"Tell me who you love most," I ask Elio one afternoon.

"I can choose two?"

"Okay," I say.

"How about three?"

"Three is okay."

"My mother, my father . . . ," he begins, then shuts his eyes to make a good third choice—"and God!"

He looks up then and asks, "Can I choose four?"

"Okay. One more."

"And . . . everybody else!"

He sweeps his arm around him to include the other people in the room, or in the church, or maybe in the Bronx, or maybe everybody in the world.

One Saturday afternoon I meet him with his mother as they're coming from a store on St. Ann's Avenue. She takes me aside next to the doorway of the store and tells me of a conversation she had earlier this week at P.S. 30 with his teacher. While we're talking, Elio is peering in the window of the store and doesn't look as if he's listening. His mother touches the top of his head in a distracted way. He looks around at his mother, then at me.

"Jonathan?" he says.

"Yes?" I say.

"Where do you live?"

"Massachusetts," I reply.

"Where is Massachusetts?"

I look up the street to think which way I'd drive to go from here to Massachusetts. Then I point in the direction of St. Mary's Park and tell him, "If you got in a car and kept on driving that direction for four hours, you would be right near my house."

He peers up at his mother. "Is that how we go to Grandma's?"

"No. Grandma's is the opposite direction," she replies.

He seems reluctant to give up his wish to find a way to locate Massachusetts in his mind. "Is that the way we go to visit Titi?"

"No. Titi didn't live in Massachusetts," says his mother.

He looks up St. Ann's Avenue, which runs in a straight line from here beyond the building in which Nancy lives, and past a sprawling, nearly block-long children's prison that was just constructed opposite a middle school, and farther north until it disappears into a maze of streets that lead into the area of Boston Road.

"Is that the way we go to see the circus?"

His mother laughs and answers, "No. The circus is the opposite direction."

She points down St. Ann's Avenue in the direction of Manhattan. His eyes follow his mother's hand. Then she sighs and tells him that it's time to go and reaches for his hand and says goodbye to me and tugs him off in the direction of Brook Avenue.

He asks a lot of questions about where I live and what my life is like. Sometimes he meanders in his questions, starting off in one direction and then starting over to explore another. Sometimes, on the other hand, he has an obvious agenda.

"Jonathan?" he asks me the next time we meet.

"Yes?" I say.

"Could you bring your dog with you someday?"

"Maybe," I say.

"When?" he says.

"Someday," I reply.

I explain to him that when I come to New York City it is usually by plane and that my dog would have to travel in the section with the bags. He seems confused about the reason why a dog can't sit beside a person on the plane.

"There's a rule," I say. "They don't allow it."

"Why?"

"I don't know why."

"I don't know why either," he replies.

I tell him that my dog can't travel with me anyway right now, because she hurt her leg.

"How did she hurt her leg?"

"Chasing another dog," I say.

"Will she be better soon?"

"Yes. Very soon," I say.

He does not give up on this, however.

"Where does your dog live?" he asks.

"In my house with me," I say.

"Where is your house?"

"I told you — it's in Massachusetts."

"What is Massachusetts?"

"It's the state I live in," I reply.

"Is it nice in Massachusetts?"

"Yes," I say.

"Is Massachusetts big?"

"Not very big, but bigger than the Bronx."

"Jonathan?"

"Yes?" I say.

"Where does your dog sleep?"

"She sleeps beside me, on my bed."

"For real?"

"For real!"

"Jonathan?" he tries again.

"Yes?" I say.

"Will you bring your dog with you when you come back next week?"

"I can't come next week," I say.

"Why not?"

"Because I can't."

He still does not give up on this entirely.

"Where does your dog stay when you're not there?"

"She stays with a friend of mine who has a farm," I say.

"Is she scared there?"

"No. It's nice," I say.

"Where does she sleep?"

"She sleeps with a pony in the hay."

"For real?" he asks.

"For real!"

This answer seems to satisfy him for a while, but he comes back to the same subject many times. Pineapple and her sisters question me about this point as well. They have tremendous curiosity about the lives of grown-ups who do not live in their neighborhood. They know that I'm not married and do not have children, and they know my parents are too ill and elderly to travel to New York with me to visit them. They seem to settle on my dog instead.

I used to edit out these questions that concern my private life when I was writing about children. I think, in part, I did this to avoid the risk of "complicating" things too much by intermingling the details of my life in Massachusetts with the more important details of the stories and impressions that the children chose to share with me. I think that this was probably connected also with the old idea that I, like many other writers, used to have of trying to remove ourselves from any situation we described in order to convince the reader, or ourselves, that we had not become entangled in these situations in a way that might affect our objectivity or have some power to affect the way the children chose to speak to us.

I think most of us recognize, however, that we *do* become entangled and that we're never really neutral in the way that we conduct a conversation with a child. Even if we try to hide some of our biases and preferences and points of view, I think the children spy us out in our disguises very quickly and that this has an effect on what they will, or will not, say to us. If they sense that we believe in God or, even if we don't, that we are stirred by *their* belief, I think they are more likely to unveil their spiritual ideas not as perfunctory expressions of conventional belief but with the specificity of revelation. If they know we're fond of animals, they are more likely to speak fondly of an animal they loved and which, as is the case with several children who have told me of their dogs, has subsequently died. If, on the other hand, we give them an impression of ourselves as people who have no particularly passionate emotions about anything at all, they often start to sound as bored as we do.

No matter how we try, it's very hard to neutralize the impact of our preferences and personalities upon the dialogue of children; and even when we tell them very little of our private life or state of mind, I think they read us well and see our happiness or confidence, or faith or disappointment, in our manner and our style and our eyes.

There are times when all of us, for a variety of reasons, are inclined to understate our feelings or disguise some of our true beliefs in talking with a child. There are also times when I am simply tired, or distracted, or too lazy to be honest, and revert to mechanistic answers to the questions children ask of me. Or, if I'm really tired, I may cut things short and slip away and maybe gravitate into the kitchen to relax for a few minutes with Katrice. On other days, when I might be depressed or worried about something that the children have no way to know about — my father's health, for instance, or my mother's sometimes anxious and unsettled state of mind — it seems unthinkable to undermine the cheerful mood of children that I'm with by giving them the slightest hint of what it is that weighs me down. On these days I often do my best to simulate a sense of gaiety that I don't feel. It's hard to fool them, though.

Now and then I look at certain of the younger ones and can imagine small antennae waving just above their heads, receiving "signals" I don't even know I'm sending. I think of an afternoon when Elio and I had gone upstairs to read a book that he'd been given by his teacher. I'd been worried earlier that week because my father had been in the hospital. I thought that I could cover up my worries, but I wasn't doing a good job.

Elio started looking at a story in his book and read the title: "Who Is Tapping at My Window?" As he turned to the first page and started reading, he looked up to make sure I was listening. I said something that I hoped would reassure him, but I knew he sensed that I was struggling to pay attention. As he turned the pages, studying the pictures and pronouncing words phonetically, as he had learned to do in school, he kept peeking up at me from time to time to study my expression.

At one point he noticed I was staring out the window.

"Jonathan?"

"Yes?" I said.

"What are you looking at?"

"I'm looking at a squirrel," I replied.

"For real?" he asked.

"No," I told him when I realized that he wasn't going to allow me to deceive him. "I was thinking of my father."

"Where does your father live?"

"In Massachusetts," I replied.

"How old is your father?"

"He'll be 92 in a few months."

His eyes opened wide at this big number.

"Is your father going to die?"

"I hope not," I replied.

"I hope not too!" said Elio.

He looked at me then for a long, long time and followed my eyes across the room and out the window into the garden of St. Ann's, as if he thought that maybe he would somehow see "the squirrel" that he knew I only had pretended to have seen.

"I knew that you were thinking about something sad," he said at last.

"How could you tell?"

"Because you looked like you were going to cry."

He patted my wrist and stroked it with the backside of his hand. "Do you feel better now?"

"Much better!" I replied.

It was the truth. I did feel better when he touched my arm. The softness of his question and the gentle gesture of his hand gave me a deeper sense of consolation than I'd felt in many days. I'd been having conversations with my father's doctors that were necessary prior to a surgical procedure, which had stirred up all the fears identified with surgery for people of his age. When Elio touched my arm, my worries didn't simply "go away," as children often say about "bad feelings," but they didn't seem so paralyzing now. Talking with my father's doctors had to do with risks of anesthesia, with percentages and possibilities that he might not awaken. Elio's hand, his two conspicuous front teeth, his flannel shirt, his worried eyes within his upturned face, his sensitive expression, had to do with kindliness, and hope, and continuities.

I had been cleaning out my father's office during the preceding week. While going through a file case that held the records of his fifty years as a physician, I had found a picture of him as a child. The picture was from 1912, when he was six years old, almost the age of Elio. He was wearing knickers and a long-sleeved shirt, leaning against his father, who was wearing an attractive, formal-looking suit, a shirt with a round collar, and a broad and thickly knotted tie. My father's hand was holding his father's hand. The photo had a brownish tinge.

My grandfather had come from Russia seven years before that photograph was taken: the start of a century that now was nearly at its end. I had hoped my father would live on to see the start of the next century. Now I knew this was uncertain, and it was a selfish prayer in any case, more for my own sake than for my father's.

My mother is older than my father. She was 93 that year and had been reasonably well, but when my father had grown ill and went into the hospital, I saw a lost look in her eyes I'd never seen before. When we were talking in her bedroom later in the week, she looked away from me, into a distance that I could not see or understand. I had to speak in a loud voice to bring her back so she would see that I was there and speak to me directly. I showed her the picture of my father that I'd found. She said, "Your grandfather was a handsome man, but no man that I ever met was as good-looking as your father!"

My grandfather grew up in a town in the Ukraine. He came from Amsterdam to Boston on a cattleboat. He was a tailor. My grandmother sold eggs and milk and ice and, later, other groceries. Elio's grandfather came from Puerto

Rico. His mother worked at a drugstore near the church. I don't know what his father did for work before he had to go away.

Late in the afternoon, when I was downstairs in the afterschool, Elio followed me into the kitchen. Once we were alone and out of sight of other children, he gave me a figure of a man, which he had made out of pipe cleaners, and a sheet of paper on which he had drawn a picture of a man, a moon, a house, and a small boy.

"When somebody you know does something nice for you," he asked me, "does it make you happy?"

"Yes," I said. "It does."

"Me too. *Very* happy," he replied.

Then he went off to play and I went off to get the train. When I saw him the next day he didn't say a word about my father or the other things we'd talked about that afternoon; but there was something different in our friendship after that.

Holy Water

"Jonathan?" says Elio.

"Yes?" I say.

"Guess what?"

"What?"

"Last night I was looking out the window of my bed-room . . ."

He says it in a prefatory way, but then he stops; and so I have to ask him what he saw.

"I saw the moon!"

I try to think of something I can say about the moon.

"Guess what?" he says again.

"What?" I ask.

"I saw that he was *happy!*"

"How could you tell?"

"I could see he has a happy mouth," he says, as if he truly thinks about the moon the way that you could think about a human being.

He asks me dozens of questions that begin in the same way: by asking me to guess something that he's about to say. I'm sure he knows that grown-ups cannot read his mind and have no way to guess what he's about to say. It's more like a game, or even something like a story-teller's "setup," to create anticipation, so that when he finally decides to tell me what he's first asked me to guess I will be properly impressed.

"Guess what?" he asks the next day when I come into the afterschool.

"What?" I say.

"I saw a bumblebee last night."

"Where did you see it?"

"In my house."

"What did you do?"

"My uncle killed him with a shoe."

A moment after that, he asks me if I know the way to draw a picture of a shoe. I find a piece of paper and sit down and try to draw a shoe.

"Is your dog still sick?" he asks me while I'm working on my picture of a shoe.

I tell him she's not really sick. "She just has to rest her leg a few more days."

"Jonathan?"

"Yes?" I say.

"When she's all better, can you bring her here to visit?"

"Maybe," I say, carefully, because he's asked me this before.

He looks dissatisfied by this.

"How big is your dog?"

"Almost as big as you."

"Do you have a picture of your dog?"

I take out my wallet and pull out a picture of my dog, a four-year-old retriever, lying upside down in my backyard, her four paws in the air. He studies the picture, running his finger along her stomach and her tail.

"Jonathan?"

"Yes?" I say.

"Can you show me how to draw a picture of a dog?"

While I'm drawing a picture of a dog, he asks, "Do you know how many ways there are to draw a picture of the sun?"

"No," I say. "How many?"

"Two."

"How do you know?"

"My teacher told me."

At my request, he draws two pictures of the sun: one of them a circle in the middle of the page with lines that radiate out in all directions, and one of them a curving line drawn in the corner of the page with four lines spreading out in four directions.

I ask him if there's any other way to draw the sun.

"I don't think so," he replies. A moment later, he's forgotten this and asks if I can make a figure that looks like an animal from a pipe cleaner.

Most of the things that seem to hold his fascination don't remain the same for very long. Ideas pass in and out of his attention like the fireflies he chases in the garden of St. Ann's on summer nights. Tomorrow afternoon, when he comes racing through the doorway of the afterschool and throws his backpack on the floor and heads directly for the kitchen to report to Miss Katrice on what he did, or didn't do, that he was supposed to do in school, he probably will not be thinking about bumblebees or of the happiness or sadness of the moon.

Elio's mother comes for him a little before six o'clock and often stays a while to chat with Mother Martha or Katrice. Her husband is, she tells me, "upstate"—which is shorthand among many people in Mott Haven for the prison system. Elio rides six hours with her sometimes on the bus to visit him on Saturdays or Sundays.

She told me earlier this year that Elio was diagnosed with a heart murmur. He's spoken of this too, but when I asked him what it means, he said he didn't know. "There's something wrong around my heart," he said, and rubbed his fingers in a circle on his chest but didn't look concerned. He has, as I have said, a round and friendly face and, while he isn't fat, his arms and cheeks are chubby. Some of the mothers in the neighborhood refer to him as "Pork Chop," which the Spanish-speaking women say in Spanish, where it has a softer sound — *"Chuleta"* — than in English.

I asked him once how frequently he prays.

He answered, "Every time I eat."

"Every time?" I asked.

He looked careful, as if there might be a trap for him in this, and he began to make exceptions.

"Not when I eat cookies. . . ."

"Not at school. . . ."

"Not when I eat potato chips. . . ."

He does this frequently, first making an impressive statement and then nibbling around its edges until it has been diminished just enough so that it's not exactly fibbing.

Every so often, when we're by ourselves, he asks me questions about God that take me by surprise because he asks them in apparent confidence that I will know the answers. I know how to draw a picture of a dog and I know things about the moon and I can multiply and I can drive a car and buy a ticket on a plane and get from Boston to New York and back again and not get lost and I can sometimes help to make sure that he gets a toy he wants. So I suppose it's natural for him to think that I would also know the answers to his questions on religion.

He asks these questions to Katrice as well.

"Yesterday afternoon," she says, "he asked me if I think that God is powerful." When she told him he should ask this to the priest, he went upstairs and questioned Mother Martha.

"Mother Martha told him that the Lord works miracles if we believe in Him with all our hearts," she says. "Later he came down into the kitchen and he said, 'If God makes miracles, how come He never helps me to pick up my toys?'

"So help me, Jonathan," she says, one hand against her breast, "I had to laugh!"

As simple as some of these questions seem, however, Elio, like many of the children here, has complicated thoughts about the relative degree of power that God exercises in his life. He also seems to see some mutuality in their relationship. He doesn't seem to doubt that God has power to affect his life, but he believes that he has power too, because his own behavior, as he seems to be convinced, can help determine whether God feels good or bad. God is pleased—"He's happy!"—when a child does what he's supposed to do. But when a child misbehaves, as he expressed it to me once, "God cries."

"How do you know God cries?" I asked.

"I can hear God crying," he replied.

"You can *hear* Him?"

"Yes," he said. "If I do something bad. . . ."

"What do you do?"

"I go to the priest."

"Who is the priest?"

"Mother Martha," he replied.

"What do you say?"

"Can you please give me bless?"

"What does she do?"

"She blesses me," he said.

"How does she bless you?"

He looked puzzled by this question and he answered first, "I can't remember."

After a while, he said, "I remember."

So I asked, "What does she do?"

"She goes upstairs."

"Why does she go upstairs?"

"To get the bowl," he said.

"What bowl?" I asked.

"A shining bowl."

I asked him if he knows what's in the bowl.

"Whole-fly water," he said carefully.

"What does that mean?"

"Special water," he replied.

"What makes it special?"

"I don't know."

"What does she do with it?"

"She sprinkles it," he said.

I've asked him to describe this ritual with "whole-fly water" several times. Each time he describes it somewhat differently.

I asked him once, "How does she sprinkle it?"

"With a big spoon," he replied.

Later that day, he changed the story slightly. "No," he said. "With a big *stick*."

Another time, I asked him where the special water comes from and he said he didn't know, but then he guessed, "From underneath the church?"

A day later, I asked him the same question and he said he thought there was "a special faucet" somewhere in the church.

The actual origins of the special water—where it comes from, how it gets into the church, and how it ends up in the pastor's bowl—are somewhat clouded in his understanding, as they are in mine as well. But his belief in blessings and his faith that there is something special in the "whole-fly water" seem not to be cloudy in the least.

"If Mother Martha blessed me I'd be talkin' nice to people and I wouldn't fight no more," he told me once when he'd been chastised by Katrice for fighting in the afterschool and was consigned again to temporary isolation on the milk box in the corner of the kitchen.

He brooded about his situation, leaning on one elbow in what seemed the deepest thought, perplexed, I guess, about the reason why he misbehaves.

"Something is making me bad," he said at last. "Make it go away."

His puzzlement and brooding seem to be assuaged by the idea of being sprinkled with the special water in the pastor's silver bowl.

I've asked other children if they know what makes the water holy. None of them has ever given me an answer that was not bemused or whimsical, or else outrightly funny. I've never dared to ask this question to the priest. I've more or less assumed the water must be given sacramental meaning through the recitation of a prayer; but whether this is done here at the church or somewhere else, and who exactly is allowed to do it, I don't know.

The big stick Elio alluded to, which I've now seen as it was being used, is called an "aspergillum" and is maybe seven inches long. The pastor dips it in the silver bowl and lifts it high above the children's heads, then shakes it many times in all directions. The ritual has less solemnity than I expected. The younger children, in particular on hot days in the summer, seem to find the sprinkling of water on their heads a mostly physical delight. They chatter like sparrows gathered near a spray of water from a fountain in a park. Elio's tears—his sorrow, anger, even his contrition—seem to be forgotten. He glows with pleasure as the water trickles down his face and soaks his shirt.

What does holy water mean to children?

Priests and ministers I ask give different answers, some of which are narrowly liturgical but most of which are more informal and impressionistic, sometimes even rather down-to-earth. Their answers often undermine my expectation that I'm in the presence of the metaphysical.

I try to ask these kinds of questions carefully because I do not want to give offense to strict believers. Most of the ministers and priests I talk with, happily, don't seem to be offended easily. They seem, in fact, to be a whole lot more relaxed than I about these matters. Perhaps because they know I'm Jewish they are being purposely informal, so as not to make me feel excluded from a Christian mystery. They seem to understand, however, why I'm fascinated by these questions, and I think they also understand the hesitation that I sometimes feel in asking for an explanation.

I once asked Elio if he could tell me what the holy water means to him. He simply said, "It's fun!" Maybe that's the whole of it; but I don't really think it is. I think my question seemed too personal and that his answer was intended to prevent me from pursuing it too far.

I asked Mother Martha once what it is like to wash the children's feet on Holy Thursday before Easter, which is done at St. Ann's, as in many Christian churches. Her answer was the same as Elio's. "Fun!" she replied, no more than that, no reference to the feet of the apostles.

I asked her whether pastors are intended to feel humbled by the ritual of washing people's feet, because she doesn't wash only the children's feet, but those of grown-ups, strangers from the street for instance, too.

"No," she said. "It doesn't have that meaning and it's not like that at all."

"What is the purpose of it, then?" I asked.

"It prepares our hearts for Easter," she said simply, and she said again, "Besides . . . it's fun!" and she would give me no more information.

I know that it annoys her when I ask too many of these questions, which I seem to do with a remarkable consistency, and sometimes thoughtlessly, I'm sure, on days when she's preoccupied with worries of which I am unaware. She gets impatient with me and is forced to cut me off abruptly.

Too often I forget how seldom she has time for speculations of the kind with which I'm able to indulge myself. Katrice once told me that she hasn't had a holiday in seven years. Only when she's with the children does she seem to let herself relax. Even on those days when she's surrounded by the unexpected crises that come up repeatedly—a teenager arrested, a family in the neighborhood evicted from their home, a parishioner in Lincoln Hospital about to enter surgery, a homeless man she first met in the subway many years ago who is about to die—the playfulness of children such as Elio elicits playfulness in her as well. When Mother Martha sprinkles holy water over Elio his face is radiant. But hers is radiant as well. Both of them are laughing.

Watching them, I start to understand the meaning of a priest in Massachusetts who had told me he believes that children minister to grown-ups quite as much as grown-ups minister to children. "Holy water blesses children who receive it, but the faces of the children also bless the one who gives it. The spirits of the children and the longings of the grown-up intertwine and wrap themselves around each other. In this way the healing that the blessing brings goes back and forth."

It's easy to believe this when you see the pastor mobbed by all the little ones as she comes down the stairs into the afterschool holding the bowl of holy water in her hands. "Of all the things I have to do here at the church," she told me once, "this is the part I love the most."

There was so much happiness and youthful expectation in her voice! Weariness and worry over tragedies and troubles of all kinds appeared to fall away. The boys and girls came running as they saw her on the stairs.

"Mother Martha! Mother Martha!"

Nancy and Katrice were watching from the side as Mother Martha raised the silver staff and shook it wildly in the air.

"Bless me, Mother!"

"Me too, Mother!"

"Don't forget *me,* Mother!"

"Bless me, Mother!"

"Bless me!"

"Bless me!"

"Bless me!"

CHAPTER 6

Bread and Wine

Lucia says her grandmother was sick last night. She doesn't tell me what was wrong but says she fell down in the bathroom and her sister had to help her to get up and brought her orange juice; so I assume she may be diabetic.

When I ask who lives with her, she says her mother, sister, and grandmother. She says her father doesn't live with them and that her mother's father died of gunshots at the front door of her mother's house when he was 32 years old. When I ask her what she loves most in the world, she says, "I love my heart."

She manages to get some reference to her heart, or to "God's heart," or just to "hearts" in general, into a lot of conversations.

"How powerful is God?" I ask.

"He's powerful to make hearts," she replies.

I asked her once to list the things she thought most beautiful in life. She jumped right into this by saying, "Hearts!" When she drew pictures of herself, her pets, or people that she knew, she generally drew them with unusually big hearts.

"God *needs* to make hearts," she told me firmly one day when I questioned her about this. It had an almost brazenly didactic sound.

Stephanie, who is older than Lucia, also speaks of "God's heart," and her own heart. When she described her mother the first time we talked, she said, "She works very hard. She does the best she can. She tries to pay the rent. . . . She's a single mother. . . . She gave us our heart."

I asked her once what she believed would make the world a better place.

"What would make the world better is God's heart," she answered. "I know God's heart is already in the world. But I would like if He would . . . *push* the heart more into it. Not just halfway. Push it more!"

Religious writers often speak of faith with the same muscularity of language. Struggling for selflessness is seen as a demanding occupation. God is asked to help believers in their effort to reject the pettiness of selfish feelings. Sometimes ministers and priests use images of "grappling" or "wrestling" with one's emotions or one's fear of losing faith, and they enlist God as an ally in a form of inner combat that sounds like a physical encounter.

Stephanie's image is a little less internalized. "God's heart" sounds like a gigantic pump that needs to be positioned slightly better in the world in order to assure a better circulation of good feelings.

Many children speak of their relationship to God in relatively passive, acquiescent ways. Stephanie sounds more demanding. "Push it more!" she says. It sounds like what a high school coach might say in exhortation of an athlete: not "an argument with God" perhaps, but certainly a friendly effort to encourage Him to do a better job.

Stephanie is a thoughtful girl with dark eyes and dark hair. She dresses soberly, in black or brown. Some afternoons, there are dark circles underneath her eyes. Her voice is utterly sincere. Her life is hard. Her mother's life is hard. Her father, like Lucia's father, is not present in her home. To "push the heart" beyond the pettiness of hate or envy or resentment is, in some ways, a diurnal job for both of them, as for too many children who grow up here in these buildings where some of the rooftops can afford a clear view of the prison colony to which so many of their older brothers and their fathers have already been consigned. Asking God to help a little more with this does not sound disrespectful.

Stephanie's almost eleven now. Lucia's only eight. When Lucia speaks about "God's heart" and draws her many cheerful pictures in which hearts are prominent, it isn't always clear to what degree her sentiments are still inhabiting the world of grade-school valentines. She wanders back and forth between the saccharine and the sincerely moving. But Stephanie's tenacious in rejecting oversweetness. She lives with far too many serious concerns to get relief out of banality.

I asked her once, "What makes you cry?"

"I cry . . . when I miss my father," she replied, "or if my mother would pass away."

Her brother, Matthew, says that when he grows up he would like to serve in the Marines or Army. Stephanie's two years younger than her brother but reacts to this as if she were his mother. "I want you to stay right here," she says. "I don't want you to die."

She has reason to be scared that people dear to her may die. "Some of my family members passed away," she says. "My grandmother's nephew, his mother, and his sister. . . ."

Matthew explains that first "the daughter and the mother died of AIDS" and "then the son"—his cousin—died from being shot here on the street.

When people pray, says Stephanie, they "don't only talk to God." They also "talk to whoever is dead in their family."

I ask if that's the meaning that it has for her to pray.

"Yes," she says. "I talk to people in my family . . . and the angels."

I once asked her what she thought the angels looked like.

"To me," she said, "they have the faces of the people that I love."

Stephanie and Matthew are two of the nicest and most honorable children I have ever known. Their religious convictions don't seem superficial. The imagery they use may be suggested by the words they hear from grown-ups or the liturgies they hear in church; but they transmute these images and make them into something of their own. "God's presence in the world" is a familiar, somewhat dulling notion, often heard in church. "God's heart" at work in pumping love into the world sounds more ambitious and, to me at least, it's more consoling.

I wish I could believe in God the way the children do; but there are many days when other kinds of "pumps"—the pump of ideology, the pump of avarice, the pump of injured dignity—appear to have a more relentless power than the heart of God. I guess the truth is that the vividness of Stephanie's beliefs—especially her nice idea of coaching God to do a better job—seems beautiful to me and yet I can't help saying to myself, "It's just a metaphor."

The effect her language has on me is not, I am afraid, authentically "religious" in the way most priests or ministers would use that word; it has to do with a desire to believe, more than belief itself. And yet the images the children use have a compelling hold that is much more, for me, than simply grown-up fascination with the various particulars of juvenile belief. Their words entangle my imagination. They "encircle" me somehow. When I reply to them I find I'm asking questions that might almost presuppose that I believe the things we talk about are real.

Teachers and clinicians comment on this now and then. They ask me if the questions I ask children in this kind of interchange are calculated in some way that will "elicit" their beliefs by seeming to participate in their imaginary world — or, as one physician put it, by "appearing to walk right into their fantasies."

I would be glad if I deserved some credit for such careful planning, but I don't think this is true. It would be closer to the truth to say that when a boy like Elio or girl like Stephanie is in a thoughtful mood and chooses to reveal a hidden place within the secret world of their imagination or belief, it feels to me as if I've just been handed a gold-plated invitation to come in and visit someplace where I've never been before. Once I look into that room, I want to enter.

I cannot receive the bread and wine when they are offered at the altar railing of St. Ann's. The state of mind in which they are received remains unknown to me and holds an element of mystery for my imagination. But there are many other mysteries to be discovered in the classrooms and the garden of an old stone church in the South Bronx, and one of the most perfect ones is when a child, for no reason you can think of, feels the impulse to unlock a secret from her soul. Sometimes it happens when we're sitting at a table in the afterschool, sometimes when we're walking in the garden of the church, sometimes in a whispered message through the heated tunnel of the child's hands placed right beside my ear.

It doesn't happen often when we're in a crowded room with other kids around. It almost never happens when a number of adults are present, or when I have just arrived here from a crowded place—a lecture hall, for instance, where I may have spoken in Manhattan, or a workshop with the teachers at a public school—and bring the sense of "busy occupation" with me to St. Ann's. The children sense the difference right away. They recognize the crispness of a public mood that comes out of a different world and may not seem to welcome private revelations.

This is true as well in visiting the homes of people in the neighborhood. I've come here with a friend, or several friends, perhaps at night after we've stopped somewhere for dinner, and it frequently has altered almost everything. It's not so much that people who have known me for a time talk differently when there are other people with us in the room; it's more the case that I am different in some way of which I'm not aware but which is evident to someone who already knows me well. It's as if, without needing to say it, we've agreed that this will be a different, less important, kind of evening and that we will save the things that matter for the next time I am here when there will be only the two of us.

A nun I know who's worked for years with families in poor neighborhoods speaks of a certain mood of "unexamined receptivity," which does not mean, she says, merely the willingness to listen carefully or patiently. "It has to do with quieting your state of mind as you *prepare* to listen. It means not pressing on too fast to get to something that you think you 'need to get to' as the 'purpose' or 'objective' of the conversation, which is what a journalist must usually do. There is a difference between 'getting' and 'receiving.'"

The distinction comes to mind when I've been visiting in public schools. I'm not usually aware of being in a "public" state of mind, or more "acquisitive" or less "receptive" state of mind, when I'm at school, but possibly I am. I do know that the way the St. Ann's children talk with me in class is generally very different from the way they speak with me in quiet situations.

When I visit in their class, the children often seem tremendously excited — it's a *big* surprise for children to see someone they already know from outside school right there beside their teacher in the classroom. They're always friendly and they answer me politely; but their answers, at least during class discussions, lack the pungent authenticity they'd have if we were in a far less public situation. They seem more like "generic answers," like set-pieces, or performances, that are the products of my unintended choreography.

Even children who, in other situations, have expressed the most engagingly eccentric points of view can start to churn out rather dull pronouncements and high-minded observations about "love" and "goodness," "faith in God" and "inter-racial understanding" when I question them in front of the full class at school: unoriginal but honorable sentiments expressed in styles that are not uniquely theirs, as if they feel somehow that this is what I am soliciting.

It may seem obvious that "school" is not the same as "church" and that a child in a group is likely to sound different from the way she does when she's alone or only with close friends; but I think the role and state of mind of the adult are factors too. The children are in a different state of mind when they're at school; but I am different also and, even if I do not realize this, the children seem to sense it every time.

There's something about silence and not being in a hurry and not being in an overly convivial or overly determinative state of mind, or one that's loaded with too much intentionality, and something also about being

unaccompanied, that seem to give a message about receptivity. I also think that children need some reason to believe that what they say will not be heard too clinically, or
journalistically, or put "to use" too rapidly, and that the
gift they give us will be taken into hands that will not seize
too fast upon their confidence, or grasp too firmly, or attempt to push an idea to completion when it needs to be
left open, incomplete, and tentative a while.

The greatest fear I have in talking with a boy or girl as
sensitive as Elio or Stephanie is of an unintended intellectual invasiveness, of entering not just the room to which I
was invited, but the next room too, and feeling suddenly
that I have stepped into a place where I do not belong and
maybe don't deserve to be. I think of the image of a "place"
or "room" because so many of the dreams and longings
and religious thoughts the children share with me have so
much structural completeness! They seem like houses—
"dwelling-places"—or like little rooms within a complicated
building. The space within them always feels mysterious.

I think of a ten-year-old I met in 1993 who knew my
beagle had just died and reassured me that I'd have the
right to visit her "on weekends" when (or if!) I went to
heaven and who also told me that "you don't need money"
to buy what you need after you die, because in heaven you
can "pay for things you need with smiles."

Faith, says the author of the Letter to the Hebrews, is
"the substance of things hoped for, the evidence of things not
seen." A friend of mine in the newspaper world who views
religion skeptically, and seems embarrassed when I speak
of the beliefs of children in a way that sounds too credulous
to him, does what he can to credit me with a degree of
rationality. "It's nice the way you play along with them," he
says—I'm sure, not meaning to be condescending. "It's
probably good for kids like them that they believe these
things because there may be little else they can believe in."

It doesn't seem that way to me at all. When children speak of "things not seen" but which they are convinced they see, I want to see them too. Theologians use a Latinate and rather fancy term, "prevenient grace," to speak of unfamiliar moments such as these. "A flash of Easter" is the simpler and less imposing way that one religious writer speaks about these moments. I think of them like tiny objects of great value that you'd never find in any store or any library or any university.

I do not intend to hint by this in any way at all, even the most indirect, that all these little kids, as they spin out their wishes, hopes, and prayers, are actually minor theologians in disguise. The tendency to seize upon a child's tender words and lift them to the level of prophetic truth is a familiar risk for those of us who like to be with children and enjoy their conversation. Some children do create their own diminutive theologies; but they are children, and not "child theologians," and it adds no halo to the head of a real child to suggest that there is something magisterial in all of this. I simply think the gifts of faith and fantasy they bring to us are often beautiful and wise in their simplicity. To me, these are the bread and wine; and I am always thankful to receive them.

For weeks, I've promised Pineapple I'd visit her at home. Finally, one Saturday in May when I am in the neighborhood, I have a chance to keep my promise.

Her hospitable sweetness is surprisingly mature. Her mother is out; she's at a neighbor's birthday party with her sisters. Her aunt is resting in one of the other rooms. She leads me to a sofa in the living room and pats the cushion where she seems to think I'll be most comfortable.

"Jonathan," she says when I seem hesitant to sit, "please make yourself at home."

JONATHAN KOZOL

As soon as I sit down, she asks if I would like something to drink. When I say yes, she goes first to a liquor cabinet and, opening the door to show me an unopened bottle of Courvoisier and several miniatures of Scotch, she asks what I would like. When I say I'd rather something that's not alcoholic, she goes to the kitchen, where she chooses a tall glass that has a "Big Bird" decal on the side, fills the glass with greenish-yellow Kool-Aid, finds a napkin and a coaster, and then brings it out and sets it all down on the table next to me.

"Are you going to sit down with me?" I ask.

She sits cross-legged on the floor in front of me. Her arms folded, her stomach sticking out, her multitudinous white barrettes arranged with artistry throughout her braided hair, she nods at me as I lift the glass, as if she's absolutely satisfied with this arrangement; but she recognizes that I feel a little shy and so she tells me for a second time, "Please make yourself at home."

I haven't had Kool-Aid in fifty years. It tastes delicious. I drink it, almost all, in one long gulp. She's eight years old. We talk of this and that. She later brings me to one of the other rooms to meet her aunt and opens up another door so I can see her bedroom, where there are two bunkbeds in which she and her two sisters sleep. The mattresses are covered with thick quilts. On one of the beds, which she tells me is hers, a family of animals is tucked beneath the quilt and linen where it's folded over.

Before I leave, she asks if I would like another glass of Kool-Aid.

"Yes," I say.

She brings me into the kitchen this time, where there are more animals with friendly faces stuck by magnets to the white refrigerator door. When I leave, she comes out to the landing in the hallway and looks down as I look up at every landing, waving to me with one of her hands.

I had asthma earlier this afternoon and had been worried about climbing the five flights to Pineapple's apartment. But once I arrived, I forgot that I was feeling bad, and by the time I leave, that pressure in my chest is gone completely. Heading down the stairs to the front door, I want to cheer out loud and tell the good news to the people on the sidewalk: "Guess what? I'm all better! I can breathe!"

A man sitting beside me in a Pentecostal service at a storefront on Brook Avenue once said to me, "You're not from the neighborhood." When I said no, he shook my hand and said I should feel welcome. "If you were lookin' to get you some church, you came to the right place."

I never forgot that phrase — "get you some church" — because it sounded like good food that you were being offered and could count on if you really wanted to be filled. I thought of those words again as I was leaving Pineapple's apartment. "Do not be conformed to this world," said Paul in his epistle to the little band of Christians who had taken domicile in Rome, "but be transformed." Pineapple's home is not a church. Her hands aren't priestly hands. But I have been changed by knowing her.

CHAPTER 7

Things As They Are

S upper at St. Ann's is served at five o'clock. The
children tend to be unruly when they're getting
settled in their seats to say their prayer. Today is no exception; but this afternoon, for reasons I don't know, Katrice's
daughter has decided it is time to draw the line against
rambunctious misbehavior.

"This is God's house," she says. "We all care for you
and love you. We have fun with you. We love to be with
you. We want you to be happy when you're here. But I
also want you to respect the food God gives you because
there are many hungry children in this neighborhood who
never have enough to eat and we are blessed to have
enough to give you and I want you to be grateful."

Katrice comes from the kitchen as the children take
their places at the tables and stands at a distance with her
arms crossed, watching certain children with particular
attention. She nods at every word her daughter speaks.

There's an easy to-and-fro between them, like call-and-response. When Nancy asks the children to be grateful for their food, her mother says, "That's right!" and adds, "They have to take their prayers more seriously too."

Nancy has a natural authority that is respected by the children. Wearing a blue sweatshirt and blue velvet hat that looks like a beret, she insists on an extended silence, which is broken only when one of the younger children, Raven, lifts her hand. Nancy looks down at her niece, who's sitting right beneath her arms.

"I have to go to the bathroom," says the child in a voice of high alert.

"Okay," says her aunt. "Be quick."

Raven dashes off, but she comes back so fast it hardly seems she's had the time to run in a small circle in the bathroom. Once she's seated with the other children at her table, Nancy leads the children in their prayer.

The older children and the staff pass out the meals, which look like airline meals and are prepackaged. Throughout the room the younger children rustle the cellophane wrappers of their suppers simultaneously.

"Everyone's doing that now," says Amber Acevedo when the children shake the cellophane. She says it in a "knowing" way, as if she were inducting me into a ritual I wouldn't understand because I haven't been here for two weeks.

I ask her why they're doing it.

"Search me!" she says.

Amber used to be a very wild little girl. Her behavior seems much calmer now. She's also dressed more neatly than she was the last time that I saw her here. Her hair, which often falls over her eyes, is parted in the middle and drawn back into a ponytail. But when I compliment her on how nice she looks and on how well-behaved she's been, she gives me a wicked look and seems to take this as a challenge to convince me that I'm wrong. First, she doesn't say her prayer. Then she doesn't eat her food but gets out of her chair and starts collecting bread from all the other children at the table. She piles the slices up between her hands, then crushes them into a ball and pats it hard and takes a big bite out of it and chews it with her mouth wide open.

"She's eating it!" says Elio.

"It's good," says Amber, stuffing more of the compacted ball of bread into her mouth.

"That's one little cuckoo girl," Pineapple says.

But Amber doesn't seem to mind. She keeps on chewing with her mouth wide open so that everyone can see the wet and messy chunks of dough stuck in between her teeth.

There are a few new children this month at St. Ann's. The littlest child in the group is six and a half years old but doesn't look much more than four. Her name is Mariposa. The older children at the table smile when she squeezes in between us. When I ask how old she is, she holds up seven fingers and says, "Six."

"She's only a baby," says Pineapple.

"I'm *not* no baby!" says the child. "I was in my mother's stomach when I was a baby!"

"What's your mother's name?" I ask her.

"Momma," she replies.

For dinner tonight the children have hamburgers. The six-year-old encounters her hamburger like an adversary. She stabs the floppy piece of meat with her white plastic fork, lifts the whole thing to her mouth and takes one bite, then puts it on a slice of bread and holds it down with her forefinger while she pulls the fork out, and then puts the other piece of bread on top of it.

There are five potato balls on the same plate as the hamburger. She tries to spear one with her fork but has no luck, then tries to scoop it with her spoon but cannot get it to her mouth before it rolls onto her lap, then to the floor. She tries another potato with the spoon, but this one rolls off also. A third and fourth potato follow the first two underneath the table. She points beneath the table with a dumbfounded expression.

When I point to the potato ball that sits alone now on her plate and ask her, "What's this called?" she doesn't know the word. She asks me, "Apple?" She doesn't know the word "hamburger" either. She does know "milk" and guesses "bread" correctly.

Nancy tells me that Miss Rosa put the child in first grade initially but had to move her back to kindergarten — "because she's just so tiny and knows absolutely nothing about *anything!*" Her mother later tells me that the child is asthmatic. "She has her pump," her mother says — Proventil, the same yellow-orange pocket pump that hundreds of the children of Mott Haven carry with them, even though there are much better products on the market now. She also has a bedside unit for emergencies. Her mother takes her to the hospital repeatedly.

I ask her mother where they live.

"Cypress," she replies, the street at the top of the hill that overlooks a large and controversial waste incinerator that went into operation here three years before.

The presence of the waste incinerator so close to the homes of people here has been a source of worry and frustration for the parents of the neighborhood since plans for its construction were revealed, which was a few years prior to the time I started coming to St. Ann's. It's a medical incinerator, burning what are known as "red-bag products" — hypodermic needles, soiled bedding, amputated limbs, and embryos—which are brought here every day from fourteen hospitals in New York City.

It had been forced upon the people of Mott Haven, very much against their will, by powerful financial interests after an attempt to build a comparable burner on the East Side of Manhattan had been stopped by people there, who rightly feared the damage it might do their children's health. The financiers, who, Mother Martha tells me, had close ties to City Hall, contrived instead to put it in the South Bronx not far from St. Ann's, where asthma rates already were among the highest in the nation.

Neighborhood activists and parents, buttressed by environmentalists and doctors, had protested the construction of the burner. The New York Times, however, had discredited the protests of the parents. In a decisive editorial, which the paper ran beneath the headline "Wasteful Protest in the Bronx" before the waste incinerator started into operation, The Times had argued that the protests were "misguided."

"It would be a tragic mistake," the paper said, if "panicky fears" of people in the neighborhood were able to halt construction and delay the testing of a "modern . . . state-of-the-art" incinerator which, it said, was then "nearing completion." Medical wastes, The Times agreed, are "dangerous" and "no one wants them in a residential neighborhood." Under zoning laws, "the only place" for these kinds of facilities, the paper said, is in an area where "residential construction is forbidden."

I don't know what information the newspaper had at its disposal that the people in the neighborhood did not have; but, on the face of it, this writing was misleading. No matter how the area was zoned, the city had for several years been sending homeless families to live in the bulidings here, some of which were city-owned and others subsidized by federal funds. More than 5,000 children and 2,000 adults lived within a few blocks of the installation; and the 80-foot-tall smokestacks of the plant spewed out its toxins to a wider area in which some 40,000 people, all black or Hispanic, were residing.

Even after the incinerator was completed and began its operation, the parents of the neighborhood sustained their protests through the next six years as children who lived close to it grew sicker. It was at last shut down in fall of 1998, while I was writing this, when government agencies confirmed the worst fears of the parents by revealing that environmental laws had been ignored or broken countless times—at least 500 times, according to The New York Daily News—by those who ran the installation. Some of the children who live close to it seem healthier today. Other children in the area still suffer from severe attacks.

In some cases, doctors theorize, a child's lungs may have been sensitized so much that other factors such as cigarette smoke, stress, and even insect-infestation might set off a chain reaction that would not take place in children who had not sustained such long exposure to external toxins in their infancy. Other physicians, like John Rosen, a distinguished clinician in environmental sciences who has discussed this with me at great length, believe that other toxic factors in the area, including a large number of waste-transfer stations and extensive sludge depositories very close to densely populated neighborhoods of the South Bronx, continue to contaminate the air that children here are forced to breathe.

In Hunts Point alone, immediately adjacent to Mott Haven, there are forty garbage and recycling facilities, one of them a plant that turns most of the city's treated sewage into fertilizer. The stench that it gives off is bad enough so children "throw up on their way to school," according to an interview with parents in the New York publication

City Limits. Dr. Rosen also notes that the exhaust from diesel fuel is known to trigger asthma and that sanitation trucks waiting to unload mountains of trash from all over the city line up in certain neighborhoods for hours with their engines running.

Even if it can't be proven that the emanations of incinerators and the odors of these waste depositories are the only causes, or the most important causes, of the asthma that so many children suffer in this neighborhood, Mother Martha speaks of the aesthetic message kids are given by the knowledge that these ugly installations, which are almost never found in upscale neighborhoods like those in which the city's civic and financial leaders live, are thought to be appropriate for places where black and Hispanic children live. "Do children of doctors, financiers, and publishers," she asks, "have to look outside their windows at trash-burners every morning? Then why should little Mariposa have to do so?"

It should not take a priest to ask this question.

Isaiah is another of the kids who live on Cypress Avenue, or close to it, and suffer chronic asthma. I met him several years ago when he was not quite eight years old. He had an episode of asthma on the day we met. He also gets severe infections in the winter. As with many young asthmatics, his infections seem to settle in his chest.

Still, he's an optimistic child and he has a charming way of making friends with almost everyone he meets. When he used to go for walks with me, he'd strike up conversations with entire strangers. He also seemed to know the names of all the dogs and cats around the neighborhood and always said "Hello" or "Hi" to each of those he recognized. At home, he used to have a goldfish and a giant panda and eleven bears. His mother told me once she had to search around the house to "round up all the bears" at night and tuck them into bed with him according to a special hierarchy that he had ordained.

"Don't ask how many times I have to kiss those bears at night," she said, "before he'll go to sleep!"

On a winter night in 1996, during the week right after Christmas, I was coming up the hill from St. Ann's Avenue to visit with Katrice. Isaiah's mother, whose name is Becky, stopped me in the street. A small woman, wrapped in a thick padded jacket with a fur-lined hood, she resembled a stick-figure doll dressed as an Eskimo.

"Is this weather cold enough for you?" she asked.

"*Too* cold," I said.

"Would you like a cup of coffee?"

"Yes," I said.

So we went up together to her warm apartment, where Isaiah was sprawled out across the floor next to the sofa, looking at the books and toys he had received for Christmas. Becky took her jacket off and threw it on a chair and threw my coat on top of hers and went into the kitchen to make coffee but kept talking through the open doorway to Isaiah, who was looking at the pictures in one of the volumes of a juvenile encyclopedia that he had scattered all over the floor.

On the coffee table was a plastic helmet with a set of dual antennas. It turned out to be a space-age walkie-talkie, which, his mother told me from the kitchen, was "one of those rarities you see now and again—a child's toy that actually *works* for a few days after you bring it from the store."

"Want to see?"

He lifted the helmet from the table, showing me the

Velcro strap you were supposed to fix under your chin to keep the headphones tight against your ears.

His mother came back from the kitchen with the coffee while he looked around the room to find a second set of headphones with a wire curving out in front of them to hold a microphone.

I asked him if it worked outside the house.

"Don't even ask," said Becky as she set the coffee cups on the low table. "He had me running up and down the street last night to try it out!"

I tried to picture Becky standing out on St. Ann's Avenue at ten o'clock at night wearing this gadget while she listened to instructions being broadcast from Isaiah's bedroom.

"I know! I must have looked like somebody from Mars," she said, "with this contraption on my head, running around in circles in the snow while he's back here in 'Houston' sending me commands. 'Mission Control! Mission Control! Mission Control to Mommy! Do you read me?'"

Isaiah insisted upon showing me the way the walkie-talkie worked. He handed me the helmet, helped me pull it down over my head, then pressed the strap beneath my chin.

"How does it feel?"

"Excellent," I said.

"It's not too tight?"

"No. It's good."

"Okay. . . ." He took the other unit in his hand and went into the bedroom, which was just about twelve feet away. He closed the door. I sat and waited for him to get organized. His mother said, "What do you hear?"

"I can't hear anything," I said.

A moment later, he came from the bedroom — "Wait

a minute"—and bent down over my head and flicked the switch.

"Sorry about that. I forgot to turn it on."

He went back to the bedroom. This time I could hear a buzzing sound, but nothing more. Then, suddenly, his voice was loud and clear: "Hello?"

"Hello," I said.

"Can you hear me?"

"Yes!"

"I hear you too!"

"What room are you in?"

"I'm in the bedroom. Where are you?"

"I'm still here with your mother—in the living room."

"Tell her I said 'Hello!'"

"Hello!" I told his mother, who replied, "Hello!"

"Okay," he said. "I'm signing off. So long!"

"So long," I said.

"Okay!"

He came out of the bedroom looking pleased. "You see? It works."

His mother laughed because the truth is that he spoke so loud that she could hear him from his bedroom through the door.

"Take that thing off Jonathan's head," she said, "so he can have his coffee."

He released the strap and took the helmet from my head. His mother and I had coffee, which was lukewarm now. We talked about his schoolwork for a time. Becky told me, "He's in Mr. Geiger's class," a reference to a teacher I admire who has been a mainstay on the faculty of P.S. 30 in the years that I've been visiting the school.

Isaiah said, "He knows."

"Well, pardon *me* for speaking out of turn," his mother said.

"I thought you didn't know," he said.

His grades were good. His attendance was uneven, but he was — and he still is — one of the better students in his class. He writes well, likes math, is good in sports, particularly baseball. His mother coaches the team he plays on in the summer, organizes a reading group of children from the building, and gives supper to a number of the boys who live downstairs when she has extra food. She's had some serious problems that were caused by years of struggle with cocaine addiction, but she's also doing several things that win her the respect and gratitude of neighbors.

She was a political organizer in her youth and says she "used to hang out" with a group that she believes "was tied up with the Panthers." She's lived in Oakland, later in St. Louis. Her husband's "upstate — way up there near Canada." She reads political writers like James Baldwin and also likes what she refers to as "trash novels." As long as I have known her, there has been a Bible, open to the Psalms, on a small end-table at the left side of her sofa.

At eight o'clock she ran the water for Isaiah's bath. I said good night and went downstairs to see Katrice, who was expecting me an hour earlier. The building was quiet. There were Christmas cards and other decorations still on many of the doors, no cries or shouts or angry words, or groups of edgy-looking adolescents in the stairs.

I told Katrice about my visit with Isaiah. She asked me, "How's he doing?" since she knew about his chest infections and his asthma. When I told her that I didn't even ask about his health, because of all the foolishness about the walkie-talkie, she just laughed and said she saw his mother in the street the night before but couldn't figure out what she was doing with "that strange thing" on her head.

It's not all fun and jokes and walkie-talkies in Isaiah's life. I've been with him when things were far less wholesome and less happy. I remember sitting with him and his mother once in church when she was in recovery from drugs and taking medication to control her nerves. Her eyes were heavy-lidded and they glistened slightly. He kept looking up at her, and then at me. He seemed to be a little scared, and possibly embarrassed.

She had told me that she was in debt to a drug dealer at the time. Her husband, who was not in prison then, had misappropriated several thousand dollars' worth of heroin he was supposed to sell and then, as she explained it, had received "a serious warning" and had therefore simply disappeared. A few nights after he took off, she and Isaiah came back to their home and found their radio and TV set demolished and their clothes ripped up and thrown across the floor. The food from their refrigerator had been strewn around the kitchen. An inky substance had been poured into Isaiah's goldfish tank. His only fish was floating on the dirty surface of the water.

Isaiah knew the threats his father had received. He knew of all the trials that his mother had endured. He knew which things it was okay to talk about with me and other grown-ups at St. Ann's, and which things to avoid. When we talked, he'd signal areas he knew he shouldn't enter by a look or word that helped him navigate around the impermissible. I think he felt that he was part of a small "team of two"— his mother and himself— who had a set of secrets they must deal with on their own. I think he knew he could endanger her if he did not respect the rules and stratagems they had agreed on. At these times I would describe him as a rather careful child: careful in release of secrets, careful in release of vigilance, careful also in encountering an unexpected situation.

These ups and downs— a period of hopefulness, an episode of illness, a season of discouragement or tension when his mother's problems surface once again or when his asthma's bad—continue in his life up to the present time. He still can be ingeniously evasive in the things he says or will not say. He still gets chest infections in the winter. He can also be morose at times. At other times he's utterly spontaneous, irreverent, and relaxed. The only constant or, at least, recurrent cause of serious discomfort in his life, as long as I have known him, seems to be his asthma.

Asthma is a miserable illness for a child. It's a misery for grown-ups too, especially the elderly. Some of the older people at St. Ann's have asthma almost every day. Women at the church speak of constriction in their chest, "a pressure . . . right here on my breast," as one of the grandmothers says when she is not quite sick enough to use her pump but has that burdened look that's so familiar among people who have intermittent difficulty with their respiration. Many people here, of course, have more than intermittent "difficulty." They'll sit there wheezing in a chair in front of me, as eighty-year-old Mrs. Santos did one day last week, before she suddenly got up and said she had to go back to her home "to use the mask," by which Katrice explained she meant an oxygen machine.

I think that asthma's worse for children, though, because play is a part of childhood and children cannot play with real abandon when they feel so bad. Even mild asthma weighs their spirits down and makes it hard to smile easily, or read a book with eagerness, or jump into a conversation with entire spontaneity. They learn somehow to live with these discomforts. Nearly a quarter of the children have to bring their pumps with them to school and church. Most don't talk about their asthma very much if I don't ask. They reach for the pump when they feel wheezing coming on. If it gets worse, they go to Nancy or Katrice, who brings them up to Mother Martha. If they're in real danger, Mother Martha puts them in her car and races to the hospital.

Isaiah is like many of the other children in the gutsy way he handles this. The kids here get inured to certain things and learn how to be happy when they can. It is their life, and they must live it. Most of them do so with considerable courage, and without self-pity.

CHAPTER 8

Ordinary
Resurrections

S tudents from colleges not far from New York City
come to St. Ann's Church from time to time to get
to know the children. More young women do this than
young men, perhaps because their consciousness of gender
issues renders them more empathetic to the women of the
neighborhood, perhaps too because some of them hope to
become teachers.

Many of these politically engaged young women comment later on the strength of character and courage they
perceive in women at the church. Sometimes, though, they
comment also on the feelings of discouragement and resignation that they sense during their conversations. Then,
fearful of assuming too much from a single meeting, they
may ask if these are my impressions too.

I find it hard to answer. I'm reminded of how risky it
can be to think you know what even people who appear to

like you and confide in you may actually feel. I've made my share of errors by assuming too much on the basis of the conversations that I've had with people who befriend me.

Still, some impressions do sustain themselves over the course of years. Even with caution, I think it is accurate to say that many of the older people in Mott Haven who have talked with me at length feel *contradictory* emotions—and, at times, a roller-coaster of emotions—in regard to the conditions of their lives and prospects for their neighborhood. Episodes of resignation and discouragement are common; but so too are periods of hope inspired by specific signs of progress such as housing reconstruction, and parental activism, and reductions in the rate of homicide. Then, however, there are times of terrible frustration when these hopes are disappointed or when promised transformations of a neighborhood turn out to be primarily cosmetic, or selective in the economic groups they benefit.

Some of the grounds for optimism seem well-founded. New housing units, some of them attractive and surrounded by small lawns and metal railings, have been going up for several years in areas that had been devastated by abandonment and arson in preceding decades. HIV infection in young women remains high—the HIV infection rate for older adolescent females in Mott Haven is, according to physicians here, the highest in the nation—but pediatric HIV has been declining since new perinatal treatments were developed. Homicide is down, as is the use of crack cocaine; but heroin remains pervasive. The mass arrests of hundreds of young men have made some neighborhoods much safer but have also left too many families without fathers, sons, and brothers.

The press refers to the more positive developments in language borrowed from theology. "Miracle" and "resurrection" are two of the terms employed sometimes to draw attention to the hopeful aspects of the story. Words such as "rebirth" and "renaissance" are often used as well. The inclination to disown an old cliché about an inner-city neighborhood — the "ravaged" and "despairing" South Bronx of the past — only to invent a new one — the "restored" and "flourishing" and "optimistic" South Bronx of the present — is a constant risk to which the press is not immune. Like all clichés, the old one never told more than a part of the full story. (There were always people in the South Bronx who led normal and rewarding lives, attended school, held jobs, stayed free from drugs, in even the most troubled periods of time.) The new one is somewhat simplistic too. (Even amidst blocks of new or renovated houses, safer streets and better-tended parks, there still are far too many children losing years of life in separate and unequal schools that are abominations of apparently eternalized apartheid, and too many children who go hungry, and too many who cannot breathe freely.)

Still, there are genuine improvements in some areas, above all in aesthetics, some in private commerce, many in housing, several in pediatric care, and some, although by far too few, in secondary education. It is, in all, a complicated and diverse scenario that warrants neither a reflexive optimism nor the morbid and reiterated incantations of despair. Between these twin polarities, most people that I'm close to in the neighborhood do what they can to steer a sane and life-affirming course.

When it comes to education, though, most of the parents of the children that I know don't buy their affirmation cheaply. Those whose children go to P.S. 30 tend to like the school, and with good reason, I believe; but, when they look ahead into the middle schools and high schools of the area, they recognize the outer limits of the opportunities that this society is giving to their children. They also know the limits of the opportunities that *they* can offer to their children; and they know these aren't the same as what another class of people in another section of the city are providing for their children. So they look at their sons and daughters with this secret piece of knowledge. They know how destinies are formed out of particulars.

A few of the mothers of the children here work as domestics in the homes of wealthy people in Manhattan. Others have done so in the past, as have a number of grandmothers. Usually they've come to know the children of these families fairly well and, in this way, have gained a close-up sense of what their lives are like. They learn about particular ingredients of life that cultivate entitlement and graciousness and opportunity and also leave these children with the likable capacity for understated recognitions of their own advantage. They aren't inert submissive stones. They see and *understand* these things. They wish that they could give some of the same things to *their* children.

Many people in Mott Haven do a lot of work to make sure they are well-informed about conditions in their children's public schools. Some also know a great deal more about the schools that serve the children of the privileged than many of the privileged themselves may recognize. They know that "business math" is not the same as calculus and that "job-readiness instruction" is not European history or English literature. They know that children of rich people do not often spend semesters of their teenage years in classes where they learn to type an application for an entry-level clerical position; they know these wealthy children are too busy learning composition skills and polishing their French pronunciation and receiving preparation for the SATs. They come to understand the processes by which a texture of entitlement is stitched together for some children while it is denied to others. They also understand that, as the years go by, some of these children will appear to have deserved one kind of role in life, and some another.

One of the mothers at St. Ann's once said to me, "My daughter should have gone to Brown. If she had had the opportunities you had in school, she would have gone there. I didn't want her to get stuck at a big public university. I wanted something special because I thought *she* was special."

I asked her how she'd come to know about Brown University. Only a few of the parents in the neighborhood had ever mentioned colleges like Brown, or even New York University, Columbia, Cornell, or other private colleges in New York State. People spoke of community colleges at times, occasionally of Lehman College or John Jay. Brown came out of a different kingdom of familiarity and expectation.

I apologized for asking this, because I was afraid she'd find it patronizing; but she said she understood exactly why I asked. "I know. . . . It seems like something that I wouldn't know about. People around here aren't supposed to be familiar with some places; but some of us are. I know what Brown is like. It's small. It's nice. It's not impersonal. My daughter's smart, and naturally polite. She would have fitted in. They would have liked her there."

She said her daughter got into a branch of New York's City University, in which she had been doing reasonably well. But something about Brown University had lingered in her mind as an idea — "a hankering," she said — a yearning, a regret, that she could not shake off.

I asked if she resented that I'd had an opportunity she never had and which she could not give her daughter. She knew I'd gone to Harvard and that Mother Martha went to Radcliffe. I used to sense at times the slightest hint of an ambivalence or holding back when she was talking with the pastor. I knew she liked her and was close to her; but I had also seen these moments when she seemed to step away into a kind of "distancing," a knowledgeable look, a recognition, that was not as sharp-edged as resentment but suggested it somehow.

"We all know certain things," she said. "We know the way things are."

I was glad she wasn't too polite to cut right through my hesitation. I was trying to be careful. She did not want me to be careful. She wanted us to have a real talk, not "an inter-racial dialogue."

Her name was Eleanor Jackson. She died a few months after we had gotten to be friends. I still remember the place we were, the color of the sky and time of day, the food that we were eating — she had a chicken sandwich without mayonnaise, I had a hamburger — on the afternoon we had that talk. I remember too the deep, deep note of un-accepted anger and of unassimilated sadness in her voice when she had said, "We know the way things are." You cannot begin to address this kind of sadness by polite, evasive conversation, or by small gestures of philanthropy, or by incantatory repetition of encoded words. You cannot talk about "a renaissance of hope" when Eleanor is telling you of broken dreams.

Eleanor's assumption that I'd had advantages unknown to her or to her daughter was well-justified. My father brought me to the Dean of Admissions at Harvard College when I was eighteen. I wanted to go to Princeton. The dean, who was my father's friend and classmate, talked me into Harvard and assured me that I didn't need to bother filing other applications. Brown would have been a third or fourth choice for most of the boys who went to school with me. To Eleanor, it was a dream deferred forever.

Eleanor was a descendant of one of the presidents of the United States. Her grandmother's grandmother was a seamstress and a slave and, she believed, the mistress of John Tyler. On a genealogy chart she handed me the next time that we met, her great-grandmother's name was listed in this way: "Mary Emma Susan Tyler Jones—born in Charles City, Va., on December 25, 1841, died in 1930 at age 89." Mary Emma's mother, Eleanor told me, made the shirt that President Tyler wore to his inauguration.

Sitting in a coffee shop two blocks from St. Ann's Church one afternoon, she showed me sepia-colored photographs of her ancestors and described their lives in slavery, and later in the segregated South after emancipation, then here in the segregated Bronx. Irony and wistfulness suffused her gloss on our undemocratic nation's history.

"President Carter's daughter went to Brown," she said in passing. "I thought my daughter ought to go there too."

Maybe, I thought later, it was this association that had led her first to think of Brown. Maybe she'd heard of it from someone in the neighborhood, a counselor at her daughter's school perhaps, or one of the women in Manhattan she had worked for as a maid. Whatever the seed that planted this idea, it had remained with her for all these years. Something about Brown University had seemed appropriate to her for the descendant of a president.

Eleanor's death was sudden; it was wholly unexpected and, to this day, it does not seem real. In the spring of the year we'd gotten together several times for lunch, and once for a long walk. She suffered from asthma, but she'd had it for at least a decade and had learned to joke about the miseries it caused her, even when she had a serious attack. She had a gift for turning miseries to satires, often at her own expense, sometimes at mine. She flirted outrageously with eligible men and told me she regarded me as "wholly eligible" and said she knew men "better than you might expect" because she had been in the prostitution business for ten years before we met. She said she wished that she had stayed in it "a few years more" so that she could have paid for private college for her daughter.

She developed a peculiar skin disease in August of that year. No one at the church was told the name of the disease, but it disfigured her and turned her face into a mass of reddish welts and open sores. I was not in New York City then, but Mother Martha told me she was rushed into intensive care and was in terrible discomfort but, at first, in no apparent danger. Then, suddenly, she told me simply, "Eleanor has died. The funeral will be tomorrow."

I asked the cause of death but, for some reason, it remained unknown to people at the church. I never found out why she died. I never found out why she had become a prostitute instead of keeping on as a domestic worker, which is how she'd earned her living when she first got out of school, or why she stopped being a prostitute, or why she had been drawn into the congregation at St. Ann's, or why religion had become important in her life in recent years.

I ought to know some of these things because we talked so many times and she was not at all reserved in what she would agree to talk about. I know a good deal, for example, of her high school years because she spoke of this when she was telling me about the hopes she later nourished for her daughter. She told me she had graduated from Jane Addams High School, which was one of the more integrated high schools in the Bronx when she was growing up. "There were still white students at the high school then," she said, "but it was segregated by curriculum. Only the white girls took the college courses." Black girls, she believed, had been discouraged from enrolling in these courses.

"I told my counselor, 'I want to go to college.' Well, I can't explain the way she looked at me, but it was like the kids would say it now, 'Yeah, right! You want to go to college!' So I got this message very clearly. What you have to understand is that they didn't even talk to you about the kinds of courses you and Mother Martha would have taken. They didn't *plan* for you to go to college and they didn't lead you to expect that it was something *you* should plan on either. They led you to expect to clean the houses of the girls who went to college."

I asked what would have happened if a student had enough determination to reject the counselor's advice.

"You could insist," she said. "Some students did. But it was like a hand went up. 'Don't waste my time, or yours, because we both know where you're going.'" She lifted her hand like a policeman stopping traffic. "'Talk to the hand because the mind is busy.'"

We were at Blimpie's, at one of the tables in the back, the time we had that conversation. It was in mid-afternoon. She was wearing a red imitation-leather jacket. She said she wasn't hungry, but she had hot chocolate. I had a cup of coffee. We were nibbling on macadamia cookies.

I asked her if she thought the counselors at school did things like this with real awareness. "I mean—that they didn't *want* you to succeed?"

"No. That's not quite it," she said. "You could 'succeed,' but in the way they *meant* you to succeed. You could succeed in learning what they thought that you were capable of learning, but no more than that. I guess they didn't think that I was capable of college."

Her mother, she told me, died when she was nine years old. She was brought up by a cousin who was kind to her—"she bought me patent-leather shoes for first communion"—but was "not aggressive like a mother, not the type to go up to the principal and fight for you and back you up."

I told her of schools I visit in which dozens of black and Hispanic women have been channeled into classes like hairdressing that don't give the credits they would need to go to four-year colleges but are viewed by educators, and sometimes by students too, as sensible accommodations to diminished possibilities. She nodded quickly and immediately followed up by saying, "Thank you!" She said this often when I mentioned something that corroborated an opinion she had held but didn't think I would believe.

Once I asked her, "What did you think your teachers and your counselors believed that they were doing with your life—or thought *you* should be doing?"

"Truthfully? I think they felt that I could do domestic work, or help out in a hospital, or something of that sort, or maybe be a secretary, possibly a nurse," although she also said she didn't think they had reflected on it long enough to call it an "intention" or an "expectation." This, she said, was why she tried so hard to give her daughter opportunities that she herself had been denied. I think she felt she'd won a partial victory. If her daughter could have gone to Brown, I know she would have felt the victory was more complete.

She used to tell me funny stories about people she'd encountered when she was, as she had put it, "working on my feet" around Times Square and, later, on Brook Avenue. During the latter period, she said that she had fallen into using crack cocaine. "Get your Crackerjacks right here!" she said, remembering the advertising pitch of dealers up on Cypress Avenue, who sold, she said, a brand of crack that came in a short vial with a yellow top and was so powerful "you'd think the radio was talking to you even if you hadn't turned it on."

She told me also that she liked having a woman priest "because I tell her things I wouldn't dare say to a man."

When I asked, "Like what?" she laughed and said, "Like, if the man you sleep with couldn't satisfy your needs? You wouldn't dare to say that to a priest that was a man. He might take off his collar and say, 'I have a solution to that problem!'"

She must have been well over 45 years old, but she seemed younger. She had a sensual-looking body, mocking eyes, and orange-colored hair. I remember the elastic bands that held her asthma pump against her wallet because it was almost always on her lap or on the seat right next to her at church.

In a letter I got from her in mid-July, she enclosed a photo of her cat. "Here's a picture of my baby, two years old," she wrote. She also included a cassette of gospel music she recorded for me.

"When we were at Blimpie's last time I was going to order a club sandwich, but I was too shy," she wrote in the same letter. "That isn't like me. Is it?" Then she said, "Next time I'll tell you when I'm hungry." She gave me her telephone number, which had just been changed, and said that she was always home by nine.

For all the wickedness that she enjoyed imputing to herself, I know she took a mischievous delight in being with the younger children at St. Ann's. "I never would have been a good schoolteacher," she once said, "because I love them most when they're most devilish."

I know the children liked her too. Elio was often sitting with her at a table in the corner of the afterschool when she was there. She used to say he was her "boyfriend." She was one of the good people who, for many years, had been out on their own and then had found a sense of safety at St. Ann's. A lot of women of about her age seem to find safety there, and a release from loneliness.

An Episcopal priest named Robert Morris speaks about the commonplace and frequently unnoticed ways that people rise above their loneliness and fear as "ordinary resurrections." He points out that the origin of "resurrection" is the Greek word *anastasis,* which, he notes, means "standing up again," and, as he puts it unpretentiously, "We all lie down. We all rise up. We do this every day." The same word, as he notes, is used in Scripture: "I am the resurrection and the life." But, in an afternote directed possibly at fellow members of the clergy, he observes, "The Resurrection does not wait for Easter."

I think of his words when I remember Eleanor. She was a good friend for a person who allowed himself to get discouraged but had never found the kinds of resurrections that are made of steel and stone and slogans utterly convincing. Sometimes, at the end of a long conversation over coffee as we said goodbye to one another, she would say, "God bless." But life itself, lived with a sense of fun, defiance, and courageous humor even at the most upsetting times, is the enduring blessing that she left behind to those who miss her and remember her.

She liked to talk about her cat, whose name was Sasha. I know his name because she wrote it underneath his photograph. I can't remember her daughter's name and I'm not even sure she ever told me. I know she had a grandson, though, because I was at church for his baptism.

She often helped to read parts of the services on Sundays. She was a member of the vestry and took pride in her position. The suddenness of her death has made it harder to accept that she is gone. Some of the younger children asked about her for a long time after she had died. "When is Miss Eleanor coming back?" one of the little ones would ask. It was a while before they understood that she would not return.

CHAPTER 9

Opportunities
for Silence

P iedad's baby brother had a bad attack of asthma.
She says she was awake part of the night because
the hospital was crowded and they had to wait for a long
time until her brother had been cared for and was out of
danger.

"How crowded was the hospital?" I ask.

"A lot of crowded!" she replies.

"How many people did you see?"

She thinks about this carefully and then replies,
"Almost a lot of people."

"What happened next?"

"They put him in a little bed."

"How little is your brother?"

"This big," she replies, holding her hands about a foot apart.

"How little was this little bed?"

Again, she thinks before she answers. "Almost like a big bed — except little," she says finally.

Like several of the children in the afterschool this year, Piedad came to New York City from a rural area in Guatemala, where she tells me her grandmother owned a pig.

"The piggy mother," she says, "had ten babies and my grandma gave me one to be my piggy and the mother pig was angry!"

"Who was she angry at?"

"At me!" she says.

"Piedad," says Ariel, who's sitting with us at the table, "was the mother piggy *really, really* angry — or only a little angry?"

"A lot of angry!" Piedad says, spreading her arms out wide as if she's wrapping them around a good-sized bag of anger.

"What's the mother piggy's name?" I ask.

"The mother piggy is named Malí. But we call her Mama Rosa."

"What do you call the little piggy?"

"Baby Piggy," she replies.

A six-year-old raises her hand and waves it in the air at me one day at P.S. 30 when I'm visiting her class.

"Teacher?" she says.

"Yes?" I say.

"I miss my dog."

"Where is your dog?"

"In Puerto Rico," she replies.

"What's your dog's name?"

"Altagracia," she says.

"Is she a puppy or a grown-up dog?"

"Older than a puppy—but not like a grown-up dog."

"How old is she?"

"Thirty-five or forty."

"What color is she?"

"Yellow."

"Is she a big dog or a little dog?"

"Big!"

"How big?"

"Fourteen hundred pounds . . . or something."

"What does she eat?"

"Well," she says, as if I've finally gotten to the point that counts the most. "She *don't* like sweet bread and she *don't* like dog bread. She only likes to eat one kind of bread."

"What kind of bread?"

"Can I tell you in my language?"

"Yes," I say.

In Spanish she says, "Rice and beans."

Another child in the class opens a folder and hands me a picture of a mouse. Beneath the picture are two neat handwritten words: "My Mouse."

"What's your mouse's name?" I ask.

"His name is Angel."

"How old is he?"

"Zero," she replies.

"Is that true? How can that be?"

"Because he had to die."

"How did he die?"

She moves her finger in a circle on the page above the mouse's head. "He died from not having cheese."

"Teacher?" says the other child.

"Yes?" I say.

"Do you know what I'm going to say?"

"No," I say. "Not yet."

"We have little people in my country."

"Is that true?"

"It is," she says. "We do."

"How little are they?"

"This size," she replies, and holds her hand about one foot above the floor.

The child's mother, when she comes to see the teacher at the end of school, tells me that the dog they had to leave in Puerto Rico was part Lab, part German shepherd, and was yellow and did not like dog food, as the child said, but ate the same food as the family.

"She's big and friendly and we loved her. When we had to leave her there we cried."

How big is "big" to someone very small? Often, talking with a child of this age, I have to remind myself of what the world must look like from the vantage point of somebody who has to climb onto a chair when she sits down to talk with me. Conversations with the children about ages of adults can also force me to slow down and try to recollect how "old" a person 25 or 30 seemed to me when I was six or seven. Elio's astonishment about my father's age, my mother's age, and mine, comes to my mind. His look of disbelief when I confessed to him that I was over 60 and the speed with which he crossed himself and ran to tell this to Katrice seemed funny at the time; but from the point of view of someone who is seven and a half I guess that "sixty-one" or "sixty-two" sounds pretty near as old as "ninety-three."

Once, when he and I and Stephanie were talking about P.S. 30, which they both attended, Stephanie mentioned that her uncle went there "many years" before and that the principal, Miss Rosa, had been principal in those days too. Elio asked, "How old is Miss Rosa?"

"I don't know," I said. "How old do you think?"

He looked carefully at me and Stephanie. "A hundred?"

"No!" I said.

"A hundred's old!" said Stephanie.

"I know," said Elio.

"Do you think Miss Rosa looks that old?" I asked. "Like an old lady?"

"Miss Rosa's pretty!" he replied.

"How old do you think she really is?" I asked.

He looked at me and Stephanie again, then took another big guess: "Twenty?"

When I was a teacher, I would sometimes work with children of about his age on what an older teacher called "location skills" for estimating things like ages, sizes, numbers, by comparing them to other things with numbers that a child might already know. The number of things you're already acquainted with, however, places limits on the possibilities for making references like these. Some of the children at St. Ann's may find it harder to make realistic guesses about ages, for example, because there are fewer people in their seventies or eighties still alive here than in most American communities. Of those who do live well past 60, it seems that a sizable majority are women.

It's also true that dozens of young men and women—men, especially, between the ages of 18 and 30—have already been subtracted from the population because they're in prison or in detox centers or AIDS hospices, or are deceased. So making guesses about ages may, to some degree, be complicated for the children by this factor too.

One day in December of that year, 96 young men and women were arrested in the early morning here on Cypress Avenue and in the streets nearby, among them several who were charged with selling cocaine from the building where Pineapple lives. It was a drug bust that had been in preparation for a long time, orchestrated by the DEA and carried out by several hundred agents of the FBI and other law enforcement agencies, accompanied by helicopters and the other pyrotechnical displays that would accompany a tactical assault by military forces in a foreign land. Some of these young people, most of whom were men, were not convicted, and a number of the ones who were have subsequently been released; but more than half of them have been in prison ever since. The absence of so many of these men, who are the fathers and the older brothers of the children, might have some effect upon their reference points in trying to make judgments about ages.

Other reference points may be affected by the demographics of a neighborhood as well. One day at a Catholic school that I was visiting on Franklin Avenue, a teacher asked the kindergarten children to describe "the Holy Family." A child raised his hand and, when the teacher called on him, he spoke of Mary, Jesus, and her husband, Joseph, as "the mother, son, and foster father." The specificity of "foster father" startled me a bit, because so many children in the area do live in foster families. The boy, I told myself, was showing "an adaptive ingenuity." The teacher told me later that this was the church's formulation, not the child's — it was an accepted usage among Christian educators, she explained — but that she gave it special emphasis so that the children in the class would feel included in the holiness of Jesus.

In spite of such considerations on the part of empathetic teachers, I become uneasy when I sense that I am making too much out of local demographics, since so many children in poor neighborhoods, as in all neighborhoods, do manage to perceive a larger context than the one determined by immediate geography. Many of the older children at the afterschool read widely, and they talk at length with

Mother Martha and with college-educated tutors who read widely, which, of course, expands the reference points for their ideas and estimations. Others acquire an expanded sense of context from good television programs — there are many very good ones now for children, and not just on PBS — which give them introductions to a world of places, sizes, distances, and other concepts that are bigger and more various than those that many of them know firsthand.

In general, I think the "differentness" of children here is overstated. Again and again, in listening to children at St. Ann's, visitors remark upon the fact that relatively little of their syntax and the intonations of their speech — and very little of their selectivity, or whimsicality, in choosing things they want to talk about — supports the stereotypes in movies, for example, or sometimes in TV news, that tend to shape impressions about inner-city children in our nation. Some of the children do make use, at times, of syntax that some people call "Black English" (not only black kids do this, the Hispanic children do as well, because so many of their playmates are black children); but it isn't done continually, or helplessly, as if they didn't know what standard English is. It seems more often to be chosen as a style suitable for certain situations or for certain listeners, but not for others.

If there is one area in which the children as a group do seem to differ somewhat, in emotional reactions, from the children that I meet in wealthier communities — and even here I would be very cautious not to overstate this — it is in their sensitivity to other children's moments of anxiety and their acute awareness of emotional fragility and of the tipping-point between exhilaration and depression. I think that they're more worried about darkness and respond more thoughtfully than other groups of children I have known to times when little candles — sweetness, solidarity—need to be taken out of secret places and illuminated quickly.

At these times, they also seem to draw upon religious faith more deeply, and more openly, than many of the children that I knew, for instance, in the public schools of Newton, Massachusetts, where I taught fifth-graders after my initial stint of teaching in the Boston schools. Here too, however, many obvious exceptions come to mind, and I've had conversations on the subject of religion with the children in suburban schools that aren't so different from the talks I've had with children here.

The emphasis on "differentness" in inner-city kids has been a part of sociology as long as inner cities have existed, I suppose. When I was a young teacher, "the culture of poverty" was an accepted phrase. Similar phrases have been canonized in decades since. There have always been sufficient differences in *some* forms of behavior and *some* patterns of expression to make large distinctions seem legitimate. The distinctions always seem too large to me, however; and the more time that I spend with inner-city children, the less credible and less legitimate these large distinctions seem.

The wholesale labeling of inner-city children was, at least, resisted strongly in the past by influential and respected intellectuals; much of that resistance has collapsed in recent years, and many of these suppositions about "differentness" go almost uncontested. Some writers even raise a question as to whether children here may constitute a group so different from most other children, with a set of problems (or, we are told, "pathologies") so complicated, so alarming, so profound, that they aren't "children" in the sense in which most of us use that word, but that they're really "premature adults," perhaps precocious criminals, "predators," we are told by those who are supposed to know. It strikes me as a dangerous exaggeration that may seem to justify a differentiation in the pedagogies and the social policies that are enacted or applied within such neighborhoods, with greater emphasis on rigid discipline than on the informality and intellectual expansiveness that are familiar in the better schools that educate the children of rich people.

One of the things I have respected most in Aida Rosa, principal of P.S. 30, and the teachers that I talk with on her staff is that they look at children here *as children,* not as "distorted children," not as "morally disabled children," not as "quasi-children" who require a peculiar arsenal of reconstructive strategies and stick-and-carrot ideologies that wouldn't be accepted for one hour by the parents or the teachers of the upper middle class. But ideologies like these are having their effect, as inner-city teachers know too well, on many urban systems now. Sticking labels — and, especially, *collective* labels — on the foreheads of the children makes it easier to treat them in a way we'd never treat the children of the privileged.

It has another effect as well, I am afraid. To some observers, it appears to justify the routine sequestration of these children in the tightly segregated neighborhoods in which they dwell, because this sequestration makes it possible to localize the "special" services that are believed to be appropriate to children who are seen as being absolutely and entirely different from our own. The children are already isolated geographically and racially. There are, as I have noted, only 26 Caucasian children in a student population of 11,000 in the elementary schools that serve this district of the Bronx. To isolate them also diagnostically, and then to concretize their isolation with a veritable formulary of prescriptive certitudes, may make it easier for social scientists and politicians to establish an assertively discriminating stance in public policy debates, but it also situates these children even farther from the mainstream of society.

It is true that the *conditions* of their lives are different in innumerable ways from the conditions of existence for more favored children in our nation, their breathing problems and the absence of so many of their fathers in the prison system being two of the most obvious distinctions; but the ordinary things they long for, and the things that they find funny, and the infinite variety of things they dream of, and the games they play, and animals they wish that they could have, and things they like to eat, and clothes they wish they could afford to buy, are not as different as the world seems to believe from what most other children in this land enjoy, or dream of, or desire.

Some of the Guatemalan, Puerto Rican, and Honduran children here eat rice and beans with many of their meals. When they have a choice, however, most will opt, alas, for hamburgers or pizza; and when Pineapple drags her little sister with her to the corner store to buy a treat between meals (which she does more often than she should), she usually reaches for the same big Hershey bars or packages of Twizzlers — reddish licorice sticks — that kids buy at the local store in my hometown in Massachusetts. Some of the teenagers watch Hispanic or black-oriented programs on TV; but they almost all watch Sesame Street when they are small, and more than half of them, I've found, were introduced to interesting rituals like hanging up your jacket in the closet and then putting on your sweater before sitting down to have a conversation by the same soft-spoken man who introduced these things to three- and four-year-olds all over the United States.

When Mr. Rogers came here to Mott Haven, there was a stampede of children wanting to be close to him. They treated him as if they'd known him for a long, long time—which, in a sense, they had. He treated them as if he knew them too. He didn't make a lot of general remarks about them later on. He spoke of individuals.

He knows so much more than most people do about the lives and personalities of children; but he didn't let himself be drawn to any overquick conclusions. He asked the children many questions. He asked the mothers and grandmothers questions too. He also gave them time to answer. I never thought about "prescriptive overconfidence" while he was here. I thought of someone walking in the woods and being careful not to step on anything that lives.

Erik Erikson alerted us, now more than forty years ago, to what he called the dangers of "destructive forms of conscientiousness." Imposing global preconceptions on the multitude of diverse personalities and motivations in a given group of children may be one of them. Rushing ahead too much to fill up silences when children hesitate while trying to explain something about their lives to us may be another. Children pause a lot when reaching for ideas. They get distracted. They meander—blissfully, it seems—through acres of magnificent irrelevance. We think we know the way they're heading in the conversation, and we get impatient, like a traveler who wants to "cut the travel time." We want to get there quicker. It does speed up the pace of things, but it can also change the destination.

Mr. Rogers told me once that he regrets the inclination of commercial television "to replace some opportunities for silence" in a child's life "with universal noise." At quiet times, he said, "young children give us glimpses of some things that are eternal"—glimpses too, he said, "of what unites us all as human beings." He also said that after forty years of work with children he does not believe that being clever is the same as being wise. These seem like

119

observations that are easy to agree with and then, just as easily, dismiss. I hope we won't dismiss them, though.

I didn't learn until two years ago that Mr. Rogers is a minister. He was ordained in the Presbyterian Church during the early 1960s with a ministry to children. Perhaps it's in the nature of his ministry, or simply of his temperament, to look with caution upon cleverness and certitude and never to be too determined to predict the destination of a journey or a conversation.

He asked me recently if we could go back to St. Ann's together in the spring. He's a modest man. He asked it rather timidly. He said he didn't know if this would be intrusive.

In the Sanctuary

A misty day. The rain's been falling intermittently all afternoon. The stained-glass windows in the sanctuary cast a rainbow of soft sleepy colors: whitish yellow, pinkish red, and bluish green.

Ariel notices that she's been sitting on her foot for half an hour.

"My foot's asleep," she says.

"Try hopping up and down," I say.

She looks up at the wooden cross and shakes her head.

"Un-uh! Not in here. . . ."

She goes out to the corridor and hops around until her foot is better, then comes back and leans against the piano, looking at the other children seated here in front of me.

Ariel seemed upset today when she and I were walking back from P.S. 30. When she learned that I was going to the sanctuary with a group of other children, she asked Nancy for permission to come with us.

When Ariel is happy she looks right into your eyes and smiles the clearest smile! She speaks with clarity as well. She has a fresh and energetic voice. "If I was very, very powerful," she told me once, "I'd have a festival for everybody on the tenth day of each month."

"Why the tenth?" I asked.

"I like the number ten," she said with a slight outward flutter of her hands, and shrugged, as if she wondered why she chose it too.

She's one of the best students in the afterschool but, like a number of the children, has a harder time with mathematics than with other subjects. She uses her fingers now and then to do arithmetic but doesn't hold them right up near her face as younger children do. She holds her hand out at a graceful distance, wrist up, and counts quickly by light motions of her fingers.

She's the oldest in the group today. The youngest one is Elio. Sitting beside him is Lucia and, behind her, Stephanie and, next to her, a skinny girl, Shentasha, who was born in Alabama and moved to the neighborhood when she was four or five.

When I try to reconstruct the first part of their conversation later on I find it hard, because there's no real continuity for quite a while. This is the way it almost always is unless I prompt them with a question of my own. Conversations with the children don't just "start" in organized and ordered ways. It takes some time before their moods and inclinations start to coalesce around a common interest. When Elio is in the group, it usually takes longer.

"Jonathan?" he says as Ariel is moving up an extra chair.

"Yes?" I say.

He twists in his seat and looks above him at the image of a woman, who may be the Virgin Mary, cradling a baby in her arms.

"I *think* about the angels. . . ."

The other children simply look at him with curiosity when he makes statements of this sort. Nobody asks him to explain himself. He makes these brief announcements, and then something in him seems to be at peace until another declaration like this wants to be released.

"Jonathan?" he asks again.

"Yes?" I say.

"How old is God?"

"How old do you think?"

"Two hundred years?"

Lucia puts her hand against her chest as if she's trying to suppress a smile. I have to struggle not to smile too, because it's just exactly twice the age he gave his principal, Miss Rosa.

Ariel tells Elio that God is "older than two hundred years" because the Bible says that "God is Jesus' father."

"How old is Jesus?"

"Two thousand years," she says.

"For real?" he asks.

"At least!"

"How do you know?"

"Believe me, Elio! I know!"

For a while he seems lost in meditation. He studies the woman in the stained-glass window and looks on the verge of saying something more about her, but does not.

The silence in the room is interrupted briefly by the sound of someone opening the door and by the voices of some children in the hallway. One of the children at the door flicks a light switch on and off.

"Hey, you guys!" says Ariel.

The door is closed. The silence is restored. The children talk but, for a time, I hear only bits and pieces of their conversation. A drowsy mood belonging to a rainy afternoon controls their state of mind, and mine.

Of the children sitting with me, two have asthma, one has a heart murmur, two have fathers who are now in prison, one has a father who has been in prison but is now at home. Two have fathers who live in the neighborhood but not in their own homes.

"I think my father is the saddest person that I know," says Stephanie, "because he doesn't live with me."

One of the children asks her why he doesn't live with her, but she does not directly answer.

"The problem is: He's *sad,*" she says.

"Where does he live?" I ask.

"You know that big, big building—over there?"

"Over where?"

"The big red building," she replies.

"Which one?" I ask.

She tries to explain it in a different way: "Next door to my grandmother."

"Where does your grandmother live?"

"Westchester Avenue," she says. "Next door to the store."

"Excuse me, Jonathan," says Elio. "I wanted to say something too."

"What did you want to say?"

"I hope no one will laugh at me for this. I miss *my* father too."

Nobody laughs. Stephanie asks him when his father will come home.

"Next week," he says.

"Elio," asks Ariel, "is your father really coming home next week?"

"No," he answers.

"When is your father really going to come home?"

"Next year," he says.

"Elio, do you know where your father is?"

"Yes," he says.

"Do you know your father's name?"

"Yes," he says.

"If your father came to visit you, how would you feel?"

"I would be proud of him," says Elio.

"Can we clap for Elio?" she asks.

Everybody claps.

Nobody presses Elio to say exactly where his father is, because the other children know. Stephanie acknowledges the truth, however, when she says her cousin is in prison too.

"I hope that no one laughs at me, because I feel the same as Elio."

Lucia says she thinks her mother is the saddest person that she knows because "she's lonely" and "she has to learn *how* to be lonely."

But Ariel says she thinks her mother's father is the saddest person that she knows because he died so long ago. "He doesn't know that I was born. He doesn't know my face."

"Ariel," says Stephanie, "I think he knows that you were born."

"I don't think so," Ariel replies.

"I think he does," says Stephanie.

"Why do you say that?" I ask Stephanie.

"I think the angels see our faces," she replies.

I ask if she believes that everyone who dies becomes an angel.

"Good people do," she says.

Stephanie's words bring up a question about God's forgiveness. Most of the children seem to think of God as a forgiving person, but Shentasha seems to see Him more as an avenging power. I ask them if they think of God as "someone stern" or "someone gentle." All of the children don't seem sure of what I mean by "stern," so I say "strict" instead, and then they talk about it for a while and at length come to a general agreement, as one of them (I think Ariel) expresses it, that God is "strict sometimes" and "gentle sometimes" but "most of the time more gentle." Only Shentasha says she disagrees with this, although it isn't clear whether she's saying what she does out of a real sense of conviction or out of the satisfaction that she gets from being in an oppositional position.

We talk into late afternoon. It isn't all high-minded, serious, and solemn. Shentasha, in particular, goes off from time to time on minor detours that subvert my efforts to pursue some of the thoughts the other children have expressed. She has a fast and funny manner of expression that reminds me of the jive talk of the ten-year-olds I used to teach in Roxbury. When someone makes a comment that appears to second-guess something she's said, she swings her head around and sticks her face right in that person's face. "You better believe it, girl!" she says.

She seems to like to say things slightly wild to stir up the dialogue when it's too tame and proper for her taste. At one point in the discussion about God, for instance, when the children are debating whether God is strict or kind, Lucia says, "I think God's . . . nice!"—a choice of words too unoriginal not to invite Shentasha's sense of the ridiculous.

"God is 'nice'?" she says, repeating it sarcastically. "Where do you get that, girl?"

"I think He's nice," Lucia says, refusing to give up her chosen word.

"God is *not* 'nice.' Un-uh!" says Shentasha. "That man is *mean!* You misbehave, you'll find it out. The Lord is a taskmaster!"

Lucia, however, holds her ground and says she thinks that God forgives us "even if we do something that's very bad."

"Like what?" Shentasha asks.

"Like . . . killing someone?"

"Sorry, girl!" Shentasha says.

"If you're sorry?" asks Lucia.

"You better be *very* sorry!" says Shentasha.

It would be misleading, though, to indicate that every child is consistently of one mood or another in the course of a two-hour conversation or that every child speaks in a consistent style. "This one's silly, this one's solemn, this one's more rambunctious. . . ." I may inadvertently leave that impression, since my own impression of a child in the first few moments of a conversation tends to color what I'm likely to retain from later portions of the conversation. It's also true that once a child like Shentasha finds a role that she enjoys within a conversation, she may purposely continue in that role and go out of her way to say things that sustain it, like a character within a play that she herself is writing, and especially if she believes the other children find her manner entertaining.

Shentasha's like a good comedian in this respect. When she gets onto a subject that amuses her, she seems to "ride" it in the way an entertainer would, or like a jazz musician playing riffs on the same melody until she's gotten all the mileage she thinks it's worth. But I've been with her also when she wasn't funny in the least, and had no inclination to be funny. I've seen her when she's been depressed so deeply that she wouldn't speak at all.

All children have these swings of mood and speak in different ways at different times. Ariel, for example, speaks with more maturity than many other children of her age, and often with a great deal more solemnity, particularly when she's in the presence of the altar and the cross.

Thank goodness, though, she isn't always on a lofty plane and doesn't always sound mature. She's still a child and says many things that are reminders of the innocence of her perspective.

At one point, for instance, she describes an incident in which her father was involved with the police. He was arrested, she reports, for driving carelessly. "It was a Sunday and I felt so bad for him because on Sundays he gets very hungry and my mother makes him a big dinner, and he *likes* to have his dinner, but he had to stay in jail all night and so he never had a single thing to eat. . . ."

The innocence in this, for me at least, is that she doesn't speak about the more important fear she and her mother must have felt about the danger that her father could have been arraigned and sentenced to a prison stay or might have fought with the police and found himself in much more serious trouble. The fact that it was Sunday and he wouldn't have his dinner may have been the only part of this that she could fully understand.

"What I want to say is this: I just felt *sorry* for my father."

The filtered light of afternoon grows dimmer in the stained-glass windows. Shentasha seldom lets up on her lively chatter. But Stephanie and Ariel say less and less and Elio begins to yawn and twist around again within the pew. On an impulse, Ariel gets up from next to me and leans against a lectern that looks like a music stand and stares into the darkened portion of the church.

I check my pocket watch. It's nearly five o'clock. The children missed their snack at four but didn't speak of this. If we don't go downstairs soon they'll miss their supper too.

Lucia asks if we can go into the gym and play after our conversation.

"I think it's too late to go into the gym," I say.

"Jonathan?" asks Stephanie.

"Yes?" I say.

"Just before we go downstairs, do we have time to pray?"

As often at St. Ann's, I find it difficult to answer when a child asks me this, because I know that I don't have the right to give permission or withhold it. Elio asks me sometimes, "Can we pray?" I'm never sure what I should say. Maybe I regret that I don't have the standing at the church that would allow me to suggest things like this on my own.

The children say their prayers, some silently. The ones who pray aloud speak softly, so it's hard to hear their words. At the start of the prayer, or at the end, some of them cross themselves. I notice that Shentasha, after all she had to say about God's unforgiving ways, has closed her eyes and clasped her hands.

When we go downstairs into the afterschool a little after five, the children seem to bring the stillness of the sanctuary with them. They don't skip steps and run and shout the way they usually do. In the bright light of the afterschool they stand apart from all the other children briefly, as if holding to a bond that grew between them in the past two hours. It's a special moment. Then the moment's over and they drift into the crowd of other children and soon join them at their tables to have supper.

It's hard, after a time like this, not to feel honored that the children would permit you to be present when they open up this way. At the same time, however, there's a complicating element in this because you know you're filling in, in some respects, for other men in whom the confidences of a child are more naturally placed and would, under more normal circumstances, be more intimately placed.

A man who is permitted this much openness and friendship by a group of children in this setting at the church, like a teacher who is granted openness and trust by students in a public school, cannot escape some recognition of the fact that he's receiving revelations of emotion that most of these children, if they had the chance, would share with their own fathers. I once told another man I know, who fills a role somewhat like mine among the children, that I felt we were like "gleaners" in the Bible, not in fields of grain but in a field of love that can't be harvested by those to whom the love rightly belongs.

I think of this in prison visits when the inmates speak to me about their boys and girls, whose photographs are often posted in their cells and whose report cards they receive sometimes and cherish even if the grades their children have been given aren't as good as they would like. Their voices are almost always filled with strong emotions of contrition and self-accusation for their inability to fill the role of father in their children's lives.

Some inmates I have met whose reading skills were low, and who could barely write a letter of real substance to their children at the time they were convicted, have received an education finally in prison. Literacy classes I've attended at the Rikers Island bootcamp, which are taught by teachers from the New York public schools, were very good. Literature classes to which I have been invited on the island were remarkable, taught by a published writer in a class the size of classes you would see at a good prep school. Class size in the prison is, on average, twelve to fifteen students, as it is at schools like Groton and St. Paul's, but half of what it is at almost any elementary school in the South Bronx.

I hope that the reflections of the children who were talking with me in the sanctuary on that rainy afternoon, or my reflections on their observations here, do not convey the misimpression that there are no stable, law-abiding, and hard-working fathers in the neighborhood around St. Ann's. There are many of such men, and several of them have important roles within the church and afterschool. Some don't have sufficient education to conduct tutorials with children but fill crucial roles providing physical and moral supervision. Others run athletic programs in the evening on an outdoor court, which is equipped with hoops for basketball, or in the gym, which is above the afterschool.

One of the most deeply trusted figures at the afterschool is a Puerto Rican man of roughly 45 who has a gentle voice and kindly eyes and fills the role of a wise uncle to the children. Another man of roughly the same age, legally blind and with a face of calm nobility tinged with the somber look of someone who has led a painful life, helps run the feeding programs at the church. The senior warden of St. Ann's, an eloquent and portly man who sometimes preaches an impromptu sermon during the announcements in the last part of the services on Sunday, stands among the children like a great old tree within a forest of much smaller trees: a reassuring presence, and a solidly affirming one.

Still, it is true that women take a more consistent role than men do in the programs that serve children here. "Women hold the sky up in this neighborhood," one of the men observed when he and I were watching Nancy and Katrice amidst the kids one afternoon. They hold it up in many neighborhoods, not just among poor people; but in these neighborhoods in which incarceration rates for men are often higher than their graduation rates from high school, the burden on the women is, accordingly, much heavier.

"My father's going to come home," said Elio this week.

When I asked how soon, he said, "He's going to graduate in June," referring to his father's time in prison as if he had been in college or at boarding school. Then, however, he seemed to indicate that this was not as certain as he'd made it sound.

"I've been giving my prayers to God," he said with a shy smile.

As he said this, he did something that I'd never seen him do before. He held his hands, with palms up, right in front of him, his elbows bent and fingers curled, and lifted his forearms in a sort of "rowing" motion, coaxingly, and did it several times, the way my father's mother used to do when she said Hebrew prayers on Friday nights. I may have revealed by my expression that this motion of his hands and arms had puzzled me, or stirred something in me, because he said, in an explanatory way, "I open my hand—like *this*—and then I close it"—and he closed it as he spoke—"like *that*."

"Why do you open it?" I asked.

"To *catch* something," he said.

"Catch what?" I asked.

"God's answer," he replied, as if this should be obvious.

I hope God sends the answer soon to Elio—the one he wants—and that he catches it. "Surrogate fathers," or "role models," or whatever other term we use, do fill a useful role, I'm sure; but it is natural that children have a longing for the real thing. Elio wants his father in his life. He misses him, and needs him.

CHAPTER 11

The Details of Life

"Peter's dog ate Jefferson's cat," says Mother Martha in a letter I received from her in the last week of May.

Peter is a ten-year-old who lives across the street from St. Ann's Church above a store on St. Ann's Avenue. His cousin Jefferson is living with him now, because the seven-year-old's mother has been seriously ill. She will be ill, as it turns out, for a long time and is, for now, according to the priest, at Lincoln Hospital.

"First his mother. Then his cat!" says Mother Martha. "When I found him here this morning he was sitting on the front steps of the church. The cat, or what remained of her, was in a cardboard box. I sat there with him and we had a long talk about animals, because I think you know that some denominations don't believe that animals have souls and he's been told a number of conflicting things.

"After our talk we found a cookie tin. Armando dressed in black for the occasion. Jefferson and Armando dug the hole. We said a prayer and sprinkled water on the cookie tin and then the little ones threw dirt into the hole. I think that he was pleased because he kept on bringing people out to see the grave. He dug her up three times to show his friends. . . ."

Armando is the sports director at the church. He tries, as do most people on the staff, to give emotional support to kids like Jefferson when they have troubles in their home. Jefferson doesn't open up to many grown-ups, though. He's rather bashful and has melancholy eyes. When things are going well with him, he likes to race around the churchyard with the pastor and her dog. When things are going bad he hardly talks at all. He gets a hunted look, like that of a small rabbit frozen by the head-lights of a car.

Mother Martha says he chose the prayer they read during the burial. Later, he found two sticks and made a cross to stand above the grave. When warmer weather came, he went back to the grave and planted flowers in the grass. "The dog who ate his cat," says Mother Martha, "is named Diesel—a good name, if you ask me, for an anti-social character who eats his friends."

Jefferson is one of six or seven children from the neighborhood who spend hours of their time with Mother Martha and for whom she sweeps away appointments with all types of visitors, to the dismay of many who have often traveled a long way to get some time with her. Four of them are boys, and two or three, depending on the season or the year, are girls who are their sisters or their cousins. Katrice refers to them as "Mother Martha's gang" and disapproves of how they pester her. "Look at how they pull her clothes!" she says when they surround her as she's coming from her car.

Jefferson brings animals he finds around the neighborhood into the garden of St. Ann's. He seems happy with the animals, more than he sometimes seems to be with people. He likes to hang around at night with Mother Martha and her dog before it's time for him to go across the street to sleep.

Why does this story about Jefferson set off some warning signals for me as a writer? Perhaps simply because I know the fairly hard-nosed attitudes that govern social policy in urban neighborhoods today and can anticipate that this, like many other stories in this book, may be perceived as a preposterous distraction from the bottom-line concerns with "discipline" and "rigor" and "job preparation" and "high standards" and what now is known as "high-stakes testing" and the rest of the severe agenda that has recently been put in place for inner-city kids. Burials for cats somehow don't fit into this picture.

Then, too, in the business-minded ethos of our age, any money we may spend on children of poor people must be proven to be economically utilitarian and justifiable in cost-effective terms. But much of what goes on around St. Ann's cannot be justified in terms like these. You could not prove to anyone in Washington that Mother Martha's talk with Jefferson about the possibilities of afterlife for animals will have "a positive effect" upon his reading scores or make him more employable a decade later.

Those, however, are the usual criteria for budgeting decisions in most programs that serve children. "Productivity" is almost everything. Elements of childhood that bear no possible connection to the world of enterprise and profit get no honor in the pedagogic world right now, nor in the economic universe to which it seems increasingly subservient.

Now and then I'm asked to go to conferences of urban school officials, corporation leaders and consultants, and the representatives of agencies that serve (or, as the jargon now requires, "service") inner-city youth. The atmosphere is very different at these sessions than it was only about ten years ago. The dialogue is mostly managerial and structural. It tends to be a cumbersome and techno-cratic dialogue, weighted down by hyphenated words such as "performance-referenced," "outcome-oriented," "competency-centered." One hears a lot of economics, many references to competition and "delivery of product" and, of course, high standards and exams. Questions that concern the inner health of children, or their happiness or sadness, or their personalities as complicated, unpredict-able, and interesting little people don't come up at all or, if they do, are often treated as a genteel afterthought and handled with dispatch and even traces of derision.

The settings for these gatherings, which business lead-ers sometimes underwrite, are generally extravagant. Guests are inundated with expensively produced materials: shoul-der bags embossed with corporate logos, loose-leaf note-books filled with corporate position papers. The feeling of a public school is far removed from all of this. The tenor of discussion seems a thousand miles away from childhood and youth. There's often an obsessive use of truly simple-minded slogans that belong to industry and marketing. Words like "replicate" and "utilize" and "implement" and "reinvent" keep coming up. The substitution of assertive-ness and verbs of many syllables for any real acquaintance-ship with subject matter is familiar.

People rarely speak of *children* at these conferences. You hear of "cohort groups" and "standard variations," but you don't hear much of boys who miss their cats or six-year-olds who have to struggle with potato balls. If a bunch of kids like Elio and Pineapple were seated at the table, it would seem a comical anomaly. Statistical decorum would be undermined by the particularities of all these uncontrollable and restless little variables.

The relentless emphasis at these events is on the future economic worth low-income children may, or may not, have for our society. Policy discussions seem to view them less as children who have fingers, elbows, stomachaches, emotions, than as "economic units"—pint-sized deficits or assets in blue jeans and jerseys, some of whom may prove to be a burden to society, others of whom may have some limited utility.

"The right kind of investment," says the former CEO of a large corporation that sells toothpaste and detergent, "from conception to age five, will pay back every dollar we spend at least four for one, plus interest, plus inflation. I don't know of a factory anybody can build that will give that kind of return. . . ." However intended, it seems a peculiar way to speak of children.

Even groups that advocate for children do not seem to feel it's safe to make an argument on their behalf without convincing us that being kind to children will be cost-effective. Money invested in nutrition programs and pre-natal care, we're told in countless publications, "saves hundreds of thousands of dollars" that might otherwise be spent to place brain-damaged children in intensive care. "Investing in Futures" is the headline of an article on the cost-saving benefits of giving inner-city children decent healthcare and good preschool, published in The Boston Globe. We invest in soy or oil futures. So we may invest in "child futures" also.

The trouble with this is that "investment values," whether in petroleum, in soy, or in the children of poor people, rise and fall. What if a future generation of geneticists, economists, or both, should come to the conclusion that the children of St. Ann's don't offer a sufficient payoff to a corporation's bottom line to warrant serious investment? We hear the stirrings of such notions even now in writings that allude to IQ differentials between racial and religious subgroups of the population. The subgroup living in Mott Haven does not stand too high within these rankings. If investment value is the governing determination here, Elio and Ariel are certain to be given less of almost everything that can bring purpose or fulfillment to existence than the seemingly "more valuable" white and Asian children who get into schools like Stuyvesant, New York's most famous high school for the academically elite.

Advocates for children, most of whom dislike this ethos, nonetheless play into it in efforts to obtain financial backing from the world of business. "A dollar spent on Head Start," they repeat time and again, "will save our government six dollars over 20 years" in lowered costs for juvenile detention and adult incarceration. It's a point worth making if it's true, although it's hard to prove; and, still, it strikes one as a pretty dreadful way to have to speak of four-year-olds. The fact that it allows a child the size of Mariposa several hundred mornings with warm-hearted people in a safe and friendly pastel-painted setting seems to be regarded as too "soft," too sentimental, to be mentioned in the course of these discussions. "We should invest in kids like these," we're told, "because it will be more expensive not to." Why do our natural compassion and religious inclinations need to find a surrogate in dollar savings to be voiced or acted on? Why not give these kids the best we have because we are a wealthy nation and they're children and deserve to have some fun while they're still less than four feet high?

Or is the point here that we don't believe this? Sometimes it seems that "having fun" is seen as a luxurious entitlement that cannot be accorded to the child of a woman who relies on welfare lest it make dependent status too enjoyable. It seems at times that happiness itself is viewed as an extravagance and that our sole concerns in dealing with such children must be discipline, efficiency, and future worth.

The problem is not only that low-income children are devalued by these mercantile criteria; childhood itself is also redefined. It ceases to hold value for its own sake but is valued only as a "necessary prologue" to utilitarian adulthood. The first ten, twelve, or fifteen years of life are excavated of inherent moral worth in order to accommodate a regimen of basic training for the adult years that many of the poorest children may not even live to know. There is no reference to investing in the present—in the childhood of children—only in a later incarnation of the child as a "product" or "producer."

"We must start to think about these inner-city children as our future entry-level workers," we are told by business leaders as they forge their various alliances and partnerships with poorly funded urban schools. It's said so frequently that it occasions little stir. Still, it's fair to ask why we are being urged to see "these" children in that quite specific way. Why are we to look at Elio and see a future entry-level worker rather than to see him, as we see our own kids, as perhaps a future doctor, dancer, artist, poet, priest, psychologist, or teacher, or whatever else he might someday desire to be? Why not, for that matter, look at him and see the only thing he really is: a seven-year-old child?

Pineapple and Elio are not "preparatory people." They are complete and good in what they are already; and their small but mystical and interesting beings ought to count for something in our estimation without any calculation as to how they someday may, or may not, serve the economic interests of somebody else or something else when they are 25 or 30. Mariposa is not simply 37 pounds of raw material that wants a certain "processing" and "finishing" before she can be shipped to market and considered to have value. She is of value now, and if she dies of a disease or accident when she is twelve years old, the sixth year of her life will not as a result be robbed of meaning. But *we* can rob it of its meaning now if we deny her the essential dignity of being seen and celebrated for the person that she actually is.

Business-minded people who come up to visit at St. Ann's and give themselves some time to get to know the children seem to find themselves relieved to be emancipated from the litanies of cost-efficiency and productivity that they might voice in other situations. Once they're here, it seems, the ideologies disintegrate. An intimate reality does often have this power to collapse or modify belief. Nobody seems to want to advocate a "lean and mean" approach to public services for children while they're sitting at the afterschool with Elio or being drilled with questions by Pineapple.

The parents and staff at St. Ann's aren't naive about the world of economic competition that their children will be forced to enter in a few more years. The pedagogic program at the afterschool is rigorous. Nelly Espina, who directs the academic portion of the program and developed most of its components, is a first-rate teacher and a savvy woman with a lot of love and hot sauce in her personality and with a realistic recognition of the academic needs of children. The church is also forced to pay attention to the newly instituted tests the children have to pass in public school. No one here, no matter how benighted they may think these tests to be, has any hesitation about working hard with children on test-taking skills, because they know that children in rich neighborhoods receive this preparation as a matter of routine, often in expensive private programs.

Intensive academics aren't the whole of what goes on here at the afterschool, however. If they were, the children wouldn't come here with such eagerness when they leave public school. Amidst the pressures and the tensions about school promotion policies (and nonpromotion policies, which recently have come to be capricious and severe) and reading skills, percentile "norms" and math exams and high school applications, or rejections, and the rest of what makes up the pedagogic battlefield, which is not now, and never was, a level field for children in poor neighborhoods like the South Bronx, the grown-ups here have also managed somehow to leave room for innocence.

The pastor has her three degrees: in economics (as an undergraduate at Radcliffe), then in law, and then theology. She also has a bracelet made of jelly beans that Jefferson's sister gave her as a present before Easter. It is, she told me once when I was looking at the brightly colored jelly beans that Jefferson's sister somehow linked together with a needle and a piece of string, the only bracelet anyone has given her since childhood—"more beautiful," she said with pride, "than finest pearls." In an age of drills and skills and endless lists of reinvented standards and a multitude of new and sometimes useful but too often frankly punitive exams, it's nice to find a place where there is still some room for things of no cash value—oddball humor, silliness and whim, a child's love, a grown-up's gratitude and joy—that never in a hundred years would show up as a creditable number on one of those all-important state exams.

Competitive skills are desperately needed by poor children in America; and realistic recognitions of the economic roles that they may someday have an opportunity to fill are obviously important too. But there is more to life, and ought to be much more to childhood, than readiness for economic function. Childhood ought to have at least a few entitlements that aren't entangled with utilitarian considerations. One of them should be the right to a degree of unencumbered satisfaction in the sheer delight and goodness of existence in itself. Another ought to be the confidence of knowing that one's presence on this earth is taken as an unconditioned blessing that is not contaminated by the economic uses that a nation does or does not have for you. What I admire most about the programs and the atmosphere of daily life here at St. Ann's is that these diverse goals are reconciled in relatively seamless ways that make it possible for children to regard the world, and life itself, as something which, though difficult and often filled with pain and tears, is also sometimes good, and sometimes bountiful in foolishness, and therefore beautiful.

I recognize that jelly beans will not be seen by all Episcopalian officials as appropriate adornments for the vicar of an urban church; but it means something to Jefferson's sister when she sees the pastor wear that bracelet as she stands before the cross to celebrate the mass. The details of life renew our faith in life. In the busy ministries of grief the detailed things — the Band-Aids and the skinned knees and the handiwork of children's fingers — are too easily dismissed or relegated to the margins of consideration. I've been thankful that the detailed things are not forgotten in the course of all the solemn matters that preoccupy the pastor of St. Ann's.

People ask me why I keep on going back to visit at this church when there are other churches in New York that operate effective programs that teach children useful skills each afternoon when they are done with school.

I don't usually answer. If I did, I know I wouldn't say too much about the writing program and test-preparation program and computer classes. They're good programs, but a "program," even one that has some provable success, would not have brought me back into a church in the South Bronx nearly two hundred times. If I had to answer, I would say that I go back for all the things that can't be calibrated by exams. Elio's imagination and his curiosity and tenderness are part of this, and Ariel's unselfishness, and Jefferson's shyness and sweet sadness, and his closeness to the priest, and Jefferson's cat.

Two years have passed. On quiet afternoons the boy with melancholy eyes goes by himself sometimes into the chapel of St. Ann's and kneels down on the floor to say prayers for his mother and his cat. Mother Martha sometimes prays beside him. I have never asked the pastor what she prays for.

CHAPTER 12

A Question of Values

Mild weather in New York. A comfortable Saturday in early June. Katrice was so exhausted by a week of minor crises at the church that she remained in bed until the afternoon today.

Raven is in her grandmother's bedroom, watching something on TV. In the living room there are a pair of easy chairs, a coffee table and a love-seat, and a long dark-covered sofa. Katrice is sitting on the sofa just beneath a wall of photographs: her children and grandchildren and her father and one of her sisters and a brother, who live in St. Thomas in the Virgin Islands.

A woman came to church this week, she says, and told her she had AIDS and needed a food supplement, known as Ensure, which many people who have AIDS depend upon, especially when they're too sick to hold down solid food. Her Medicaid and food stamps had been cut without her being given any reason, an old pattern in

New York but one that's grown more common in the past two years. The woman cried, according to Katrice, because she said her daughter was afraid to touch her.

The reaction of the woman's daughter — her withdrawal from her mother — troubled Katrice greatly. "For a stranger to be scared of you I understand. But for your own to turn away from you?" The woman told Katrice her daughter wouldn't let her hug her. "She didn't ask if I would hug her, but I thought God *wanted* me to do it," Katrice says.

After holding the woman, and consoling her, Katrice went back into the kitchen, found her keys, and opened up the closet where she keeps supplies for the food pantry. Food supplements have been in scarce supply this year, she says, but one half-empty case remained. She counted out a dozen cans and put them in a cardboard carton for the woman to take home. Then she brought her up to talk with Mother Martha.

Many people in this woman's situation end up at St. Ann's in times of panic after they've been turned away from other places. The city's emergency unit for the homeless, which is twelve or fifteen blocks away, is not a hospitable place. I've been there on a freezing winter night when scores of children and their mothers have been sleeping on the floor with all of their belongings packed in plastic garbage bags beside them. But dozens of families who show up there without proper documents are turned away and told they first must call a number from a pay phone in the street in order to be "certified" as homeless. Sometimes the pay phone doesn't work. Even when it does, the number often comes up with a busy signal.

You see desperation there on winter nights. Mothers standing with their children on the corner beg for change so they can use the phone, or try it for a second or third time, or for a few dollars to buy supper for their children at a take-out place nearby.

The emergency unit—"EAU," as it is called—is run with either military harshness, and defensively, like prisons under lockdown, or else with haphazard sloppiness, depending on who happens to be running things from one night to the next. I spent two hours talking with some children and their mothers there one night before someone who looked like an official even asked why I was there. Another time, I came with Mother Martha but the woman running things refused to let her in because, she said, "We can't allow just *anyone* to walk into this unit and endanger people," even though the priest was dressed as always in her priestly dress and collar and does not look dangerous.

Families who are not admitted to the shelter sometimes stay out in the street all night and find their way to churches like St. Ann's the following day. Katrice sees many people therefore when they're close to giving up. Often, she says, their kids are wheezing but, because of the disorder and confusion in their lives, no longer have their pump. Infants may be soiled. Mothers may not have the money to buy baby formula or Pampers.

Other families show up very late, after the kitchen door's been locked. "No one's there but me and Elsie," says Katrice. "So we unlock the door and look in back and find some food. The bread and rolls come from suburban churches, or from restaurants, or bakeries downtown. It could be a few days old by then. They see the bread there in the box. I say, 'It's stale.' They stare at it as if they're scared to ask.

"Sometimes I find them standing outside near the door in cold or rain. If it's late, the lights are out. They see the door's been locked. I find them when I'm leaving. So I open up again and bring them back into the kitchen to get warm."

Some, she says, are families that have just been placed in an apartment but don't have the money to buy food.

147

JONATHAN KOZOL

"We give them soup in cans, maybe a jar of peanut butter, can of beef stew, tuna fish, maybe a box of cereal or pasta, jar of cooking oil, bag of rice. Some don't have a pot to cook the rice. Whatever I can find back there I give them."

After coming here in need of food, she says, a woman sometimes is embarrassed to accept it. "I'll say, 'Don't be embarrassed. This is here for you to have.' They'll say, 'I don't have any way to thank you.' I tell them, 'You don't *need* to thank me because this is what a church is for. That's why we're here.' They'll say, 'You didn't need to open up the door.' I tell them, 'Yes. I did. I *had* to open up. This is a church. God doesn't close the door.'

"A woman was at church two weeks ago that had two little ones in hand. One was a baby that had just made two. The other had made four. Onliest thing that I can't stand is see a child hungry and her mother so embarrassed that she's scared to ask. Picture children to a table sitting and their mother doesn't have a thing to feed them. . . .

"All the women down there, me and Elsie, Mrs. Santos, Margarita, all us women are grandmothers. So we're in another generation now and some of us don't have the strength we used to have. But grandmothers have to be there, whether you feel good or not. If a child's mother's using drugs, or sick, or in the hospital, or in some other trouble, and she can't sustain, you have to take her place. You have to be the mother *and* grandmother. Not just for your own. For all."

She often says "sustain" like that without an object for the verb. It stands alone. Other mothers use the word in the same way. "I'm tryin' to sustain," a woman in the neighborhood might say if she's been going through a time of crisis or depression. The word "maintain" is used like that as well. It's as if the object of these verbs is so amorphous and so large, or maybe so self-evident, that there's no point in naming it.

148

On Sundays sometimes during the soup kitchen, Katrice will see an older person who has finished eating but is looking at the food she's serving as if he's still hungry and would like a little more but is afraid to ask. If there's enough for everyone she'll ask if he would like a second helping. At this point, however, many people are reluctant to accept it. They truly do not want to take what someone else might need. This balance between need and hesitation, between wanting and accepting, between dignity and pleading and abasement, is a matter that involves a lot of care in choice of words and manner of expression for the people who on any given day are in the role of giving or receiving.

I've been in large soup kitchens run by charitable agencies or churches where it seemed that a degree of self-abasement was assumed to be appropriate by some of the traditional providers who were running everything with an impersonal and vaguely punitive efficiency. Catholic Worker houses, on the other hand, tend to be governed by a mood more like the one I sense here at St. Ann's. I don't think that sensitivities like these can be established by a set of rules or regulations. They have to do with personalities and styles of the individuals involved.

"Would you like some more?" Katrice might say.

The man holds back, fearful perhaps that there is something impolite or inappropriate about his hunger.

"Go ahead!" she'll say. "God knows, it's there! It's there for you. If you don't take it, it's just going to be thrown away."

That isn't actually true. No matter how much food the church prepares, it's almost always gone before Katrice goes home. If there's still some turkey and some sweet potato left at a Thanksgiving dinner, for example, she may make a final plate and wrap it up in foil and deliver it to someone who's too sick to come to church; or else she'll send it with a child who may live in the same building as the person who is ill. The efforts she makes to guard a stranger from the dangers of humiliation are, for her, I think, not simply matters of religious duty. She knows the risks because she's been on both sides of the table.

Generally, when she and Margarita and Miss Elsie are preparing dinner on a Sunday, they're so busy that they don't have time to go upstairs for mass. Mother Martha comes down to the kitchen on those days before the service starts and serves communion there. The busy preparations for the Sunday dinner and the holiness of the communion do not seem in conflict with each other. "The Sabbath was made for man, and not man for the Sabbath," says one of the passages of gospel that the pastor cites when people question her about the informality of certain practices that she adapts to meet the needs of her parishioners.

Katrice worked twenty years ago at Hunts Point Market, cleaning chicken parts. In subsequent years, like Eleanor, she also worked as a domestic in Manhattan. She told me once, however, that when she was a young woman she had had a dream of owning her own restaurant. "I had this imagination in those days of growing up to run a restaurant and doing 'fancy foods.' I never had another wish but own a restaurant where I could cook and see the people coming in to find good food there on the table."

It came into my mind that, in an unexpected way, she did end up running a "restaurant" of sorts, not one she owned but one that did, at times, serve fancy foods, which were leftovers from elaborate parties and receptions in Manhattan. The strangest foods have shown up in the boxes that arrived here from Manhattan: little hot dogs wrapped in cheese and bacon, mushroom pies that looked like quiche, and other elegant-appearing items that had been prepared perhaps for weddings or bar mitzvahs, or for cocktail snacks at an expensive restaurant.

An overeagerness to search for ironies, I am afraid, is one of the afflictions that I picked up as an undergraduate in college. Katrice does not have time to hunt for ironies. Where I might think I've found an irony, in any case, she is more likely to see God's intention. I feel foolish sometimes when I point to something that appears to me to be a grand, ironical coincidence — she wanted to run a restaurant and now, in a sense, she does — but she just nods and tells me that whatever she is doing is, she has no doubt, exactly what God must have planned for her to do from the beginning.

Irony, I have to say, did come to mind one afternoon when I was looking at a box of diet biscuits, decorated with small bits of salmon, that had just been sent up to St. Ann's. Katrice did not have time to play with this idea. It was a busy day. Shentasha's mother had come to the afterschool because her electricity had been cut off. Katrice went out into the walkway by the garden so the two of them could talk without the children overhearing. Then the woman went upstairs to talk with Mother Martha, and Katrice came back to put away the food. She tried one of the decorated biscuits to make sure it wasn't spoiled, said it tasted fine, then wrapped them up in cellophane and stored them in the big refrigerator in the kitchen.

Shentasha's mother trusted in Katrice. It was to Katrice that she had turned for help one day when she was standing in the street in tears in front of Blimpie's and Katrice had happened to come by. "She just looked scared of *something*," said Katrice; so she had stopped to find out what was wrong and then had talked with her about the programs for the children at the church. Soon Shentasha started coming to the afterschool. Then her older brother started coming to the church as well. After a time, her mother started coming Sunday mornings for the mass.

Sometimes when she tells me narratives like these, Katrice's eyes begin to fill with tears. She often holds a crumpled piece of tissue in her hand. Stories that have happy endings seem to make her cry as easily as sad ones do. Her voice chokes up. Then she goes out and stands alone in the fresh air in order to compose her feelings.

The children love Katrice. They trust her judgment and her goodness and her common sense. "Their worries should be my worries," she says of the ones who have the greatest troubles in their homes. It seems an ordinary thing to say; but living your life as if this actually were so is not as common as it ought to be for most of us.

"Katrice is a fisher of souls," says Mother Martha.

Of all the many sad and happy souls Katrice has brought into the church, Shentasha may well be the liveliest. As I have said, however, she's not always in a jubilant and foolish mood. In a neighborhood where almost everyone is poor, Shentasha's mother is the poorest of the poor. Heat and water and electric power are repeatedly cut off in their apartment. On those days, Shentasha's mother cannot wash her clothes. I've seen the nine-year-old come to the afterschool in clothes so smelly that her friends would not get close to her.

Shentasha and her family live in three constrictively small rooms that smell of sewage backup, and sometimes of kerosene or gasoline, in an unpleasant building less than two blocks from St. Ann's. The building has no elevator, no bell, and no buzzer system. When I go to visit them I have to yell up from the street. One of them has to lean out of the fifth-floor window and throw down the key to the front door.

On one occasion when I had to go to see them on short notice I was with a friend who had been visiting the church. When we left the apartment, he said something that I've now heard several times from people who were in the neighborhood for the first time. "I didn't know that people live in places like that in the South Bronx anymore. I felt embarrassed. I was sure they must have known what I was thinking."

I don't write so much about these aspects of existence in Mott Haven now. You say these things for six or seven years, or fifteen years, or thirty years. You say them to a Senate subcommittee or a House committee. You say them in a talk to college students or a sermon to the always sympathetic Unitarians. You say them in your writing and get slapped down by the routine arbiters of culture in New York, who wonder why you're angrier than they are. After a time you start to feel worn out by your own words. You grow sick of being angry — sick, as well, of being isolated by your anger. Perhaps, in time, your narrative grows more subdued.

Then something happens to stir up your sense of anger once again. A child is telling you about the bus ride that she takes to see her father, far from New York City, in one of the huge state prisons. She speaks of the mixture of emotions that she feels — for him, herself, her mother. Then Shentasha, who is sitting there beside you, lowers her defenses and describes the rides that *she* takes to see *her* father as well. Then another child adds her contribution, and an older boy adds his; you realize with dismay that this is one thing all the children at this table have in common.

They speak of being searched by prison guards and being stamped with an electric imprint of some sort before they can go through the metal gates. They talk about the almost normal-seeming hours that they spend there with their fathers, getting snacks from a machine, or making friends with other children they may meet, or playing on the swings and slides that now are found at many prisons, where so many children come to see their fathers on the weekends. But they also speak of the anxiety they feel when they

153

are told it's time to leave, and of the sad leavetakings, and the grimness of the long ride all the way back to the Bronx.

Nearly a quarter of the children see their fathers, or have seen their fathers, only under these conditions. It wasn't like this in our country when I was a teacher. Vans and buses run directly from New York to prisons several hundred miles away. The children fall asleep on the way home. Six hours, seven hours, sometimes even more. A devastating way to learn American geography.

I am reminded of this every time I leave New York because the planes leaving LaGuardia take off over Rikers Island. In daylight hours you can see the inmates on work duty. The buildings on the island are so crowded that some inmates have been housed in huge balloonlike structures that resemble metal mushrooms. There's a prison for teenagers out there also. I met a guard there once, a Puerto Rican man who grew up in Mott Haven near St. Ann's and introduced me to a number of the boys who came from the same area. They told me where they lived and where they went to school. Some of the streets on which they lived were streets I walk when I go from the subway to St. Ann's, or from St. Ann's to someone's home. Some of the schools they mentioned were the schools I visit.

Across the water from the prison island, next to yet another sewage plant and trash-deposit station in Hunts Point in the South Bronx, there's a multistory prison barge that has been used in recent years for children in detention. Several thousand juveniles thirteen years old or older have been held there at one point or other in a given year—about one hundred at a time—while they awaited transfer to more permanent facilities. It's a tremendous structure, with six floating floors of prison cells, one of them under water. From the sky, however, it looks decorative. It's painted in clean colors, blue and white, and looks as if it might be some sort of a pleasure craft, a cruise ship possibly.

The city spends $64,000 yearly to incarcerate an adult inmate on the prison island. It spends $93,000 yearly to incarcerate a child on the prison barge or in the very costly and imposing new detention center built on St. Ann's Avenue. That's about eleven times as much as it is spending, on the average, for a year of education for a child in the New York City public schools during the last years of the 1990s — *eighteen* times what it is spending in a year to educate a mainstream student in an ordinary first-grade classroom in the schools of the South Bronx. There are countless academic studies of allegedly "deficient" social values in the children of the poor, but I do not know any studies of the values of the educated grown-ups who believe this is a healthy way to run a social order.

I don't think of things like this — not often, certainly — when I'm with children at St. Ann's. I'm more likely to be thinking of what's happening in front of me right now, or something I just heard a child say, or looking at a drawing that a child's brought me or a book a child's shown me. I'm thinking of Pinocchio or Charlotte's Web, and not the number of the children's relatives in prison.

It's later on, in other settings, that I'll be reminded by some memory or detail of the sadder aspects of their lives. I try to counter these discouraging reflections. I think of all the good work being done by teachers that I know at P.S. 30. I think about the good work being done by many doctors in the area. I think about the good work being done by Elsie and Katrice and Nancy and the other people at the church. I think of people working hard at all the other churches in the Bronx. I look continually for reasons to be hopeful. I just want them to be genuine.

PART TWO

CHAPTER 13

A Sense of Scale

When Elio was in first grade, he misbehaved and didn't do his lessons and when springtime came, his teacher said he wasn't ready to go on to second grade. So, on a day in early June, Miss Rosa had to tell his mother that he couldn't be promoted.

Elio and I were not acquainted at the time. I'd seen him at the church but didn't get to know him until maybe about eight months later — it was in the last part of the winter, I believe — when he came up with me and Stephanie one day to the computer room.

"What grade are you in?" asked Stephanie.

"I had to repeat," he said in an unhappy voice.

"What grade did you repeat?" she asked.

"First grade!" he said. "How do you pass first grade?"

"It's hard," she said.

"Yes. It *is*. It's hard," he said. "All that work! And now I have to do it all again."

Stephanie tried to find some words to reassure him that he wouldn't have to stay in first grade his entire life; and, as it turned out, he did much better on his lessons that year and passed all of his exams and, being small, he didn't seem to suffer quite as much as other children might for being one year older than his classmates.

I remember that discussion, though, because it served as such a sharp reminder of how very big, and hard, the "big world" seemed to him — the world of reading tests, of school promotions, and the world of second grade — and of how minuscule his status seemed to him to be, and actually was, when placed before these necessary checkpoints, which are part of life for children everywhere.

The first time that I really got to talk with Elio at any length was in the spring of 1996 when he and sixty other children from the neighborhood went on a trip to Washington and Mother Martha and the parents asked if I'd like to come too. The idea of the trip was for the children and the parents to participate in a large demonstration organized by people who were hoping to discourage Congress and the White House from approving legislation that would bring an end to federal welfare benefits for children. I was asked to help to supervise the children on the ride, which took about six hours and turned out to be a test of patience for the grown-ups, on my bus at least, particularly in the final hour of the trip when many of the older kids were getting restless. It still was fun and gave the children glimpses of a small part of the nation that they'd never seen before. Some had never been outside New York up to that time. A few, I found, had never been outside the Bronx.

The kick-off for the trip involved the usual amount of chaos and confusion and excitement, but was also interrupted briefly by a moment of alarm. The children were about to climb into the first of the two buses parked out-side the church on St. Ann's Avenue when gunshots rang out somewhere to the left of us. The shots were loud and came in sequences of several blasts—perhaps three shots, then silence, then three more. Elio was standing with me and his mother on the sidewalk, waiting for the driver of the second bus, who was rechecking his directions with the priest. The older kids were doing what they could to keep the younger ones from drifting out into the street.

Katrice was standing with a clipboard, counting off the children, at the moment when the shots were heard. She threw down the clipboard and began to run in the direction of the shots, which seemed to come from Beek-man Avenue. A number of children at St. Ann's lived on that street and on the two adjacent blocks. It was early evening and some of their mothers would be outside at this hour with their babies on the sidewalk before going in for supper. Katrice was 53 years old, but she was run-ning up that hill like a teenager. Seven young people she had known, or whom her children and grandchildren knew, were murdered on that block in the preceding years. Once she was sure that no one had been killed or injured she came back and found her clipboard and con-tinued checking off the children.

Elio and his mother sat across the aisle from me on the second bus. He was drowsy by the time we left but grew alert as soon as we crossed Harlem and the Hudson River and began to head south through New Jersey. Half standing and half sitting, with his right hand pressed against the window, he asked questions about every little thing we passed and never really stopped for the first hour.

"Are we still in New York?"

"No," his mother said. "We're in New Jersey now."

"Is that tree there in New Jersey?"

"Yes," his mother said.

A man was standing by a car beside the highway, looking in his trunk.

"Is that man in New Jersey?"

"Yes," his mother said.

We passed a number of big buildings.

"Are those buildings in New Jersey?"

"Yes," she said.

Soon we passed an area of airline runways, part of Newark Airport. An aircraft that was landing flew directly over us.

"Are we still in New Jersey?"

"Everything you see around you is New Jersey," said his mother.

He looked at the sky, in which the sun was setting low behind a cloud of pinkish red over a flat and smelly area of giant metal tubes and oil tanks and such. "Are those things in New Jersey?"

"It's *all* New Jersey," said his mother.

As darkness came, he started humming to himself while sucking on the bare end of a stick that held a lollypop a few minutes before. His mother took away the stick, and soon he started to get sleepy. In her bag his mother had a pillow that was decorated with the face of Mickey Mouse. Inside the pillow cover was a blanket, also decorated with the face of Mickey Mouse. She handed him the pillow and he held it for a while against his chest. Then she took the blanket out and tucked it in around his shoulders as he curled against her on the seat.

He woke up more than an hour later, when I think that we were somewhere close to Philadelphia, and crawled across his mother's legs and came to sit beside me. He had a bag of peanut-butter snacks and offered some to me. When I said I don't like peanut butter he took out a package that held slices of bologna, which he shared with me until the bus pulled off the highway for a stop at a rest-area.

The other bus, which we'd been following, was parked already and the kids were heading for the bathrooms and Roy Rogers and the other food shops there.

"Guess what?" said Elio to Mother Martha, who was waiting for us as we climbed down from the bus.

"What?" she said.

"We're in New Jersey!"

"I don't think so," Mother Martha said. "I think we're supposed to be in Pennsylvania."

"Un-uh!" he said. "We're in New Jersey."

"I don't *think* so . . . ," Mother Martha said.

He turned around and looked up at his mother.

"That's enough," she said.

He ran off through the darkness with the other children to the bathroom. Once we got back on the bus he fell asleep again and didn't wake until we got to Washington at one A.M.

The bus got lost as we were looking for the church in which the kids were supposed to sleep for the remainder of the night. Some of the teenagers, sitting in the back part of the bus, were hollering and hooting in the last half-hour as the bus driver would stop, back up into a narrow street and turn around, or park there briefly, hoping that the driver of the other bus would notice that we weren't behind him and would come and find us.

The driver complained about the noise. I soon was shouting at the older boys to quiet down. Nelly Espina, who was sitting in the front, said later that she was "intrigued" to notice I was capable of getting really mad.

Elio slept through it all. The following day he and several other children held a purple banner with the name of St. Ann's Church as we walked in the line of march with children and adults from all over the nation. Standing on a patch of grass by the reflecting pool, Elio went wild with excitement when he saw that Mother Martha had come out on stage to read an opening prayer.

"Yay! Yay!" he kept on shouting.

"Elio!" said Stephanie, who stood beside him in the sun.

"It's not a baseball game," his mother said.

But he was too excited to contain himself and cheered throughout a series of long speeches.

I had to return to New York City to attend a meeting in the Bronx. I left the children and the other grown-ups on the walk back from the mall, found a subway station, and got to the airport just in time to catch the shuttle to New York. Ruth Westheimer, who had come here for the rally with her daughter and grandchild, was in line ahead of me. Irwin Redlener, a children's advocate and doctor working in the Bronx whom I had met the year before, was just behind us; so we sat together on the plane.

Both doctors were concerned about the pending welfare legislation and its implications for the children of New York. Dr. Ruth is not so widely known for her political beliefs as for her humor and her sexual irreverence; but she's a stalwart advocate for children, and she told me she had tried to get in touch with me a year or two before and scolded me because I'd missed her message somehow and had never called her back.

Dr. Redlener was in the early stages of developing a comprehensive program to address respiratory problems among children in the Bronx. He spoke about the causes of these problems and described some of the obstacles he faced in finding the resources to address them; but he didn't seem discouraged. He's a powerhouse of energy who won important victories for homeless children in New York during the 1980s and has recently been chosen to direct a children's hospital now in the planning stages in the Bronx. He has a skillful way of finding allies and constructing coalitions without compromising his beliefs. I got back to New York exhilarated by our conversation.

The gunfire that broke out near Beekman Avenue as we were getting set to leave for Washington the night before was a reminder of the past. When I had written Amazing Grace in 1995, I listed all the boys who had been murdered on that block in an obituary at the end—ten young men, in all, were killed there or in nearby blocks during the previous four years—in part because one of the mothers on the street said that their children never got obituaries.

There hadn't been so many incidents like those in recent years as in the first part of the decade—mostly, as Katrice believed, because the cocaine trade had been much quieter. The drug trade never really stops, however. Driven from one block, as an agent of the federal Drug Enforcement Agency who was responsible for the Mott Haven neighborhood observed to me while we were having lunch one afternoon, it moves around the corner to another. Driven from the streets entirely now and then, it moves indoors. This leads at times to unexpected confrontations.

On an evening about twelve months after that, as I was coming down the stairs in the apartment building where Isaiah lives, which is Katrice's building too, I turned a corner in the stairs between the fourth floor and the third and walked into a drug deal taking place a step or two beneath the landing. The dealer was standing on the stairs. Five of his customers were in a line in front of him. He looked at me with curiosity but didn't show concern and went on counting money from a wad of bills to make change for the man in front of him.

I later told Katrice I was surprised that he did not seem bothered by my presence. She said he'd surely seen me there before, or at the church, or in the street nearby; and nobody, she said, would have mistaken me for a narcotics officer or a policeman. I think that my reaction at the time was irritation, maybe even injured dignity, that my appearance in the stairs had been of little interest to these men. When I mentioned this to Mother Martha at the church, she said, "You sound insulted!" She may have been right. The incident, in any case, seemed trivial. It had to do with oddity and accident and a coincidence of timing, not with any sense of dread or danger.

Some of my friends who live outside the Bronx believe I take these incidents too lightly. "Is it smart," a friend from Cambridge asked, "for someone of your age to walk around the way you do at night in places like Mott Haven? Did you ever actually sit down and think this through?"

Others ask if I may, consciously or not, be trying to relive the years when I was a young teacher and was living in the segregated neighborhood of Boston where some of my students lived.

"You're not 29 years old. This isn't 1965."

I hear that comment, or one like it, frequently.

Usually these comments are not based on firsthand knowledge of the neighborhood but are derived from the impressions of the South Bronx given by news stories on TV or by a single frightening event that isn't typical of what goes on but is sufficiently dramatic to awaken fears. A young schoolteacher, for example, to whom I was introduced one night at dinner in Manhattan and who said that he was teaching English at Taft High School in the Bronx, a likable man whose father was a well-known figure in New York, was murdered six months later in his own apartment by a boy who'd been his student. My mother heard of this because it was a front-page story in The Times and was reported widely on TV.

The teacher happened to be white, and Jewish, and had gone to Trinity College, where I had been a teacher once. His first name was Jonathan. My mother remarked on this coincidence. Inevitably, she also took the opportunity to lecture me, as she has done repeatedly since I was 25 years old, about my thoughtlessness in forcing her to worry and "stay up all night" with her anxieties, which is a potent weapon in the hands of mothers even when the son whose actions worry them is over 60.

In this case, of course, my mother had no context of experience in which to place this frightening event. This is not the case with everyone who questions me, however. Some of the friends who show concern about my wanderings are speaking from their own experience.

"Stereotypes about these neighborhoods may overstate the dangers," says a friend who lives in the South Bronx, was once a heroin user, and knows almost all the streets around Mott Haven and East Tremont—another South Bronx neighborhood where I have friends. "There still are inescapable realities, however. Drugs are down from six or seven years ago, but drugs have not evaporated from these neighborhoods. Beekman Avenue seems quiet now, but Cypress is still dangerous and the section of East Tremont that you visit is notorious, and rightly so, for hard-core heroin addiction.

"Liberals may think that they can contradict a stereotype," he notes, "by walking off into a neighborhood where they do not belong" and may believe they'll "be protected" by their ideologies or sentimental loyalties. "It doesn't work like that," he says, "and you'd be unwise to believe it."

It's difficult to answer these concerns without pretending that you're braver than you are or making coy denials that imply a reprimand to those who voice these worries. If I say—what is, in fact, the truth—that I don't usually feel frightened, it sounds almost like self-praise to some. To others it suggests a fatuous bravado. I have never figured out a dignified and reasonable way to deal with this. The truth of the matter, though, is that these questions about danger almost always seem unreal.

The time I walked into that group of men as I was coming down the stairs of the apartment building where Isaiah lives, I was briefly startled, but my main reaction was annoyance. I had to ask one of the guys to move so I could pass him on the stairs. The look he gave me had a mocking quality, but it conveyed no sense of threat.

A sense of danger, frankly, is not something ever-present in the streets around St. Ann's, and certainly not something that you think of constantly when you're with children here. If it does come to your mind, you feel embarrassed when you realize you can leave at any time you want but that the children *can't,* that they'll still be here when you're gone. These complicated feelings are made even more complex by the protectiveness the children tend to show for *you* — a grown-up — which is a familiar role-reversal that takes place here between children and the visitors they get to know.

Anthony Bonilla, a sophisticated, deeply intellectual teenager whom I met near Cypress Avenue when he was twelve years old and who attends a secondary school in Massachusetts now, often goes for walks with me when he's home with his mother in Mott Haven for vacation. He has a way of reaching for my arm at times and indicating that we ought to cross the street, or take a different street, in order to avoid specific corner-lots or buildings that he thinks to be unwholesome.

"I don't think this street is good for you," he'll say.

"What do you mean?"

"Let's just say it gives me an adverse reaction," he replied once when I asked, showing off, as is his frequent pleasure now, one of his newest items of arcane vocabulary.

Even Elio can be protective in his way. I ran into him late one night in June when he was walking with his mother and a friend of hers on St. Ann's Avenue and I was coming out of the apartment building of a friend with whom I had had dinner.

"Where are you *going*, Jonathan?" he asked, appearing truly shocked to see me there so late.

"I'm going to the subway," I replied.

"Which one?" he asked.

"Brook Avenue," I said.

He looked at his mother, then at me, and asked if I would like them to come with me. When I said it wasn't necessary and assured him that I'd made that walk repeatedly, he tapped me on the arm, as if he were a very wise old-timer, and he said, as I am sure his mother must have said to him a good number of times, *"Cuidate!"* — which means "Careful!"

His mother nodded at his words and seconded his good advice. "Be careful, Jonathan. . . ." Then I went to the train; and all went well, as usual.

I hope these comments don't seem to romanticize the situation in the neighborhood, as Mother Martha notes that visitors are prone to do. These children do not live in a green valley. Shootings still take place, not only late at night but in broad daylight too; and even the solicitude and innocence of children and the mantle of protectiveness they cast on those they love, and which their mothers also cast on them, cannot work miracles.

Innocence cannot stop bullets. It cannot eradicate disease. It can't put books and well-paid teachers into underfunded schools. But innocence has power. It undercuts obsessive fears. It tames anxiety. It brings things down to manageable size. It also helps to separate the little fears from big ones.

On some occasions, if I'm leaving her apartment very late at night, Katrice insists on walking with me to the subway station. If the trains aren't stopping at Brook Avenue, she'll walk another three long blocks to Alexander Avenue in order to be sure that no one bothers me while waiting on the platform. It's more a matter of her sense of courtesy, however, than of physical protection. I think she simply feels that walking with me to the subway is the proper thing to do, no matter what the hour.

Katrice has firm ideas about politeness — basic rectitude, traditional gentility — and is unfailingly observant of proprieties. She sends me greeting cards on Jewish holidays. She asks repeatedly about my mother's health. She says prayers for my mother and my father. She also has a sense of scale about the dangers that mean most in life. She knows which ones are real, which ones are overstated, and which ones can never be escaped.

Her shrewdness about life and her realism in the face of death have helped me greatly in these years as I have had to watch my two best friends, those I have known longest and loved most, slipping by inevitable stages from a world in which I am afraid to live without them. By her basic sanity and her unselfish love, she casts a spell of goodness on the world, a sense of grace, a vision of eternity.

Her friendship means the world to me.

CHAPTER 14

A Reunion

Autumn in New York. It's nearly four months since I've seen the children. It seems even longer. My mother's been sick. I've been preoccupied with finding people to take care of her and trying to convince her not to fire them more rapidly than I can hire new ones.

Elio sent me a birthday card two months ago. His mother bought it for him and he signed his name and she signed hers beneath it. But I haven't seen him since the last week in July.

When I walk into his class at P.S. 30 on a Monday in November, he appears a bit confused at first and seems unable to decide what he should do. I find it confusing too, because we know each other pretty well by now. We've spent a lot of time together at St. Ann's and in the neighborhood and on our trip to Washington. I know his mother and I see her at the drugstore where she works and also at St. Ann's. He knows about my dog. He knows her name.

But this time he's in class, in second grade, and I am a class visitor. Do school rules still apply?

A protocol exists in elementary school about the way a visitor is introduced. The visitor's relationship, initially at least, is with the principal or teacher. Usually the teacher asks the class to say "good morning" to the visitor. The visitor says "good morning" to the children. Then the teacher tells the children something that may lend the presence of the visitor an aura of importance. Sometimes the teacher asks the visitor if he would like to tell the children who he is, or what he does; sometimes she invites the visitor to ask the class some questions.

All this protocol goes out the window when a child shyly climbs out of his chair and takes your hand. Elio's teacher, an affectionate woman who has been here fifteen years, asks him if he'd like to introduce me to the class.

"This is Jonathan," he says.

"But who is Jonathan?" the teacher asks.

He looks perplexed. "Someone I know!" he finally says.

"What does Jonathan *do?*" the teacher asks.

Elio looks stumped by this. The teacher smiles, tells the class that I was once "a teacher too," and then tells Elio that he can go back to his chair. I follow him across the room and take a chair beside him.

The teacher, whose name is Frances Dukes, was doing a reading lesson when I entered. The story she's reading is a fable about animals with simple pastel illustrations.

"There once was a wolf who loved to eat," she reads. "As soon as he finished one meal, he began to think of the next." The wolf, she says, elaborating on the story as she holds the book for them to see, developed a craving for chicken stew one day and went into the forest looking for a chicken. He found the chicken, she says, but it occurred to him that she was not quite fat enough to make sufficient stew. "So he decided he would feed her first," and he went home and made "a hundred scrumptious pancakes," then "a hundred scrumptious doughnuts," then a cake "that weighed a hundred pounds."

After three days of cooking good things for the chicken, says the teacher, he decided it was time to make his stew. So he put his "stew pot" on the fire and set out to find his food. When he came to the chicken's house and looked inside, however, says the teacher, he discovered that her house was full of baby chicks who had been feasting on the pancakes and the doughnuts and the cake and who were overjoyed to see him. "The baby chicks gave him a hundred kisses and they told him that he was the best cook in the world."

The wolf decided against making chicken stew, the teacher says. An illustration shows the baby chicks climbing all over him, their tiny beaks wide-open, and the wolf appearing to be flummoxed, and embarrassed, by their gratitude.

Miss Dukes writes out the title of the story on the blackboard. The children's homework for tonight is to "pretend you are the baby chicks" and "write a letter to the wolf to thank him for the food." While Elio copies the instructions in his notebook, I go to the teacher's desk and ask her if she has an extra copy of the story. She apologizes that she doesn't and explains that there are not enough books for the children in the class and that she therefore cannot let them take the story home, which means that they will have to write their letters to the wolf from memory.

This is a familiar problem in the New York City schools. Textbooks are scarce; so many classes have to double up and teachers often have to buy books on their own, using their own salaries to supplement the skimpy rations that the school board gives the children of poor neighborhoods. In richer neighborhoods, the parents of the students frequently raise money independently to purchase books or even hire extra teachers to reduce the class size for their children. But, because they do this only for the school attended by their children and don't bring the same aggressive energy to bear in fighting for a higher spending level for all children in all neighborhoods, their efforts militate against the opportunities of children in poor neighborhoods, whose families do not have the money to add private funds to compensate for public parsimony. In the richest sections of Manhattan private money keeps the class size relatively low, sometimes as low as 21 or less; Miss Dukes has 29.

She seems devoted to her class and it is obvious she's fond of Elio. "I'd love to take him on a holiday someday!" she told me once. "I think it would be fun to take him to the South and show him where I lived when I was growing up."

A black woman in a school that serves a mixture of black and Hispanic children—more Hispanic now than black—she spends as much time as she can developing relationships with parents of her pupils. "My children are grown up," she says. "I live alone now. So these children are my family." She says she comes to school an hour early and stays late most afternoons, often as late as five o'clock. "I walk around the neighborhood and visit them at home or at the church. I like to stay as close to them as possible."

While we're talking, Elio comes up to me again and, with the unselfconsciousness I've seen in him so often at St. Ann's, he puts his arms around my waist and rests his head against my side. He doesn't seem concerned about the children who are watching him. When I was his age I was afraid to hug my father or my uncle or another grown-up man with children watching me. But Elio, it seems, has no such inhibitions. With his head against my side, he looks up at his teacher, and she smiles at him and reports that he's been "trying very hard this year" and "doing very good" in mathematics, but "he does talk out of place in class" and knows that this is unfair to the other children "and we're working on this—aren't we?"

A little before two o'clock, she puts subtraction and addition problems on the board; the children do a few of them, some at their desks, some at the board. Some of the children don't say "borrow" anymore, or "carry over," when they do subtraction and addition. They say "re-group," "exchange," or "redistribute." Elio introduced me to the first of those three words last year when he was doing two-column subtraction at the afterschool. He was subtracting 28 from 90 and was temporarily befuddled by the zero. I asked him, "Can you borrow something from the nine?" But he did not know what I meant by this. I asked him, therefore, "What do you do when eight is more than zero?" He tapped the troublesome zero with his pencil and at last announced, "Regroup."

Elio's teacher tells me that this is a word the teachers have begun to use, but that she uses both the new word and the old ones because parents and grandparents, when they help the children with their homework, use the terms they know from their own schooling. She beckons to Elio and calls him to the board. He does a number of subtrac-tion problems that require him to show he understands how to regroup. Other children come to the board to show the teacher that they understand it too. Elio returns to his desk and whispers something to the girl who sits beside him. Then he copies down the problems on the board.

"Okay, boys and girls," the teacher says. "It's time to get your coats."

The children go politely to the closet and bring back their coats and hats and backpacks to their desks. Elio wraps his long wool scarf three times around his neck and ties it with a careful tuck beneath his ear. Then he lifts his big thick hooded jacket, which says "BOSS" in large white letters on the front, staring at the ceiling as he tries to get his hands into the tunnels of the sleeves. Then he puts his notebook and his workbooks in his backpack, zips it shut, and wrestles with the straps to get his quilted sleeves into the proper slots. Then he lifts his chair and turns it upside down and places it as quietly as possible upon his desk. Then he holds a woolly hat with eyeholes for the child who sits next to him while she zips up her coat, her chin pressed down so she can see the zipper as she pulls it towards her throat.

The teacher stands beside the door to guide the children into lines before they file out, then walks beside them to the stairs. After the last child has departed, I remain for a few minutes in the empty room. On the blackboard are the twelve subtraction and addition problems that the class has copied down. To the left of the problems is a square in which the teacher's written "Writing Homework" and, beneath those words, instructions for the letter they are supposed to write about the wolf and baby chicks.

The children are gone, the teacher with them, making sure they file down the four long flights of stairs in proper order as they head for the front door. The sudden absence of so much vitality transforms the silence, but the empty space does not feel desolate or lonely. It's flooded still with memories of scarves and voices.

I take down Elio's chair and sit on it to make some notes and copy down the writing on the board. When I'm done, I lift the chair and put it back where it's supposed to be. The clock on the wall says two forty-five. A bell rings somewhere. The corridor outside the room is empty.

P.S. 30 holds 900 children. It's not an ultramodern building (one part of the school was built nearly a century ago), and it does not have many of the academic extras that you'd see in schools in rich suburban neighborhoods; but the building's clean, the corridors are decorated with the artwork of the students, and the doorways to the stairwells have been painted in bright-colored images of animals and landscapes by the children. Despite the size of classes, teachers for the most part seem to keep things calm and orderly; and, by and large, the mood within the school is happy and familial. The lunchroom in the basement, unlike many lunchrooms in the other inner-city schools I visit in New York, is spacious and attractive.

On a day in mid-November, three of the children from St. Ann's are sitting with me at a table in the front part of the lunchroom before going back to class. One of them is Maricruz, an eight-year-old whose photograph I took four years ago when she was with her mother at a picnic in St. Mary's Park. One is Vanessa Tompkins, who was born in Arkansas. Another is Soledad de Jésus, whose family comes from Puerto Rico.

The three who know me are possessive of the right to answer questions that I ask about the school and get a bit competitive when other children try to talk to me. When I ask their teacher's name, for instance, a good-natured girl I've never met begins to give the answer but is silenced by Vanessa.

"You don't even *know* him!" she says to the one who tried to answer.

She reaches for my pen and paperpad and spells her teacher's name. "There," she says, capping the pen. "Ask *me* things, instead of her. She doesn't even know you."

"Ask *me* things too," says Maricruz as she gets up to go back to her class. "You don't need to ask someone that you don't *know!*"

Vanessa brings me to the doorway of the cafeteria to meet her teacher, who invites me to come back to class. I walk upstairs with her but then decide to visit her another day because I promised Stephanie I'd visit in her class today.

I get to Stephanie's class at one-fifteen. One of the other St. Ann's children in the room, a boy named Damian, waves at me as I come in and, when I pass his desk, he says, "Hi, Jonathan," and slaps my hand. The teacher, however, who is finishing a sandwich, isn't very friendly.

"How many students do you have?" I ask.

"Thirty-one," she answers listlessly.

I ask how many years she's been here.

"Thirteen years," she says.

"How's Stephanie doing?"

She says something that I can't hear, but doesn't sound enthusiastic.

I ask her where the children in the class will go for middle school next year.

She looks at her sandwich, chewing slowly. "I didn't know that I was going to be interviewed," she says, then names four of the local middle schools, but none of the good selective schools outside the neighborhood, and nods her head as if to say that's all the information she intends to give me.

I can see that I'm not welcome; so I stay for only fifteen minutes to observe a reading lesson and then make a quick retreat. As I'm heading for the door, Damian makes a "V" sign with two fingers. Then he brings his hand down with the palm extended, like a vaudeville comic asking, "So, what can you do about this situation?"

The situation seems more optimistic in Isaiah's classroom, which I visit next. The students spent the morning in a section of the Bronx called Bedford Park, where they attended a ballet at Lehman College. As I come in, they're taking turns reading reviews they did of the performance. Isaiah is the third to read.

"It was a very good ballet," he says. "They had a lot of pretty girls. The dancers were barefoot, but their costumes were too tight. . . ."

Other children also comment, somewhat indirectly, on the sexual suggestiveness of the ballet. "There was this girl and this strange-looking boy," one of the children says, "and they were dancing with their bodies very close. . . ."

The teacher asks her why this bothered her.

"The way they posed did not look . . . *right*," she says.

Isaiah explains the problem more directly: "The girl was reaching for his privates." Turning sideways to me, with his hand before his mouth, he fills me in on what he means: "Her hand was going for his zipper. . . ."

The teacher explains the starkness and the mild, stylized eroticism of the dance as "something not unusual in modern dance performances," and he contrasts this for the children with traditional ballet. A former businessman who switched careers last year to be a teacher, he talks to the students as a father might explain something a trifle awkward to his children, in a serious and cultured voice. Miss Rosa tells me that he's had some problems with instructional techniques, because this is his first year in the classroom; but the children seem to like him and pay good attention.

Schools in inner-city neighborhoods are under a persistent scrutiny these days. Some teachers therefore feel a little threatened at the sight of visitors, especially of school officials, who seem predisposed to find their weaknesses. This has always been the case to some degree in public schools. I'm reminded of the way I felt in Boston when the teachers on my floor received a note from the school office telling us there would be people from the school board in the building and that we should be prepared to be observed, which was a way of asking us to be on high alert and do our "foolproof" lessons and keep tight control of all the kids until the visitors were gone. The scrutiny of teachers by officials isn't something new; it's simply gotten more judgmental, less collegial, than it used to be.

One of the teachers here at P.S. 30 whom I've known for several years is Louis Bedrock, who has taught a number of the children from St. Ann's when they were in fourth grade, including Stephanie and Ariel. Like all the teachers here, he's seen a lot of school board delegations come and go within the building. I can often hear a hint of irritation in his voice when he describes the many visits he receives. I used to worry that he'd feel the same uneasiness about my presence in his room and view my visits as intrusive.

I don't have this worry any longer. I think he views me as a friend and likes it when I visit. Still, I know he's disappointed with himself if I'm in class on one of those bad mornings that almost all teachers have when children who behave well almost every other day decide that this is a good time to misbehave. It pulls me right back more than thirty years and I remember how I used to feel about the visitors who came into my classroom to observe what they'd been led to think would be a confident and innovative teacher but would somehow always manage to show up on days when children were most restless and unruly or when I was the most cranky, typically at one P.M. on Friday afternoons in nice spring weather! I knew it ruined the illusion of enlightened pedagogy for observers when they heard me raise my voice and talk like an old-fashioned classroom tyrant. I'd be mad at them for being there, mad at myself, mad at the kids especially for their bad timing.

It's never easy for a visitor, whether you were a teacher once or not, to understand how hard a job a man like Bedrock has and what he's up against each Monday morning when he looks out at the children in his class and wonders which one spent his Sunday visiting at Rikers Island with his father, which one went to Bedford Hills to see his sister or his mother, and which one simply did not sleep the night before because his mother had no food, or was upset, or had been given an eviction order.

Bedrock is a sensitive and empathetic teacher. The children in his class confide in him and grow emotionally close to him. He comes in early every day to do a thirty-minute study hall for kids who haven't done their homework. He stays late in the afternoon, as many of the P.S. 30 teachers do, to give some of the kids a little extra time to be with him. He spends some of his Saturdays with students also, taking them to a science learning center in New Jersey, which most of these kids would never get to visit otherwise and which he pays for out of his own salary.

Like many good teachers, he's considerably better at relating to the children than to figures of authority. I gather that he's had his run-ins with some people from "the district," which is how the teachers speak of local school headquarters in the Bronx, maybe also with Miss Rosa. I think she finds him hard to figure out; and yet I also know she likes him. "What can I say?" she asked me once when I came down into her office after I had been in Bedrock's class much of the day. "The man is an eccentric. He's an intellectual. He talks about Noam Chomsky! He could teach in college if he wanted. But he's chosen to stay here at P.S. 30 so that he can drive me crazy. Why does he stay? One reason: He loves children."

Many people with the competence to teach in college *choose* to teach in elementary schools, including schools in urban districts like Mott Haven. I feel grateful that some of these teachers and their principals encourage me to visit freely in their classrooms without making me jump through the bureaucratic hoops of asking for permission every time from school officials, which can be a time-consuming and frustrating process. Now and then a teacher lets me take a class and teach a lesson, which is a real pleasure (and can be a bit intimidating too) for somebody who hasn't taught in public school for many years.

It is, quite frankly, a luxurious experience to have this opportunity: to be allowed to be a casual and informal visitor in someone else's class when you know that you have no obligation to accomplish anything that can be judged or tested later on by someone else. Visiting is easy. If you know a number of the kids and some of them sneak little nods and smiles at you when they see you in the stairs, or in their room, it's more than "easy." It's a joy and a reunion and a covert celebration.

It's another thing to be the one who has to teach the class day after day, to plan the lessons, fill out school department records, put up with the messages that blast out of the intercom in many schools or are delivered by a student from downstairs, make sure there are books for every child in the room, cope with tensions, arguments and tears, clean the boards, arrange the chairs—in short, perform the real work of a classroom teacher in a good but poorly funded and entirely segregated public school.

I hope I don't lose sight of this distinction, which is easily forgotten when we make these periodic visits and imagine that we understand the situation in a classroom far more quickly than we do. This is one reason why I hesitate to speak too much of situations like the one that I encountered when I entered Stephanie's class. The teacher was in a sour mood today. She may have had a reason that I'd have no way to know. She may not be like that tomorrow. Miss Rosa tells me that she grew up in the neighborhood.

How does she feel when someone who, she knows, writes books and is a friend of other teachers in the school comes in to visit her and seems to know a number of her students? If I were the teacher in that situation, I suspect that I would be defensive too.

One of the hardest-working teachers at the school is Carmen Suarez, who has taught bilingual kindergarten here for many years. In the afternoon, she teaches some of the same children in a supplementary program called "extended day."

Twenty-eight children file in as she and I are standing in the hallway just outside the door at three o'clock. She shows them where to put their hats and coats and gives them each a cookie and a half-pint milk container. While the children have their milk and cookies, she arranges books with simple stories on their tables.

"Read with your eyes, not with your mouth," she says.

She tells the children in English everything she's doing. "I write on the board. . . . I give you a snack. . . . I take attendance. . . . Uh-oh! Somebody talks!"

She takes attendance. As she reads each child's name, the child says, *"Presente!"*

When she's done she says, "Okay. Thank you for being here."

When they finish their milk and cookies, they assemble on a carpet in the middle of the room. A very big and lifelike panda, twice as big as any of the children, sits there on the carpet with them like a member of the class. His head leans forward on his chest, like a real panda in the zoo.

The teacher stands in front of the children by an easel that contains a set of pictures illustrating words with different vowel sounds. As the children say the vowels with her, she encourages the ones who seem too shy to speak. When a child says a vowel wrong, she leans way down and looks into the child's face and says, "Excuse me?"

The children repeat the first five vowels several times, and then she swings her head and makes a big loop with her hand and tells them, "Also! *Sometimes* . . . 'y'!"

They go through all the vowels, now including "y," a couple times again, and then she does the consonants, then the entire alphabet. Each letter is named, then sounded, and then illustrated with a word.

Most of the children in the room are dressed in uniforms: the girls in navy pinafores and light-blue blouses, boys in trousers, light-blue shirts, and ties.

The teacher does the lesson once in English, once in Spanish. Then she asks the children, one by one, to come up to the blackboard to write words in Spanish starting with the letter "r." When a child named Rosita comes up to the board, Miss Suarez chooses *rosa* and goes to her desk and lifts a real rose in her hand and lets the children smell it.

Later she does the letter "g"—starting with *gusano* (worm), and then *guitarra,* and then *gato.* A child named Marisol who comes up to write *gato* turns around to face the class after she writes the word and, without the prompting of the teacher, puts her hands next to her face to look like whiskers and says, "Meow. . . ."

"Aplauso!" says the teacher, and the children clap.

"Carlos — venga!" says the teacher.

A boy comes up and writes *gallito* and then imitates a rooster's crow, and once again the children clap.

Miss Suarez then begins a reading lesson, using not a textbook but a story book about a lamb who's looking for his mother. She reads it in Spanish first, repeating certain words in English.

"Caballo, caballo," says the lamb, "will you be my mother?"

"Yo soy un caballo," says the horse. "I cannot be your mother."

The lamb asks the same question—"Will you be my mother?"—to a bull, a hen, a rabbit, and a boy. Each of them tells the lamb, "I cannot be your mother." When the lamb is told this by the boy, however, and begins to cry, the boy changes his mind. In the final pictures of the paper-covered book, the lamb is following the boy into his house and then is being held by him and fed by him.

"Bueno, bueno," says the boy. "Yes, I will be your mother."

The story, which is printed in two versions, one in English, one in Spanish, is narrated without pathos. There are six or seven lines at most on every page. The illustrations, richly drawn, are pastoral and reassuring. When the children read a word with good pronunciation, she says, "Good!" When they do it wrong, she says again, "Excuse me?" When a child seems confused about an English word the teacher used, she talks to her in Spanish. The teacher passes back and forth between the languages in conversation, repeating almost every Spanish word in English.

When children want to speak, she says in Spanish and in English, "Raise your hands." When she wants them all to say a word with her, she says in Spanish, then in English, "Say it! Everyone!" When one child tells an answer to the boy beside him, she leans down and asks him, "Do you think you're helping him by whispering the answer?"

She's firm in making children follow rules but has a warm maternal manner and seems always on alert for times when children's faces stiffen up with fear or look as if they're fighting back the possibility of tears. One little girl, named Lidia, who used to be in special education class and came into this room only a week or so before, *does* break out in tears during the class. The teacher stops the lesson, gets down on the rug, and rocks the child in her arms. Two of the other children kneel beside her and stroke back her bangs and whisper in her ears.

"Every day in every class we have a crisis," says Miss Rosa later, trying to explain to me why she regards some of the politicians in New York as selfish and shortsighted — "ignorant," she says — in failing to restore the services of counselors and school physicians who were taken from the city's elementary schools, along with art and music teachers and librarians, during a budget crisis more than twenty years before and haven't ever been restored.

Many teachers are obliged to be physicians, counselors, psychiatrists to students in this school, in which a number of the children are on medication for depression, or anxiety, or for other reasons. Miss Suarez draws upon a deep reserve of lived experience and seasoned intuition when she puts her arms around a child who is crying out her heart over an unknown sadness that she is too small and scared to translate into words. Schools like P.S. 30 do not get enough of the expensive things that wealthy districts lavish on the schools that serve their children; but there's lots of love and tested loyalty among the teachers in this school.

Another teacher with a gift for bringing back the children's smiles when they're feeling sad is Miss Reistetter, who has been at P.S. 30 teaching first grade for two years. She has a merry disposition, and she seems to get excited by the same small things that are exciting to the children.

When I visited the first time in her classroom during April of the year before, there were three children in the room named Jonathan. When she introduced me to the class, she said, "And — guess what?" and she told them that I was "*another* Jonathan!" The idea that there were now four people in the room with the same name seemed pretty near amazing to the children; but it seemed to be impressive to the teacher too.

Today, when I come in, the children have already had their lunch; but when they stand to say hello, some of them start to say, "Good morning. . . ."

"*Is* it morning?" says the teacher.

"No!" the children say.

"Is it night?" she asks them.

"No!"

"What do we call this time of day?" she asks.

"Afternoon!" the children say.

"What do we say to Mr. Kozol, then?"

"Good afternoon!" the children say.

After they sit down and I get seated in the back, she teaches an impromptu lesson about hours and days.

"What is today?"

"Today is Friday!"

"What was yesterday?"

"Yesterday was Thursday!"

"What is tomorrow?"

"Saturday!" the children say.

When one of the children fools around during a lesson about numbers, Miss Reistetter leans across his desk and says, "Remember, Daniel, we're first-graders now! What does that mean?"

The boy seems scared to speak.

Stooping down beside him so that she can press his hand, she says, "It means we have to *act* like big first-graders!"

When the child answers a question that she asks a moment later and his answer is correct, she cheers him on. "Good going!"

When she asks another question and his hand goes up again, she circles right around to him. "Let's see! Has everybody got their light bulbs on?" When he gets the answer right again, she says, "Good boy! We're on the ball!"

To make a transition from a period of classroom conversation to a quiet period of writing, she stands very straight beside her desk and tells the children, "Simon says, 'Touch your nose!'"

The children touch their noses.

"Simon says, 'Touch your ears!'"

The children touch their ears.

"Simon says, 'Pick up your pencil!'"

The children pick up their pencils and in this way she has led them into the next lesson without needing to announce it in advance.

She writes in big neat letters on the blackboard, tapping the chalk against the board each time she dots an "i" or makes an exclamation point. She does it fast — "tap-tap!" "tap-tap!" It's like instructional gunfire. When she's done she draws a line beneath it all and makes two final exclamation points.

When she turns to face the class again, she notices a boy whose head is buried in his arms. She goes to his desk and strokes his head. "What do we do when someone's feeling sad?" she asks the class.

"We give him a smile!" say the children.

"Can we give Livio a nice big smile?" asks the teacher.

The children smile at Livio, who opens up one eye — reluctantly and tearfully at first — and sees the teacher smiling at him too, then opens both his eyes and wipes his hands against his eyes and looks at last as if the cloud has passed.

At the end of the day the teacher does a lesson on the months and seasons, and she asks the children to describe the ways that winter differs from the spring. When a child speaks about "the green leaves in the trees," the teacher lifts her arms above her head and does an imitation of a tree and asks the children to stand up and do the same. She shakes her hands to show what happens when the cold winds come in autumn and the leaves fall from the trees. She has a willowy figure and the grace of a ballet dancer. In a long print skirt and soft black jersey, she seems frolicsome and at her ease and seems to fill the room with happiness. The little ones look captivated. Some teachers have to work so hard at this! Some do it almost without trying.

CHAPTER 15

Pineapple Takes Control

A little more than half the children in the St. Ann's program go to P.S. 30, which is just around the corner from the church. Most of the others go to P.S. 65, which is three blocks away on Cypress Avenue. P.S. 30 is the better of the two schools. Mothers who know something of conditions in these schools do what they can to send their kids to P.S. 30.

Pineapple's mother, however, is an immigrant from Guatemala and does not read English well and may not understand the way the schooling system works as well as other parents do. She's a diligent parent, and she works long hours as a health attendant, taking care of children who have HIV infection; but I have the sense that she's cut off from information that more knowledgeable parents have at their disposal. In poor communities, as in most middle class and wealthy ones, there is also an informal loop of inside information, which is one of several reasons why the heavily promoted notion of "parental choice" involves a lot more choice for certain families than for others.

Pineapple, in any case, has been attending P.S. 65. I met her there in 1994 when she was six years old. She was in kindergarten then and wrote her letters and her numbers in reverse. She still does it now and then for fun — to show me that she still knows how to do it — or on some days from forgetfulness. Even when she does make real mistakes, she gets on top of things quite easily. Her gift for reestablishing a sense of domination over almost any awkward situation is one of her qualities that grown-ups at St. Ann's remark upon repeatedly.

I think of this again when I go up to P.S. 65 to visit classes and to meet the principal — a new one, who was put in charge of P.S. 65 two years before. The principal does her best to organize my visit, which most principals would do when they have visitors, but maybe with more diligence than usual, in order to restrict what I may see. P.S. 65 is on a list of troubled schools, and she may not be eager for me to observe the school as freely as I am allowed to do at P.S. 30. Her efforts to control my visit are confounded, though, by Pineapple's assumption of her right to steer me where she chooses.

I start the day in one of the fifth grades and don't get to Pineapple's third grade until noon. As I come in, the children are about to do a mathematics problem that requires them first to divide and then to multiply.

"If five nickels make a quarter," asks the teacher, a young woman in her second year of teaching, "how many nickels would it take to make a dollar?"

The children at Pineapple's table try to calculate the answer with their fingers but become befuddled and come up at first with "fifty." Some of them draw lines in groups of five, perhaps a way they have been taught to multiply; but this approach yields only more confusion.

Pineapple finally asks me if I have some nickels. I have a few and she combines them with some nickels that the other children have. The teacher adds some nickels of her own. After a period of moving nickels back and forth across the surface of the table, they arrive at the right answer.

The lesson continues until twelve-fifteen. Then the children line up at the door for lunch and recess; but, because there are four other classes waiting in the hall to go downstairs, the teacher has the children sit down on the floor outside the room and wait their turn to file to the stairs.

I sit beside Pineapple on the floor; but she becomes impatient with the time that's being wasted and at last goes back into the classroom, finds a book, and brings it to the hall. The book looks much too easy, and she seems to realize that I'm thinking this, because she tells me, "This is only Level One."

"What level are you reading at?" I ask.

"I read at Level Two."

I'm eager to ask her why she didn't choose a book at "Level Two," but I don't have the chance because the atmosphere becomes chaotic in the hallway as the children in the class grow restless and the teacher has to scold them.

"Are you hungry?" asks Pineapple.

"Yes!" I say.

"You can come and eat with us," she tells me.

"I'll come down with you, but I don't think I'll eat right now," I say, because the principal did not give me permission.

"Why not?" she says.

"Because," I say, an answer she has heard from me before when there was something I decided not to tell her.

The stairwell that the children have to use to get down to the lunchroom isn't the main stairwell. It's extremely dark and narrow, with a metal grating on one side. Another class is coming up the other way at the same time, and there's a mob scene near the bottom, where the kids are halted by a man who seems to be a teacher or administrator.

"I don't want to hear a word from *you*—or *you!*" he says, his finger pointed at some boys beneath us in the stairs. "Yes, I mean *you*," he says, to which a girl beside me says, "I hope you don't mean *me!*"—a flip remark which, luckily, he doesn't hear.

The lunchroom, a medieval-looking place I've visited before, is packed with other classes when we finally get in. Pineapple and her classmates file to a group of tables and sit down—"You sit here," she tells me—but are forced to sit and wait again for a long while. Hungry and impatient, several of the children start to bang things on the table.

"We always be bad in the lunchroom," says a child named Samantha, who sits opposite Pineapple in the classroom.

Other children imitate the rhythmic banging on their tables on both sides of us. "Yo! It's beeper music," says one child.

When he sees me write this down, he says, "You like the word I used?"

"Yes," I say.

He leans across the table to see what I wrote.

Samantha gives a stick of bubble gum to Pineapple, then hands me one as well. I look at my watch. It's getting close to one P.M.

"I hate this noise," Pineapple says.

The boy who asked me if I liked the word he used before sees that I'm scribbling again.

"Did you write all those words?"

"Don't answer him," says Pineapple.

The long delay goes on and on, for maybe 10 or 15 minutes more. The noise within the room is deafening. It reminds me of the chaos in the crowded inner-city school in which I taught fourth grade in Boston. It doesn't seem quite accurate to call this "lunch," because we've been here nearly twenty minutes and the kids aren't eating. It's more like a holding-action to contain a couple hundred over-heated bodies that should either be in class learning to read and write and do arithmetic or else be outside hav-ing fun.

Class by class, the children are allowed to go and get their lunch; but, because the lunch attendants need to keep the room under control and get each table to be silent before children are allowed to have their food, the process seems to take forever.

"I've got a stomachache," Pineapple says.

"When did it start?"

"Right now," she says. "When I don't eat my food at the right time it gives me gas."

At last the children file to the kitchen to receive their lunch. The food looks good: pizza, green beans, slices of canned peaches, little apples for dessert, and chocolate milk. "I'm thirsty," says Pineapple when we come back to the table. She swallows all her chocolate milk, tells me she's still thirsty, and then drinks the juice from her sliced peaches.

The pizzas come in two shapes. Some are round and some are long and fat like sandwiches. The children com-pare their pizzas and discuss the shapes and ask each other whether they taste different and decide they taste the same.

"I like the inside, not the outside," says Samantha.

Pineapple makes no distinctions. She devours it all, then goes to work on the sliced peaches.

I ask her if they're good.

She holds her hand up like a grown-up lady who is trying to converse while swallowing a canapé at a reception, chews ferociously and shuts her eyes to swallow, and then opens her eyes brightly and provides an uncommitted statement of opinion with her hand, which flutters slightly in the air to indicate her limited appreciation for canned peaches.

It's past one-twenty now. The children have finished eating but are being held here longer for some reason. Pineapple fiddles with her red plaid scarf. To break the tedium I ask her where she got it.

"Ninety-nine Cent Store," she says.

"What did it cost?"

"Ninety-nine cents!" she answers.

"Does everything they sell there cost the same?" I ask.

"Only almost everything," she says.

Bored by the wait, she studies my suit and asks me if these are the only clothes I have. I tell her I have two suits but they're both nearly the same.

"Is that your only sweater?"

"No."

She plucks some bits of paper that look like confetti from the front and holds one of the pieces up and studies it and asks me where it came from.

I tell her I was in a kindergarten yesterday at P.S. 30. The children there were making pictures out of dots of colored paper and some of them got stuck in my sweater. She picks away the dots of paper. Some of the boys begin to bang more on the table.

"Why are we still sitting here?" I ask.

"Because we're bad," replies Samantha, which is not really correct. Children anywhere would get impatient if they had been doing little more than lining up and sitting still for well over an hour.

There is only one child at the table who appears to be resigned to the delay: a quiet girl with long dark hair who has a rather mystical expression in her eyes, serene, detached, but vaguely troubling somehow. "She doesn't like to talk," Samantha says.

Pineapple studies this quiet child for a moment. She then gets up and walks around the table and surrounds the child's head with both her arms and smiles down at her. The child smiles up at her but still says not a word.

At last, around one-thirty, they're allowed to go outside. The boys race off in all directions in the schoolyard while the girls form in a group around three older girls who have a double length of rope. They give the younger girls a chance to jump and Pineapple shows off her skill at double Dutch. Her short and pudgy legs skip up and down and, as the girls increase the speed, her feet move very fast, not only up and down but also slightly outward to the sides, which, as she tells me later, is the key to doing it successfully.

Recess turns out to be brief, however. After waiting all this time, the children get about twelve minutes to relax and play. Then a whistle blows and they line up again to go back to their rooms. Even then, there is another maddening delay to hold them in these lines: A bell rings. "It's a fire drill," a teacher says in obvious frustration.

The classes that already went back to their rooms start filing out again while those that are still here remain in line for several minutes more. By the time the drill is over, it is close to two o'clock. It's hard to see what Pineapple has learned since twelve-fifteen except the patience to remain in line.

I agreed to spend the last half-hour of my visit in another third grade, where the teacher is a friend I met here at the school four years ago when I was visiting for the first time. She was a first-year teacher then, but must have had good preparation because she was teaching with a sense of self-assuredness. She also seemed to be right in her element amidst the kids and seemed to be as inexhaustible as they were.

The teacher, whom the children call "Miss G," is still a dynamo. She's wearing jeans, a loose blue workshirt, and a bright-red headband holding down her hair. Always in motion, reaching out repeatedly to different children, she maintains a comfortable discipline without the need to sound severe.

I've tried to visit with Miss G—her real last name is Gallombardo, which the kids do not find easy to pronounce—when I've gone back to P.S. 65. Her classes are exciting and her students do a lot of writing and, unlike some of the other teachers in the school, she doesn't have the slightest hesitation about being visited. I wish Pineapple could have had her in third grade because I think their personalities would have ignited one another. I also think Miss G would have been good at coping with Pineapple's inclination to manipulate the grown-ups that she knows, although it's possible no grown-up that she ever meets will be successful in that effort.

Pineapple later asks me why I didn't come back to her class with her after the fire drill. Like the children from St. Ann's who go to P.S. 30, she assumes that, when I'm visiting her school, my loyalties and my affiliations are primarily with her, not with the school—which is correct.

A reporter from a New York paper leaves a telephone message at my home a few days later, saying she has heard that I've been looking at the school restructuring of P.S. 65 and asking my reactions. I don't call back, because I haven't been there long enough, or seen enough, to give a thoughtful answer; and the visits that I've made to P.S. 65 were not, in any case, what education writers would refer to as "site visits." They've been too informal and I wasn't looking at curriculum or methods of instruction. Anything I said to the reporter at this point would have been too selective.

I do visit schools in ways that are more organized and make more comprehensive notes on lessons that seem interesting and teaching methods that appear to be unusually effective. In those cases, naturally, I visit several classrooms. In this case, however, I was only in three classrooms, one of them because I knew the teacher, and another because it was Pineapple's third grade; and I honestly don't think I would have visited the school at all, or not this month in any case, but for the fact that Pineapple and both her sisters were enrolled here and she had been pestering me for many weeks to promise I would come and spend part of a day with her in school, and I had finally promised that I would; and it was nearly Christmas now, and so I did.

I do think the school is poorly organized. The building's gloomy to begin with, and it isn't fair to children to be herded in and out of lines all day, or forced to wait so long for food or play. It's not fair to teachers either to be forced to *make* the children wait and have to fill the role of traffic cops for so much of the day.

I wouldn't have said this on the basis of one visit, but some other visits in the next two years convey a similar impression of constrictiveness and of chaotic scheduling, which make it hard for teachers to behave with normal friendliness to children. The relatively comfortable way Miss Gallombardo manages her class has much to do with her unusual self-confidence and independent personality. It doesn't surprise me when I later learn that she does not plan to remain at P.S. 65. She will, in fact, have left the school before this book is published.

Miss G's departure from the school, one of several such departures of good educators from the faculty of P.S. 65 in recent years, continues a longstanding pattern that has been disruptive to the continuity of education for the children here. Already, in the fall of 1997, at the time I made this visit to Pineapple's class, there had been a high turn-over rate within the faculty. Many of the newer teachers in the school, moreover, were not merely unprepared for what they had to face but wholly inexperienced: Of 50 teachers on the faculty in the preceding year, 28 had never taught before; and half of them were fired or, unhappy with conditions at the school, decided not to come back in September.

Some things at the school appear to have improved during the two years since. Virtually all the classrooms have been fitted with computers. A genuine library now exists and is well-stocked with books. Math and reading scores rose slightly in the spring of 1998, although they would decline again within another year. Some of the young teachers seem enthusiastic, and a number of the older teachers, some of them admired highly in the neighborhood, have chosen to remain; but the high turn-over rate has been a real disaster.

In her fourth-grade year, in 1998 and 1999, Pineapple told me recently, she had four different teachers in a row. She can still recite the names of each, and why each of the first three didn't stay more than a couple months or weeks. "One was only a helper-teacher and she said she needs a 'paper' job. One of them was a man who liked us, Mr. Camel, but he said he needed to earn money, so he found a better job than teaching kids. One of them used curse words. She said, 'Sit your A-S-S-E-S down!' And she had yellow teeth that looked like fangs. And so they fired her. The other one was nice. . . ."

Pineapple's older sister, Lara, who was with us when we had this talk, corrected part of what Pineapple had reported. The name of the teacher who, Pineapple said, had liked the children wasn't really Mr. Camel. "It was Mr. Campbell, like the soup," her sister said. The teacher who, Pineapple said, had teeth that "looked like fangs" had actually been fired, it turned out, because she had been smoking at the school, which is against the law, and, said Lara, "wasn't a good teacher." Two of the other teachers at the school confirmed that this was so. They also explained what Pineapple may have had in mind in saying that one of these teachers was "a helper teacher"— she may not yet have been fully certified — and they noted that the class had lost a good deal of the year because of the confusion caused by having temporary teachers prior to the time when a fourth teacher, who appeared to be effective and related well to children, was assigned to them.

All these are familiar problems in New York, where nonwhite neighborhoods routinely are assigned the largest numbers of uncertified or inexperienced instructors, with predictable results in classroom chaos and curricular discontinuity. Still, the relatively stable and effective faculty at P.S. 30 demonstrates that these calamities can be diminished greatly by a capable administrator, given optimal conditions, if, as in Miss Rosa's case, she is the kind of person talented young teachers *want* to work for.

I don't like describing situations like the one at P.S. 65. But children in the neighborhood have paid too high a price for staffing and administrative problems at this school; and, even though Pineapple and her schoolmates sometimes get a couple of the details wrong when they're describing things, I think Pineapple is, in general, an accurate reporter. Children know when something at a school is seriously wrong; and their critiques, in my experience at least, are usually on target.

P.S. 65 was taken over by the chancellor of New York City's schools in 1996 and has been going through a process called "reconstitution." The chancellor, an able and politically resilient man, has done perhaps the best that any good administrator could, given the pressures he has faced from City Hall, the limitations of low salaries that cannot draw sufficient numbers of already-proven teachers to the school and keep them here, and the archaic infrastructure of the building. It's hard for me to speak of this impartially, because I know so many of the children here and also know the chancellor, and like him, and was sorry to be told, as I was writing this, that he was soon to be dismissed. He's won some major victories for children in the New York City schools and held his own in a political arena like no other in the nation. Some of the schools he's taken under his direct control may have made larger gains; but P.S. 65 is still a school in which I doubt that he, or any members of the Board of Education of New York, would let their own kids be enrolled. It isn't fair that Pineapple should have to go here either.

An element of what appears to be regarded as "acceptable unfairness" is built into things, however, by the economic class that sets priorities and shapes public opinion in this city. It represents the precondition for whatever else one wants to say about the lives of children and the larger numbers of the schools that serve them in these neighborhoods. It would be accurate to say that P.S. 65 is probably a better-disciplined and, possibly, a more efficient segregated and unequal school today than it was several years ago. In these respects, Pineapple and her classmates are perhaps a little better off than when I met her first in kindergarten. In other ways, however, with the loss of many independent-minded and creative teachers like Miss Gallombardo, they're worse off than ever.

The children don't complain too much. They trudge along and do their work and have their fun and make their comical remarks about the things they find peculiar or frustrating. They line up on the sidewalk to buy coconut icies after school when it's nice weather. A woman sells them from a cart with an umbrella that she wheels to Cypress Avenue each afternoon a little before three o'clock. There's plenty of sweetness in the details and the sun that shines on children in the richer quarters of the city shines on children here as well. There are at all times, and in every season, these reminders of democracy.

CHAPTER 16

Benjamin

B itter cold. In the streets around St. Ann's small children are wrapped up like Russian dolls, their hands in mittens sticking out of padded jackets buttoned to their throats, scarves wrapped around their faces. Three boys in woolen hats pulled down over their eyes and mouths stare out at me through eyeholes as they wait outside the big doors of the afterschool.

"Hi, Jonathan!"

"Orlando?"

"Nope!"

"Davis?"

"Nope!"

"Elio?"

"Nope!"

He pulls off his cap. It's Damian. The other two are friends of his that I don't know.

The decibel level in the afterschool is quite spectacular for a few minutes when the public schools let out. Katrice's daughter, Nancy, often stands close to the door beside the row of hooks where children hang their backpacks and their coats, steering them to different tables or to different groups according to their ages, some of which will go upstairs to the computer room or other rooms, while others stay down here to do their homework first.

During a week when I can be here almost every day, Nancy picks a group of children who need extra help in math or reading and assigns us to one of the smaller rooms upstairs, where it's much quieter than in the big room on the ground floor. If I want to follow up with children I've been working with already, Nancy lets me choose the group myself.

One day in January, she suggests I go upstairs with several of the boys I know from P.S. 30. Elio wants to come with us, but Nancy wants him to remain downstairs because she says he hasn't done his homework. It's probably just as well, because the other boys are slightly older and it's hard enough to get them settled down to do their work without the added pressure that I feel when Elio is with us.

Benjamin, the oldest in the group, lives in the same apartment building as Pineapple near the end of Beekman Avenue. Eleven years old in the fourth grade, he's repeated once and, with the tougher nonpromotion policies the school board now is putting into place, he may be required to repeat again. A tall and skinny boy who sometimes picks on younger children and can be sarcastic when he's speaking to adults, he finds it hard to sit still in his chair for more than a few minutes at a time. He doesn't disturb the other boys; he just keeps getting up and going to the bookcase to examine the bookcovers, standing at the window to look out into the street, then coming back a moment later with a kind of loping rhythm, and then slumping down into his chair.

Damian, the smallest of the boys, is ten years old and doing well in school, where he's a year ahead of Benjamin. A bright and lively boy, he never leaves his seat as Benjamin keeps doing; but, even while he sits there in his chair, his energetic little limbs perform the most remarkable gymnastics. It's as if he were connected to the chair by a ball bearing or a universal joint that links him to his seat at one spot only. The most advanced boy in the group in verbal skills and mathematics, he explodes with words, with unexpected answers, with unusual and funny comments about things the other children say. Although I'm sitting just three feet from him across the table, he raises his arm repeatedly and waves his fingers in my face to capture my attention when he has something to say.

"Ooooo! Ooooo!" he keeps exclaiming when an urgent thought comes to his mind.

When I turn to him and say his name, he's so excited he forgets what he had planned to say. "Think for a minute. I'll come back to you," I say.

As soon as I call on someone else, he waves his hand and tells me, "I remember!"

Orlando, who is also bright and nearly as excitable as Damian, doesn't squirm as much, but he too waves his fingers in my face and, with theatrical exaggeration, makes it sound as if he's on the point of death from intellectual combustion.

"Oooooo! Ooooooo! I know! I know!"

Some of the children call me "teacher." Others speak to me by my first name. Damian calls me "Jonathan" because he's known me for three years. Davis is Nancy's son and sees me at his home. He calls me "Jonathan" as well. Orlando and Leonardo call me "teacher," but they rarely say it only once. They double it up—"teacher! teacher!"—so it comes out twice, but like one word.

I look forward to these sessions; and, quite honestly, when children call me "teacher" I feel happy, even though I know they say this somewhat automatically, because they know I'm not a teacher anymore and not a member of the staff here at the church. Sometimes, too, I feel a little guilty when I think of their *real* teachers—Miss Reistetter, Mr. Bedrock, and Miss Suarez, for example—who are with these children every day at P.S. 30, and I think, "Good God! Real teachers have to work like this all day!"

I worked hard too when I was teaching school, and even harder after I was hired by the parents in an inner-city neighborhood of Boston to direct a freedom school—an afterschool and evening school—based in a church that was involved in organizing for the civil rights campaigns. Nearly 150 children had to navigate the narrow stairs and passageways of that small building every time they moved from one room to another. When class let out at period breaks, the noise within the stairs was like the rumbling of thunder.

I must have had a lot more energy in those days—and, I'm sure, a better sense of humor—than I've had in recent years. I had a white Volkswagen bug in 1966. When one of the kindergarten children didn't show up for a class and teachers had searched everywhere, in every corner of the church, and even in the pastor's study and the space behind the altar where a child now and then would hide, or curl up for a nap, I would simply run out to the street, get in my car, drive around the corner to the child's house, pull up on the curb, and ring the bell, and climb the stairs. If the child wasn't sick and nothing serious was wrong, I'd lift her right up on my back and bring her downstairs to the car and, minutes later, would "deliver" her like a reluctant present to her teacher.

But I was only 29 years old that year; and I was in good health, and thin, and wired with the hyperactive hopes and the romantic sense of possibilities that were so common among activists and organizers in those days. Thousands of young men and women in the schools and freedom schools and civil rights campaigns in Boston and Chicago and New York and in the rural neighborhoods of the Deep South lived and worked in the same way, with not much sleep and little pay and often without ever sitting down to have the normal meals our parents would approve of. It seemed that we could go for weeks on little more than coffee, cookies, candy bars, and the exhilaration of the children and the solidarity of their enthusiastic parents and grandparents.

Many people teaching in the South Bronx have that kind of wired energy and live and work like that today. I find it harder to keep up the pace. Having asthma doesn't help; I'm not as good as I once was at climbing six or seven flights of stairs, although there often is no choice. Some buildings in Mott Haven have no elevator. In the ones that do, as Damian once said, "it doesn't always want to come to the first floor." Then too, I often feel my energy collapsing in the last part of the day, especially if I did not have time for lunch, which may be why that look of weariness in Mr. Rogers's eyes the afternoon he visited St. Ann's struck a familiar note for me.

It seems to be around that time in the late afternoon when energy levels are the lowest for adults that children are becoming the most restless and determined to get recognition for the things they want to tell you and the most competitive with one another in attracting and commanding your attention. The persistence of some of the younger ones in doing this is like a force of nature.

"Jonathan! Jonathan!" Damian keeps saying while I'm trying to get Benjamin back to his chair.

"Yes?" I say.

"Somebody tried to steal me!"

The other children are immediately silenced by this statement. Benjamin stops his prowling in a distant corner of the room and comes back to the table.

"Where did this happen?" I ask Damian.

"Near my uncle's house," he says.

"Where does your uncle live?"

"Near Willis Avenue," he says.

Benjamin takes his seat and looks at Damian with real concern as Damian begins to tell the story of the man who tried to steal him.

"My father gave me a glass of orange juice," he says, which turns out to be unrelated to the story. "So then I was walking to my uncle's house and saw a man who looked at me a funny way, because I think he was a drunkie. And then the drunkie man came up and mumbled something and he *grabbed* me! And he mumbled something else and then my uncle came out of his house and saw him and my uncle has a knife in his back pocket because he knows how to throw it, because he takes throwing lessons. And he threw it in his back! And then the man was running up the street. So he fell down and so I hit my head—like that! bam!—because I fell and he fell down on top of me. So then my uncle chased him and he ran away. And that's the way I got this bump here on my forehead."

He stands halfway and turns his body back and forth to show his bump to everyone.

"Did your father find out why he tried to steal you?"

"No," he says. "Nobody knows."

"Why do you think?"

"I think he didn't have a son."

"Some people can't have babies," Davis says.

"Maybe he wanted to have his own son," says Orlando.

"I think that he was lonesome," Damian says.

The children move from this into a brief discussion about having babies, and they talk about the good things and the bad things that result from having little brothers in their families.

"The good thing is they got fat little legs and rubber toes," says Damian.

"They follow you around the house," Orlando says.

"And you got somebody to play with," Davis says.

"You can take their toys from them," says Benjamin.

"The trouble is," says Damian, "when your mother has another baby, sometimes she forgets to feed you. You say, 'I'm hungry,' and she says"—he imitates his mother's voice—"'Don't bother me right now! Can't you see I've got to feed your brother?'"

The other boys agree that this is one real disadvantage about having babies in their homes. Even Leonardo, who does not have any siblings—nor a mother to take care of him, at least not in New York—expresses his agreement with the other boys about the disadvantages of babies.

After a time the boys take out their writing and we get some work done for three quarters of an hour. Benjamin is the only one who never settles down. He stays by the bookcase looking at a book he's taken from the shelf, but in a way that seems halfhearted. He opens it and holds it in his hand, but it's not clear how much it interests him. When the other boys finish their work and go downstairs, I ask him to remain for a few minutes more and let me see the book.

It turns out to be a book by Langston Hughes I've never seen before, poems written about animals, that someone must have given to the church. He shows me a poem that he's been looking at and asks me if I know "the man who wrote it." When I say I never had a chance to meet him and that he died long ago, the boy seems disappointed.

At my request he reads the poem aloud. It's a short poem, but he reads it with some difficulty. At the end, however, he seems pleased and reads the first four lines a second time, then reads it all again in a clear voice:

> A lion in a zoo,
> Shut up in a cage,
> lives a life
> of smothered rage.
>
> A lion in the plain,
> Roaming free,
> Is happy as ever
> A lion can be.

The only word he can't pronounce is "smothered." Once I say it for him and he understands it, he goes back to those four lines and reads them with real feeling. Without the other boys around to serve as foils for his foolishness, he seems more willing to allow himself to take some pleasure in the poetry. He sits in his chair, leaning on his elbows with his upper body draped over the table. Holding the book with one hand, he runs his other hand over the surface of the page.

Benjamin had been in special education for the first few years of elementary school—a category that includes developmentally delayed and "troubled" children but has also sometimes been a dumping ground for problematic students in New York, black and Hispanic children being far more likely than the other racial groups to be perceived as "problematic." He's in a mainstream classroom now but still has difficulty with his basic reading skills and math. Having to repeat a year had been embarrassing for him, especially because he was already taller than most children of his age. If I hadn't had this opportunity to talk with him alone, I don't know if I'd have gotten past my first impression of him as a rather loose-limbed, casual, and superficial boy who seemed to laugh too easily at other kids' mistakes.

It is the real respect with which he grapples with the poem, the way he looks down at the page and touches it, the patient, labored way he moves his finger on the page from line to line, and the apparent satisfaction on his face when he arrives at the last line, that leave me thinking of him as a very different person from the boy I thought I'd known before.

"How did it go?" asks Nancy when she sees us coming down the stairs.

"Fine," I say.

She gives me a discerning smile. "Tell the truth," she says. "They wiped you out!"

Benjamin gets settled at a table where the other boys who were upstairs with us are sitting. Nancy blows a high-pitched whistle, like the ones gym teachers use. The eighty children seated at the seven wooden tables quiet down and fold their hands to say The Lord's Prayer before dinner. Elio signals to me from his table just before he says his prayer: a timid gesture of his hand, perhaps a way of making sure I still remember that he's here. Pineapple is sitting with her sisters at another table, closer to the door. Ariel and the older girls, as usual, are clustered at a separate table near the far end of the room.

Once the children start to eat I slip outside to get some air and stand there for a while by the railing that divides the walkway from the garden. After several days of snow the weeping willow at the high point of the hill looks like a picture on a Christmas card. Its branches are bent down beneath big clumps that look like soft white comforters.

The children in the afterschool having their supper now are far more fortunate in some respects than many of the other children of Mott Haven. They have this church in which to play and do their homework, with the help of tutors, after school. They have good books and toys, and games, and crayons, paints, and paper. They have supper. They have physical and moral safety. They have prayer. They have the fierce allegiance of the mothers and grandmothers. They have a priest whose vigilance is not flamboyant and whose loyalty is unconditional.

The ones who go to P.S. 30 also have the powerful allegiance of a principal who is a specialist in what one of the teachers there describes as "heavy-duty love" and fights on their behalf the way a mother lion fights for her endangered cubs. They also have devoted teachers who, in the majority of cases, would be welcomed into faculties in good suburban districts but have personal commitment to remain in this community.

Still, the math and reading scores for kids at P.S. 30, even though they tend to be among the highest in the district, are extremely low compared to those of children in the suburbs and to those of children in more favored sections of the city. Few of the children in this neighborhood are given preschool opportunities. Only two of every ten preschoolers in Mott Haven are admitted to the underfunded Head Start programs in the area. Miss Rosa runs a preschool, but it's small—she's limited in space and funds—and two thirds of the eligible children can't be served. Low education-levels among parents, many educated in this neighborhood fifteen or twenty years before, limit their ability to reinforce instruction taking place in school, especially in crucial areas like mathematics and linguistic skills, which makes the lack of preschool all the more injurious.

Many children, too, go hungry; many have a hard time sleeping because of anxieties and illnesses at home. Kids with asthma wake up wheezing. Usually their siblings wake up too; the whole house wakes up when this happens. Sometimes children don't get back to sleep until the morning. So their mothers keep them home from school, which interrupts the continuity of their instruction. Many fall behind their class and never do catch up and cannot be promoted.

Most damaging of all the factors that are truly in society's direct control, at least in my belief, is the large size of classes here, especially for kids who have so many worries on their minds and so much natural desire to receive a big share of the adoration and attention of a grown-up. Suburban schools get worried when a second grade has more than 21 small bodies in one class; people who send their children to expensive private elementary schools in New York City and New England grow concerned if class size rises much above 16 or 17. But Damian's class has 31, and fourth- and fifth-grade teachers in the fall of 1999, as I was finishing this book, began the year with classes ranging up to 35.

This is not unusual in elementary schools in inner-city sections of New York. There are classes in the city that begin the year with 40, even 45 or 50. I've also been in classes in the Bronx that don't have classrooms of their own but share a large and noisy space with several other classes, maybe 80, 90 children in one room, or else are held in basement corridors or storerooms, closets really, without windows.

If Miss Rosa had the same per-pupil budget as an elementary school in wealthy Great Neck or Manhasset, and the same extensive and uncrowded physical facilities, every class within this school could be reduced to 18 pupils, every four-year-old within the neighborhood could be provided with a full-day program of developmental preschool, and Miss Rosa still would have sufficient funds left over to bring in a full-time doctor, full-time art and music teachers, and a counselor for children with emotional disorders. To those who ask us, with the loaded phrasing that is used too often on this issue, whether money really is "the only answer" to the problems faced by schools serving the poorest children in our cities now, I think it is fair to answer, "No. It's not the *only* answer, but it often is a precondition for most other answers." If it weren't, we would be hard-pressed to explain why schools in affluent districts spend so much to guarantee that class size remains small.

In spite of all these systematic inequalities, the children from St. Ann's who go to P.S. 30 are well-loved and carefully protected by their priest and principal; but when they leave this school, and leave the afterschool, and move into the more anonymous milieu of secondary school, and do not have these women, and the others working with them at the school and church, to watch them closely every day, things often change dramatically.

Most of the children go from here to one of the four middle schools in the Mott Haven area. Although, in principle, they have some other choices outside of the area, few children ever hear about these choices and the ones who do are generally unsuccessful when they file an application. The largest numbers end up at the middle school across the street from P.S. 30, which the pastor of St. Ann's and many of the parents bitterly dislike because they see how rapidly the gains made by the younger children in their years at P.S. 30 have been canceled out after a year or two in this historically dysfunctional and chilly institution. (There is a better middle school less than a half-mile to the north on St. Ann's Avenue, directly opposite the newly built reform school; but when I visited this school in

1998, I learned that competition and selection patterns more or less assure that only a few kids from P.S. 30 have a chance of getting in.)

From middle school, a small number of children go to high schools in some other sections of the city or to small and innovative schools in the South Bronx; but the largest numbers go to Morris High, a school I visit every couple years and where, each time I do, I find myself peculiarly surprised when I am told that the statistics are no better than they were the last time I was there. Approximately 1,900 boys and girls are still enrolled each year at Morris High, about 1,200 of them in the ninth-grade class alone; but there are seldom more than 65 — out of 1,900! — who get to the twelfth grade and receive diplomas.

In principle again, the kids have other choices; but, again, these choices prove repeatedly to be beyond their reach. In 1997, for example, students in the eighth grade at the middle school across from P.S. 30 made out applications, as they were instructed, to eight different high schools they had chosen, some of which were not in the South Bronx; but virtually none of them, Mother Martha told me, "were assigned to *any* of the eight schools they had chosen," with the consequence that, by default, most ended up at local schools like Morris High. A meeting was held. Katrice was there. Some of the kids, she said, were given one more chance to file an application elsewhere. Most of them, by that point, didn't dare to try.

There are a number of ways to break the will of those who have a fleeting notion of escaping from the destinies a social order seems to have in store for them. Attrition and confusion and misinformation and alleged computer errors are a few of many ways in which the sequestration of these children is achieved. Some of the children from St. Ann's escape these patterns now and then; having a pastor who was once a litigator helps them to kick down a couple of these doors. It's too selective, though. It calls for too much elbowing, too much manipulation, and too much last-minute intervention. It's not the way a fair-minded society should function.

Most of the children come to all of this, initially at least, with a degree of trust that they are going to be treated fairly. The way the social order kills that sense of trust is cumulative, quiet, sometimes subtle, sometimes not so subtle, usually a little complicated, so it seems that it could be an oversight, not something consciously intended. Intentional or not, however, all these processes have powerful effects.

Snow begins to fall again around five-thirty. I decide to walk up to Ali's, the corner restaurant close to St. Ann's, to get a cup of coffee. Since I didn't eat today I get a doughnut while I'm there. By the time I get back to the church it's after six o'clock. Most of the children have gone home. Benjamin is shooting baskets in the gym with several older boys who come here in the evening. Davis is downstairs with his mother and Katrice. A few of the younger children are still sitting at the tables, playing games or reading books while waiting for their mothers. Even on the days when I've run out of steam I never like these afternoons to end.

CHAPTER 17

Esperanza

Benjamin's reaction when he read the poem about the lions in the zoo surprised me. I thought I'd figured out what he was like. Then I realized that I didn't know this boy at all.

Damian's story about the man who tried to "steal" him had surprised me too. I thought of Damian as a light-hearted boy whose life was filled with carefree thoughts and easy victories in academic work at school. I'd never pictured him in situations like the one he had described; and, even if he had embellished the knife-throwing story, which I think he did (it sounded too much like the action videos that boys his age enjoy), I still came from his telling of the story with some very different thoughts about him than I'd had before.

Every time I think I've got the personalities of certain children "fixed"— "established"— in my mind, something new is said or something unexpected happens that dismantles my assumptions and compels me to go back to zero and start over.

It would, of course, be easier if children would agree not to revise their personalities each time they reappear. Children play a game called "Freeze!" I wish at times that I could play it with them too. "Stay right there where you are with that idea, that mood, that tendency, that disposition, which I'm almost sure I can explain or sound at least as if I understand! Don't make things hard for me by being someone else tomorrow afternoon."

It's possible I've sometimes even left a situation prematurely, not quite by intention, but perhaps with the unconscious thought that I could thereby cut the *risk* of learning "something more" and get down something that I think I know already into words. "Children learn best under X and Y conditions," I might finally conclude. "Children tend to cope best with a painful situation" if they have "this body of beliefs and attitudes" or are endowed with that particular compendium of "resources and values." It all seems quite convincing if you didn't stick around too long.

Obviously, you can't write books if you cannot convince yourself at certain times that you know *something* with finality. At some point you tell yourself, "I know enough! If I learn one thing more about this child, or these children, or this situation, or this church or classroom, or this school, I'll never dare to write a word." The education writer John Holt once surprised me when I questioned him about some confident assertion he had made in one of his first books about the ways that children learn, which were received somewhat like sacred texts by people of my generation when I started teaching school. He thought a moment, smiled sheepishly, and said, "You know what? I was wrong!"

One reason I admire Robert Coles so much is that he keeps on going back to talk with the same children over a long period of years, and *still* is careful about summarizing his conclusions even after that. I used to get impatient with his hesitations and self-questionings because they didn't give you quick and finished answers that could spare you the untidiness of ambiguity. I'm glad now that they didn't. I'm glad he didn't make the world of childhood appear more simple, or more simply comprehended, than it really is.

One day in Pineapple's class at P.S. 65, the teacher is about to introduce a lesson, but the lesson hasn't yet begun, and several of the girls who sit around Pineapple in the second and third rows are passing something back and forth to one another. I find that my attention is distracted by a solemn-looking girl who's sitting at a separate table in the back part of the room, perhaps a dozen feet from almost all the other children. I'm seated three or four feet from her at a large round table. The teacher is checking some papers at her desk; there's a hum of whispering among the children.

The solitary child sits there looking at me with her big brown eyes, so serious, and with the strangest look of curiosity and friendliness, but also hesitation. I get the feeling that she thinks she knows me and that possibly we've met before; but I'm not sure that this is true, and if it is, I can't remember where.

At last, she gets up from her chair and comes across to me and asks me, "Can I tell you something all alone?"

It's hard to make the context for this moment clear because, of course, we're not alone at all. There's a student sitting near us who, I think, is being isolated by the teacher because he was misbehaving; and there are the other children in the room, which isn't large, and there's the teacher too, of course, although her presence isn't felt right now because she's doing something at her desk, which is, I think, in preparation for the lesson.

"What's your name?" I ask the child.

"Esperanza," she replies.

She comes closer to my chair and whispers, "This is kind of crazy."

"I won't think it's crazy."

"I don't know my father's name."

"His last name or his first name?"

"I don't know either of his names."

"Where does he live?"

"He lives in Florida."

"Where were you born?"

"In Florida," she says.

"Did your father have to go away?"

"No," she says. "*We* had to go away."

"Where did you go?"

"We came here to New York."

That's all she says at first. She leaves my side and goes back to her chair.

The teacher starts to introduce a lesson about rice production. After a time, she notices that Esperanza isn't listening. The child's arms are folded on her desk, her body bent way over, and her face against her arms. Someone from the office stands outside the door and gestures to the child. The teacher says, "I'll have to call her mother. . . ." I realize that the little girl is crying.

Some minutes go by. She finally sits up and tries to pay attention. The teacher passes out a page of information about rice production. The children read it silently. Then the teacher asks them to describe the subject of the page.

Several children answer, "Rice?"

It's not a very interesting lesson. Some of the girls who sit together in the front part of the room are whispering about a picture on the cover of a magazine about the Spice Girls.

The teacher finally notices the girls, who don't appear to realize that she's watching them.

"Ayeesha!" says the teacher.

"Yes?" the child says.

"Which is more important, Spice Girls or your work on rice production?"

"Spice Girls!" says Ayeesha.

"Rice is boring," says Pineapple.

The teacher gets distracted once again by someone at the door. Esperanza finally gets up and comes back to my table.

"Can I tell you something else?"

"Yes," I say.

"Can I say it in your ear?"

"Okay."

I turn my head so she can whisper in my ear.

She says, "My father loves me."

I ask whether he visits her.

"No," she says. "I haven't seen him since I was a baby."

"Does he write you letters?"

"No. He calls me on the phone."

"But you don't know his name?"

She shakes her head.

The teacher finally turns to face the class. Seeing Esperanza standing at my side, she nods at me: a very casual gesture of permission.

A smile gradually comes across the child's face. "I'm going to tell you something nice," she says.

"Okay," I say.

"My father gave me something beautiful."

"What did he give you?"

"It's a music box," she says.

"What kind of music does it play?"

"Lullabies," she says.

"How does it work?"

"You wind it up and open up the top," she says.

She looks down at the floor. "My father says to play it if I'm sad. . . ."

"Is that what you do?"

"I pretend he's singing to me," she replies.

After a pause, she says, "I'm going to tell you something else."

"Okay," I say.

"I think you met me once."

"Where did we meet?"

"Downstairs," she says.

"I don't remember. When was that?"

"It was in the cafeteria," she says.

"Now I remember."

"You were *here* — and I was *here*," she says, explaining how the table was arranged.

"I was sitting with Pineapple?"

"Yes," she says. Then, after another pause, she asks me, "Can I tell you one thing more?"

"Yes," I say.

"My father's name is Alejandro."

"You remembered!"

"No," she says. "I knew it all along. . . ."

Her presence at my side attracts the notice of the other children, but she seems oblivious to their attention and continues talking softly. She tells me that her mother has a boyfriend who lives "in our house with us," but says she doesn't like him.

I ask, "Why don't you like him?"

"Because," she says, "I have to make his breakfast."

"What do you make him?"

"Pancakes," she replies.

"How many pancakes do you make?"

"Only two."

She studies me again for a long while.

"Can I tell you something else?"

I turn my head so she can whisper in my ear again.

"I have the beauty of my mother and the braveness of my father."

I turn my paperpad to write down what she said, which does not sound immodest, but mature and slightly tremulous. "Did you say 'bravery' or 'braveness'?"

"Braveness," she replies.

Her reference to her mother's boyfriend, and her obligation to cook breakfast for him, leaves me puzzled—worried also, to be truthful; but our conversation ceases to be serious when Pineapple gets up and comes to sit beside me. The class seems to be doing little work. The teacher is involved again with something at her desk. The lesson about rice production seems to be forgotten.

Esperanza reaches around behind her back and pulls her long thick braid in front of her and holds it in both hands.

"She has a cat," Pineapple says.

"You do?"

"Yes," Esperanza says.

"Guess her name," Pineapple says.

"I can't guess."

"Guess anyway," she says.

"I can't."

"Dimitri!" says Pineapple.

"Is that so?" I ask the child.

"Yes!" she says. "And, guess what?"

"What?" I ask her.

"She's a girl!"

"Dimitri is a boy's name," says Pineapple.

"What color is Dimitri?"

"Black," says Esperanza.

"How long have you had her?"

"All my life," she says.

"How long is that?"

"Eight years," she says.

"I'm older than she is," Pineapple says.

"How much older?"

"Six months," says Pineapple.

The teacher seems to have evaporated as a presence in the room. It's an odd situation. Someone from the office is in front with her again, bent down beside her desk. Children don't get up and move around the room and chat with me in classes in which teachers exercise authority. Only when the teacher tells the children that it's time to line up for dismissal is her presence in the classroom re-established.

On Cypress Avenue outside the school Esperanza shows me where she lives. Her house is opposite the school, a few doors from St. Mary's Park. There were some killings in that park a few years earlier. It's safer now, although Katrice tells me another man was brutally assaulted there—his throat was slit—as I was writing this. It seems safe enough during the afternoons, especially on weekends when it's filled with families having picnics.

Esperanza waves goodbye to us from her front door before she goes inside. I've seen her a few times since then—twice in the playground at the school, and once on an evening at the corner store. She's never seemed to have the wish to talk like that with me again. Sometimes a window like this opens briefly. Then it closes and you wish that it would open up once more but also wonder why it opened up the first time.

"Do you know Esperanza well?" I asked Pineapple as we walked down to St. Ann's.

"No one knows her well," she said.

"Does she cry a lot?"

"A lot!" she said.

"Do you think of her as an unhappy child?"

She made a wavy gesture with one hand, her way of indicating a mixed feeling on the child's situation.

"Complicada," she said finally.

Some children who have troubles in their heart don't talk a lot at first but, when they finally do, the things they say can be so beautiful. I've had several conversations in which children told me that they didn't know their father, or his name, or where he lives, but then would add an extra piece of information that transformed the story and transcended what had seemed like undiluted sadness at the start. It's as if they save these "extra" things until a special time when everything seems right, then hand them to you for no reason, on an impulse, and without conditions.

It's hard to explain the slightly nervous way I felt when Esperanza asked if she could tell me "one thing more." The innocence in all of this just made me scared that I would not know what to say, or what to do, about whatever confidence she was about to share with me.

She told me something else, which I did not write down at first, because it didn't seem important. After she had told me about making pancakes for her mother's boyfriend, I did not know what to say about this; so I asked her, "How do you make pancakes?"

"Well," she said, "first you take a cup of flour. Then you mix the eggs and then you pour some milk into the bowl, but not too much. And then you stir it all around and then you pour it on the pan and then it's cooking on the pan and then you look at it until it gets a little brown and then you start to see the little bubbles"— she looked up and smiled when she said "the little bubbles"—"so you turn it over and you wait and then you go and turn it off, and then you put it on the plate."

It's insignificant compared with what she told me of her father. In the past, when I was writing stories about children, I would skip these frivolous digressions. Now it seems to be the moments of digression I remember with most interest later on. I think about the "interruptions" longer than the things they've interrupted.

The part about the bubbles you're supposed to look for in the pancakes seems so ordinary and inconsequential. Still, she took a detailed pleasure in describing that to me, and little bits of detailed pleasure are what much of life is made of for the children when they're happy, and the medicine for pain when they are not.

Most of the things that I remember longest from the stories children tell me have this detailed and inconsequential quality. Smallness of range, tenderness of tone, sometimes a particularity of sorrow, at other times an easy merriment of mood, at almost all times a determined insignificance, are very much a part of the majority of conversations that I have with children here, as with most other children that I talk with almost anywhere.

I often feel a curious inclination, possibly some kind of academic "obligation," to add something that will make these moments more important than they are. How do you do that with the bubbles in the pancakes? What of a child's hands around her long thick braid? The braid has small white beads in it. Her hands hold on to it in an engaging way. She's eight years old. She has braveness, beauty, sadness. She has a cat. She has a music box. "That's it!" as Pineapple says often when she feels a subject has been given the attention it deserves. She doesn't belabor things like this. She says what needed to be said; then she moves on to something else.

CHAPTER 18

A Nice Week in the Neighborhood

Pineapple's little sister, who is named Briana, tells me that she spent the weekend in the country, in a town called Woodcrest, at a Protestant community known as the Bruderhof, where people lead a simple life in an idyllic setting. "I sat on a horse and carried a bunny and I went on a horse-ride in a carriage and I held a Woodcrest baby. And I touched a Lassie dog!"

Katrice says that she went to Woodcrest with the children and that they were treated beautifully. "When we got off the bus, their children came with flowers they had woven into garlands. They put flowers in our hair!"

The dogs the children played with at the Bruderhof, according to Pineapple, were "not *really* Lassie dogs." They were golden retrievers, she reports, some of them newborn puppies. To Briana, though, they're Lassie dogs and she seems happy to remember them this way.

The mild-natured child also tells me that she fell at recess while she was at P.S. 65 today. Another child pushed her in the schoolyard and she landed on her face and hurt her chin and scraped the skin. She asks me if it ever happened to me and I say yes. She asks me if it hurt and I say yes. She asks me if I cried and I say yes. Then she nods, as if she knew I must have cried, and says that she cried too.

Yesterday afternoon I sat with her while she was having supper at St. Ann's. She made a terrible expression when she opened up her milk container.

"You can have my milk," she said.

"You don't want it?"

"It smells bad," she said.

I sniffed the milk container. "I think it's okay."

"Un-uh," she said.

I offered to trade milk with her.

She shook her head and pushed my milk away.

Pineapple got into an unattractive altercation with another child earlier this week. She stood in the middle of the room, pointing her finger at the younger child.

"She says that her dog *talks* to her!"

I asked the younger girl if that was true.

She said, "She does."

"What does she say?"

"She doesn't use words," she said. "If she's hungry she goes to her bowl and barks. If she wants to go outside she stands next to the door."

"That isn't talk," Pineapple said.

"If she wants to say she loves me," said the child, undeterred, "she comes up on my bed and licks me. If she wants a drink of water, she runs to her water bowl and does quite a number of things."

Pineapple was stern in making clear that she was not convinced by this. "That isn't talkin'! Don't be lyin', girl!" she said.

"I *ain't* lyin'!" said the younger child.

Nancy, who was standing right behind Pineapple, instantly reproved her. "I don't want to hear you talking in that tone of voice to anyone!" she said.

"Excuse me," Pineapple replied, but in a voice that did not sound contrite.

She later approached me near the kitchen door and said, "She only *thinks* her dog is talking."

Absolutely positive about the younger child's misconception, she remained there with her two feet planted on the floor, her two hands on her hips.

"To me, that isn't talking. . . ."

I was at P.S. 30 the next day and spent some time in Ariel's fifth grade. Her teacher, Mrs. Harrinarine, was talking to the children about "structure" in expository writing. After explaining about "Introduction," "Body," and "Conclusion," she said that their homework was to write the first draft of an essay about problems they might face if they're encouraged by another child to experiment with drugs.

Ariel, who has a way of asking for unusual precision when someone is giving her instructions, asked the teacher to be more specific.

"Let's say you're doing a first draft and make a very small mistake — or *two* mistakes," she said. "Is it okay to cross it out or do you need to copy over everything you wrote?"

Mrs. Harrinarine seemed amused by the preciseness of the question. Ariel's wording made it sound as if there were a law about first drafts. Two mistakes perhaps could be crossed out, but maybe three mistakes could not.

"Just write it neat enough so I won't get a headache," said the teacher.

To get the children interested in the subject of their essays, she began a brief discussion about drugs and various choices that young people might be forced to make. She asked, for instance, how they might respond if they received an invitation to a party but had reason to believe that people who used drugs had been invited too.

"You have to think it through and scale the consequences," Ariel replied.

The teacher knew the word that Ariel was looking for. With the pacing of a practiced teacher, she watched Ariel to see if she was going to reword this on her own, then asked her whether "scale" was really what she meant to say. Ariel bit down on her lip, then understood her error and said, "Weigh?"

"Yes," the teacher said. "We 'weigh' the consequences of decisions that we make." When it comes to drugs, she said, "we want to weigh them *very, very* carefully."

Ariel's meticulous determination to refine a question to specifics is familiar to me from a number of our conversations at St. Ann's. There's a crisp lucidity about her search for the right word or right idea or proper connotation, which is one of many reasons why it's satisfying to converse with her, although her teacher notes that the same need for absolute precision which is so refreshing in her conversation also functions as an inhibition in her writing. "Wanting to know exactly how to get from Point A to Point B hasn't *always* been a positive for her," according to the teacher, who admires Ariel tremendously and has high hopes for her to go to college.

Elio was having tea with Aida Rosa when I stepped into her office around one o'clock today. When I saw him sitting with her at the table that extends almost the full width of the room, I more or less assumed that he'd done something wrong and had been sent here by his teacher; but Miss Rosa said this wasn't so. His class had done well on a math test and, as their reward, were being shown a movie he'd already seen. So he had asked if he could spend the time here in the office with Miss Rosa, and his teacher had agreed.

The two of them were sitting there like two good friends having a social visit with each other. Elio was sipping tea with milk out of a coffee mug. Miss Rosa was drinking coffee from a Styrofoam container. There was a plate of cookies on the table.

The office at P.S. 30 is a friendly and inviting place for children and, no less important, for the parents of the neighborhood, who often feel an understandable anxiety in visiting a public school. Some of them went to the same schools and do not have good memories. Many never finished high school and don't think of schools as places of remembered victories. Miss Rosa tries to make each contact with a child's parents welcoming enough so they'll be eager to return.

Some of the parents come here, as they also come into St. Ann's, at times of crisis in their lives. Some are having bad financial problems and will tell Miss Rosa frankly that they have no food. Other people from the neighborhood stop by impulsively sometimes and leave containers of hot food they may have cooked initially the night before. I've never been in a school office anywhere that quite resembles this one in its informality.

Teachers or parents stick their heads into the office now and then to say hello or ask a question. "Not now, *Papí*," she'll say quickly to a teacher — Mr. Bedrock, for example, who is often stopping by to query her about some regulation he dislikes — "call me tonight." She stays here almost every night until well after eight o'clock, sometimes as late as nine.

Elio seemed bashful with me in Miss Rosa's presence. He munched on a cookie and looked down and sat there silently while she was showing me some papers I had asked for. Running into him in unexpected situations like this often lets me see an aspect of his personality I've never seen before: in this case, his sense of reticent politeness and his recognition of the way he should behave while grown-ups were discussing grown-up matters that he maybe didn't think he was supposed to hear.

Isaiah's class was having a discussion about Roman history this afternoon. I was sitting beside him during the discussion. A girl who sat across from him was looking at him shyly, then kept turning to the girl beside her, who appeared to know something about the interest she was showing in Isaiah. The girl beside her wrote a note and gave it to her, and the two girls smiled.

She wasn't as shy as I thought, however. At the end of class, after Isaiah got his coat and was collecting papers from his desk before the children lined up at the door, she walked right up to him and asked him if he'd give her his phone number.

"Sorry," he said. "I don't give out my number. I'll call *you*."

She seemed offended then. "You don't have my number," she replied, "and you *won't* have it either!"

Isaiah looked at me and gave a shrug, as if he didn't care. As it happens, however, he could not have given her his number anyway, because his mother's phone had been cut off. Isaiah's skill at keeping up a front before the other children in his class seems to come easily to him. He's popular and funny; and the other kids look up to him. Still, his vigilance is carefully maintained. He's watchful always for those situations that could open him to too much close examination.

Occasionally, at lunch or near the end of school, after a day when he's appeared to be as carefree as he usually is, he'll come up to me and whisper that his mother wants to talk with me and asks if I can come to his apartment after school or when I'm finished at St. Ann's. At times, it turns out to be something entirely unimportant. At other times, it's something serious.

Six months ago, he asked me during school if I could come and visit in the afternoon. Late in the day, as I was coming up the stairs of his apartment building, I could see from the stair-landing that there was an order of eviction taped across the door of his apartment. On the coffee table in the living room, next to the Bible, there was a big pile of prescriptions that Isaiah's mother said she had been given by her doctor. She handed them to me so I could see the medicines she was supposed to take.

One was for Xanax. I don't recall the others, but the point is they had all remained unfilled because, she said, she hadn't been "recertified for Medicaid." The details were confusing and, although this happens often in New York with Medicaid these days, she wasn't clear about the reasons; and, because of what is known as the "deterrence" policy enacted by the mayor to keep people in need from getting benefits of any kind, she probably was not given a reason.

She also said that she'd been out of food the night before but borrowed twenty dollars "from a guy up on the corner" who had some involvement with her husband. When I asked if it was dangerous to do that, she assured me it was not. "He's a friend. I've known this guy for years," she said, but said it very fast.

She had a rapidly articulated way of stringing sentences together when she wanted to convince me, or herself, that she was in control. At those times she'd often fall into a patter of quick-witted statements that were meant, it seemed, to demonstrate a sense of confidence that she could handle things. When I asked about the debt to the drug dealer, for example, she replied, "Would you believe it, Jonathan? That's all resolved! I take care of my business. . . ." She said my name more frequently than usual when she was in that state of mind.

Isaiah, perhaps, had learned from her some of his artfulness at rapid repartee. He used my name a lot in slightly nervous situations too, as if to simulate connectedness and openness between us even at those times when I did not feel sure that he was being open. Still, there is that other side of him: adaptable congeniality, delightful humor, and well-targeted irreverence. He doesn't make his mother kiss his panda and eleven bears at bedtime any longer, and he doesn't play with children's toys like walkie-talkies anymore; he's still fun to be with, though, and still seems capable of walking through some very messy situations without losing his self-confidence or forfeiting his sense of pleasure in the uses of sarcasm.

The word "resilience" may be overused in writings about inner-city children. It's become a kind of catch-all term that doesn't give much specificity in any given situation. To call Isaiah a "resilient" child would, in any case, not do real justice to his talent for strategic ingenuity. He doesn't just "sustain" the difficulties of existence. He steers *around* them in inventive ways that give him the defense he needs. I see him often in the streets around St. Ann's. He's always neatly dressed. He carries an attractive leather briefcase. He speaks politely with well-chosen words. He never seems like someone who's agreed to be defeated.

There were cheerful days and troubled days this week at St. Ann's Church. Jefferson came into the churchyard Monday with another wounded animal he'd found. It was a pigeon that appeared to have a broken wing. He had placed the pigeon in a box that he'd been given by the owner of a store. He opened the box in front of Mother Martha on the steps beside the church and showed her that the pigeon was alive but couldn't move. I don't know what happened after that because I had to go downstairs. When I left, the two of them were studying the pigeon's wing.

Pineapple cornered me downstairs and told me that she's on a diet and cannot have candy anymore. "Don't tell this to *anyone*," she said in a loud whisper. "I can't have milk. I can't have cookies. I can't even have dessert."

"Why not?" I asked.

"I'm on a diet — 'high cholesterol,'" she said.

"I think you mean the opposite," I said.

"Uh-uh," she said.

"I'm *sure* you mean the opposite," I told her.

"Whatever!" she replied, tossing it off as if the point that I was making were unworthy of additional consideration.

On Tuesday afternoon I had an inconclusive conversation on the subject of religion with Pineapple and a girl named Jennifer, who is her cousin. Jennifer said she had a dream that she was visiting with God. "There were no stores or restaurants," she said. "You had to call out to get food, and someone would deliver." She also said God had brown hair, "dark-brown, like mine," and that she found out God was married, because, while she visited, "His wife came in and kissed Him."

A boy who was sitting with us said he had been told that God is "with us in the world" and "not above us in the sky," but Jennifer said it wasn't so, that God "stays up in heaven" but "He breathes into the world."

When I asked her to explain this, she was unable to do so, but Pineapple said, "It's easy! Look — like this." She filled her cheeks with air, then pushed them in like a balloon with both her hands and said, "Kapoof!"

Then she laughed and said, "I'm sorry. I was fooling."

"I knew you were," I said.

"We're only children," said Pineapple, and she handed out grape-flavored sourballs to everyone — her diet, it appeared, already forgotten.

Late on Tuesday afternoon, a nineteen-year-old girl who has been helping Mother Martha in the office told me that she went to Morris High School until dropping out about three years ago after a friend of hers was murdered while he walked across a playground near the school. She showed me a memorial card that had been printed for his funeral. The boy's name was Roberto. She'd been close to him, she said, and sat beside him in an English class. After his death, she had decided to leave school.

She's a very pretty girl with a flirtatious smile. In warm weather she wears jerseys that are too provocative to satisfy Katrice and other mothers at the church. She says she'd like to get a GED (a high school equivalency degree) so she can go to college. A year from now she will be pregnant and will have to leave St. Ann's in order to get ready for her baby. Her education plans will have to be postponed. For now, however, she's a great help in the office, where she handles correspondence for the priest. The little boys are fond of her. Some of them sit there and just stare at her.

One of the girls I met four years ago when she was still at P.S. 65 is working as a tutor to the younger children at St. Ann's this year. Her name is Timeka. She attends a middle school on Morris Avenue that's named in honor of Paul Robeson. I try to draw her out a bit about Paul Robeson, but she tells me she has no idea of who he is. I ask if it's a school that emphasizes music. She says no and seems perplexed that I would ask.

"It's a medical school," she says, but this, as it turns out, is not strictly correct. It's actually one of the so-called theme schools in New York that emphasize careers, part of the school-to-work momentum that has come to be familiar in the past few years in urban areas. The theme of the Paul Robeson School, according to a school brochure, is "medical careers," which does not mean that children there are being given a regime of education likely to prepare them for a university and then a medical degree. Those who become interested in the healthcare field are likely to end up in other roles within the medical profession — medical assistant, nursing aide, or lab technician — if they stay in school for long enough to graduate.

Eleanor and I had talked about the way black and Hispanic women used to be "tracked down" in high school when she was a student in the Bronx. We had talked about the way they used to be directed into classes such as "cosmetology" — a standard course in inner-city high schools for as long as I've been visiting in urban schools. Some of them, of course, still are. The programs in health sciences are more demanding and may lead to steadier employment; but skin color and class origin are still determining curricular provision for these children.

It's disappointing to realize that Timeka's options have been circumscribed already at this age. "School-to-work," an idea President Clinton favors, makes considerable sense with older children who are certain that they won't, or cannot, go to college. Imposing terminal training on a fourteen-year-old student seems unjust, however, especially when we observe how often programs of this sort are targeted at young people of color.

In a wholly different setting like that of the affluent white suburb in which I grew up and later taught, Timeka would in every likelihood be on her way to a good academic high school, then to college, and, if she so wanted, would be able to prepare herself to be a doctor, which, in fact, is the career to which she actually aspires. She seems

239

unaware of what is happening to her. When I ask her what she'd like to be, she says "a pediatrician." But when I ask her where she hopes to go to high school she says that she plans to go to Morris High.

On Wednesday afternoon, I came down to the after-school at six o'clock when almost everyone was gone and found Pineapple's sister sitting on the bench beside the door. The six-year-old was crying because she had some-how lost her Giga Pet. Katrice was standing there with Pineapple beside her.

"She lost her Digital Doggie," said Pineapple, who ex-plained that she was scared her mother would be angry.

I asked Pineapple what it cost.

"Ten dollars," she replied.

Katrice assured Briana that her Giga Pet would prob-ably be found and that her mother probably would not be mad. Pineapple, however, felt obliged to disagree. "Un-uh!" she said. "She's going to be *mad!*"

Katrice had to remain there with Briana to subdue her tears while Pineapple, who thought that she was going to be blamed for this, continued to make grim predictions of her mother's wrath.

All in all, it was a good but complicated week. Pine-apple's sister found her Giga Pet on Thursday. Elio did his homework every afternoon and said his prayer each day before he had his supper and did not get into any heated battles with the other children, so the overturned blue milk box in the kitchen stayed unoccupied for five days in a row. There was one sad piece of news, however. I learned on Thursday afternoon that Elio's cousin had committed sui-cide on Sunday. Elio had been crying early in the week and spent part of an afternoon alone with Mother Martha.

Nancy knew the twenty-year-old man who'd killed himself. She was shaken by the news and gave a stirring lecture to the children in the afterschool before they had their supper.

Maybe "lecture" isn't the right word. It was less a lecture than a heartfelt pleading. She begged the children never to permit themselves to hide their feelings of depression but to come to her or Mother Martha, or Miss Elsie, or Katrice, "and tell us what's inside of you," and "trust us always at your times of sadness," because "you will always know that we can help you with these feelings" and "we all know times like that, because we all become depressed and sad. I know that I do and I'm sure that Mother Martha does as well. We *all* get scared. We *all* have times when we would like to end our lives, and when we feel that way, we know we need to turn to someone that we love.

"And so I beg you, children, each and every one of you, to come to me and tell me when you're feeling sad and never think you need to be alone with your own thoughts. I'm *always* here for you. That's what our church is for, that's why we're here, because we love you and we want you to be happy and we always have you in our hearts.

"So now let's fold our hands and say our prayers. . . ."

The week did not end on a somber note, however. By Friday Elio was smiling again. Pineapple's little sister was her old light-hearted self. Pineapple told me that she thought she was in love with Felix, a fifth-grader. She stood with me on Friday afternoon and pointed out the boy but said that he did not reciprocate her feelings. "He doesn't even know that I *exist*," she said. I asked her if she thought that she was old enough to be in love. She thought about it, then conceded, "No. It's probably not love." But, looking at the handsome dark-eyed boy across the room, she put her hand against her chest and sighed.

"He sure is cute!"

On Sunday she and both her sisters wore white robes and served as acolytes. Jefferson was an acolyte as well. Isaiah's mother was at church that day. She and Isaiah sat beside me. When it was time to take communion they were first in line. There was a festive mood that morning at St. Ann's. Pineapple carried the cross in the procession of the acolytes. The cross looked heavy, but she held it in both hands and almost managed to look dignified.

CHAPTER 19

A Pastor's Ministry

W hy is it that some children seem to be so strong and full of energy and hopefulness about their lives and manage to do well in school despite the most discouraging conditions in their neighborhood while other children facing the same obstacles appear unable to prevail?

For people who write on education, as I do, there is a premium on coming up with neatly packaged answers to this question; but the actual answers, as we generally concede to one another when we're not advancing a particular agenda, tend to be as unpredictable, and various, as life itself, and character, and chance, and personality.

For some of the kids I know whose parents have led troubled lives, the greatest source of moral strength may lie in a grandmother, though the problems that the children face as they become teenagers often overwhelm even the strongest of grandmothers. In other cases, it may be a deep religious faith that keeps a child in a positive and optimistic frame of mind. In still others, it's a potent sense of humor that enables children to turn sorrows into smiles. Many times, it's simply pure good luck in running into an extraordinary teacher, doctor, minister, or priest. If I had to narrow it to one, I'd likely point to the religious factor; but that is probably because I have been spending so much time with children at the church and so I see that little light glowing particularly brightly.

There's a student at the afterschool, named Leonardo, who asks frequently if he can talk with me alone in the computer room. He often has a glum look on his face. He gets depressed about the situation in his home, which isn't good. His mother is in Honduras, and the relatives he lives with aren't affectionate to him. He wears a dreary-looking U.S. Army jacket every day to school. It's like his "uniform," the badge of his perpetual depression.

On Sundays, though, he stands beside the pastor at the altar as one of her acolytes. On that day he gets to wear the wonderful white robe and ties the rope around his waist and looks resplendent there beside Pineapple and Briana and the other kids who also serve as acolytes. Sometimes he hands the wine to Mother Martha in the moments just before communion. Other days, he carries the censer or the cross. He waves to friends when he thinks Mother Martha isn't looking. It's the only time that I can think of when he seems entirely happy.

"The bread is good!" he told me once last year when he had noticed that I didn't take communion. "It's *good!*" he kept repeating, as if it were not a tasteless wafer but a slice of buttered pumpernickel. "Try it!" he said. "You'll like it!"

Leonardo, like the other children, knows that I am Jewish, so I asked if he was trying to convert me through my appetite. He said no but kept on coaxing me for several days whenever he ran into me downstairs. "The bread is *good!*" he'd say with teasing laughter in his eyes. He sounded like a salesman for communion — or a bakery.

"Try it! You'll like it!" he would say without the need to let the other children know exactly what this was referring to. The fact that there was now a private joke between us seemed to be the thing that made this fun for him.

He didn't take communion lightly, though. I can't think of any children at the church who do. Even the teenage boys who slip into the church after the service has begun and slouch in one of the back rows, with baseball hats still on their heads, as if this were a boring duty or a sullen favor for their mother, don't look sullen in the least when they kneel down to take the wafer on their tongue at the communion rail. All of the teenagers do not pray; but when they do most of them seem to pray devoutly.

Prayer, of course, is a pervasive part of life among the children at St. Ann's and isn't limited to services that take place at specific times and are mandated by church calendars. Many services take place unplanned when children wander up into the pastor's office at a time when they're upset and simply ask if they can pray with her. These services are held most often in the smaller chapel that is also used for tutoring on crowded afternoons. Vespers, which are quiet early-evening services, are held there too.

The pastor holds two services and gives two sermons Sunday morning, one in English, one in Spanish. She stays up late on Saturdays to write her sermons, which are crafted carefully, but not ornate, and seldom driven by exaggerated rhythms of rhetorical momentum. There are even silences at times, not big ones — hesitations really — when she's talking to the congregation. I don't know if they're intentional; and, if I asked, I think that she'd deny this. But they do have an effect. They seem to open up some "space." That's just about the only way I can describe it.

I know nothing of theology; but it occurs to me that modest hesitations—normal ones, like those in ordinary conversations—may allow a bit more space than a relentless speaking style does for people in a congregation who may feel the world has tried to clip their wings and that the powers and the principalities of their society might actually prefer it if they didn't fly too high.

This idea of leaving, or permitting, open spaces that another person, who has never been to college or to seminary, has an opportunity to fill is not something that the priest has ever spoken of. If I actually did question her, I'm sure she'd tell me not to read so deeply into random hesitations on a morning when she's simply tired or distracted. Still, I think it does reflect an aspect of her personality and represents, even unconsciously, an element of pedagogic style that may have an unexpectedly empowering effect. Whether on a weekday morning in a fourth-grade classroom or on Sunday in the sanctuary of a church, I think that passages of normal hesitation and, at times, a searching pause that speaks of a respect for silence can accomplish things that flashier and more inexorable performances cannot.

Thomas Merton said once of the contemplative life that it should offer those who enter it "an area, a space of liberty, of silence," in which "possibilities are allowed to surface and new choices . . . become manifest"—a space in time, he said, "which can enjoy its own potentialities and hopes." Silences, however, in monastic life or any other area of life, need not be abdications. In her sermons at St. Ann's, the pastor's words, though often stated softly, can be charged with adversarial intensity. When she speaks of the endemic inequalities of education, health-care, recreation, and aesthetics in New York, she doesn't simply say, for instance, that rich people "have advantages." She words it with a sharper specificity. She says, "They *take* advantages," refusing to accept the too convenient notion of injustice as an accidental consequence of unintended processes—"the way things are"—but making clear that *these* injustices, at least, are consequences of decisions people make to benefit themselves at the expense of others.

New York City has for decades shipped some of its ugliest and smelliest waste products to be burned, recycled, transferred, or just piled up and stored in the South Bronx, and Mother Martha is convinced, as are so many doctors, that this is a direct cause of the respiratory illnesses of people of all ages at St. Ann's. The city also sends much of its sewage to West Harlem to be processed at a plant that brought the stench of excrement into the homes of thousands of black and Hispanic families in the area for several years. Mother Martha never speaks of this the way the mainstream press tends to describe it as a mostly technical dilemma that might prove at worst to be "misguided" or "unsound." She speaks of it as social and environmental theft, as she did recently in an unsparing sermon titled "Stealing Air."

The idea of unauthored evil, of inert and agentless injustice where advantages and disadvantages are doled out more or less by chance (clean air and charming neighborhoods with nice boutiques and outdoor restaurants on one side of the city, children wheezing from their asthma, waking up each day to odors of incinerators and of burning trash and plastics on the other side), may be appeasing, and is certainly exonerating, to the powerful. The pastor does not swallow this mythology.

When the press rejoices, for example, in the "cleanup" of Times Square—a reference to the banishment of beggars and the homeless and the prostitutes and sex shops that were once familiar there—she notes how many of the homeless people banished from Manhattan have been moved to shelters or substandard housing in Mott Haven and how many wait in line at the food pantry at St. Ann's, which has run out of food for the first time in 1998 and 1999 as more and more of those who have been hidden from the sight of tourists end up in this neighborhood.

The privileged, as she observes, are not the passive beneficiaries of these policies and plans. "These actions are *not* agentless. They're planned, devised, and engineered by those who also have the means to win the acquiescence of the poor by holding out rewards for not complaining."

The suppression of this kind of language and the substitution of a terminology of falsified consensus are a part of what some of my journalistic friends in New York City call "civility." Mother Martha calls it "suffocation" and "the false peace" of the privileged. One seldom sees those kinds of words in the newspapers, as one seldom sees a word such as "injustice" or "oppression" or, as Mother Martha notes, "an unambiguous, plain-spoken word like 'segregation'"—not, at least, in reference to New York—unless these words are placed within quotation marks in order to suggest that language of this sort is unacceptable.

"Rome's peace is not God's peace," as she stated it one Sunday morning—bravely, I believe, because her reference was to institutions of the press that many people with so little power might not wish to challenge so directly. "False prophets cry 'peace, peace' where there is no peace," she continued, or where "there's a false peace" that has been established as "a cover-up for the intimidation of the poor." Jesus, she said, came to earth "in order to disturb the false peace of the Romans and to free God's people once and evermore."

I asked her once why she said "evermore," because the "false peace" she had spoken of seems constantly—indeed, hypnotically—to be restored. "The struggle goes on," she said, sounding more like a Black Panther, or one of the radical Young Lords for whom she used to do pro bono work, than like the woman she once was who rode her bike through Harvard Square en route to class among her fellow-students at the university, where legacies of opportunity are handed down routinely from one generation to the next.

How are the social loyalties of someone who was treated well by our society when she was young so radically transformed? The Brazilian educator Paulo Freire, whom I came to know in 1969 when he was living temporarily in Cambridge and I used to bring some of my students to his home on Sunday afternoons, would sometimes speak of people "dying from their class" to be reborn with a new loyalty to other social classes that they may have scorned, ignored, or even viewed as humanly dismissable before. "To break the ties, to step away from all the benefits our birth afforded us, to see the world in a new way and take our vision not from books *about* the poor but from the poor themselves," he told me once with a great smile in his eyes, old socialist and Christian and sweet person that he was, "*this* is their Easter!"

I don't know what prompts a woman born to privilege and polished to sophistication in the finest schools and given rapid access to considerable opportunities for wealth and status by her competence in law, to give it up, already in the middle of her life, and choose instead to be ordained a priest and then accept a vicarage at an impoverished church. I do know there's no maudlin piety or philanthropic sacramentalism in her style. The pastor is, thank

God, more fun to be with, and more humanly transparent, and a great deal more defiant of established power, than a number of the philanthropic ones who end up in church windows.

Above all, she does not pretend to be what she is not. An educated woman in a neighborhood where education levels are extremely low, she never pretends *not* to possess the tactical and verbal and forensic competence she really has. Ever since the 1960s, I have known white people who were so determined to conceal their educational attainments in the presence of a poor community of color that they'd even undermine their syntax and adopt street phrases, or would shade their phrasings with Latino accents, in an effort to defend themselves against those ever-present local demagogues who might attack them otherwise for their skin color or their education.

I am very much aware, uncomfortably so, that I fell into this peculiar habit too, because good friends in Roxbury at last gave me a talking-to. "We don't *want* you with arms tied behind your back," a very kind and candid local leader named Paul Parks told me one day when we were coming from a meeting. "That doesn't equalize the game. We know your education. *Use* it for our children!"

Perhaps, like other young white activists, I had the strange idea that I could circumvent racism if I hid or manacled my actual effectiveness in areas in which I did have skills, because I felt I had attained them in an unjust social order. To leaders in the black community, however, this was, in itself, a racist exercise — and an unhealthy one.

Mother Martha doesn't waste her time with rituals like these. Her sermons, as I've said, do often leave a pause of hesitation, and they're usually understated, and they're worded plainly (half the congregation on most Sundays are young children, so plain language is good pedagogy too); but in the actions that she takes, and in the confrontations she does not avoid, she draws on every bit of knowledge that she has, including what she knows about the ways in which a meritocracy of money can perpetuate itself.

Eleanor had some knowledge of these things from secondhand familiarity. The pastor knows about these things—the "test preps," the small classes around maple tables, and the playing fields, and the expensive science labs, and the exquisite elm trees at the private prep schools—from her own experience and that of her brother and her father; and she compares this constantly, sometimes explosively, with what is given to the children of Mott Haven.

This "dual vision," as I would describe it, adds a layer of political and moral texture to the way she analyzes certain of the challenges faced by the children of St. Ann's; but it also adds a constant sense of tension between struggling for piecemeal victories on one hand and envisioning a larger and more sweeping challenge to the structures of injustice on the other.

As unprotected as she seems when she speaks from her heart about these issues of class privilege, the pastor is not frail. "Mother Martha," says the poet and historian Juan Castro, who lives very near the church, on St. Ann's Avenue, and knows the pastor well, "is tougher than any six men that I know," a statement that I know he means admiringly, although a hint of chauvinism in his choice of words has now and then led to a verbal fray between the two of them. Others, including powerful black leaders like the Reverend Jesse Jackson, who has visited St. Ann's and knows the priest, have voiced a similar reaction.

Religious activists from other cities who have met the priest have made allusions to Dorothy Day when speaking of her fearlessness and willingness to take the blows and not do too much dodging and evading. She pays a price for this, however. Some years ago she did some legal

research and discovered that the CEO of one of the prestigious TV networks was a partner and investor in the company that owned the shamefully neglected buildings in
which dozens of the St. Ann's children were residing. "I
want you to come to the neighborhood and see the way
your tenants live," she said when she was able to get
through to him. He indicated that he'd like to come someday but could not do it then because, he said, "My chauf-
feur's on vacation." Clearly, you do not endear yourself
to someone with enormous wealth and, in this instance,
with the power of retaliation when you try to make him
see some of the suffering from which he's managed to
obtain a valuable tax-shelter.

Some ministers are forced by indigence to be accomplished courtiers. They learn to navigate between two
worlds, excoriating money-changers in their sermons Sunday morning and then having lunch with them perhaps on
Tuesday to obtain a badly needed contribution. Some
establish what are known as "partnerships" with business
leaders or with business corporations and essentially go
into business with them as developers of real estate or in
related local projects of this sort. Pastors of the poor are
frequently accorded more esteem by the newspapers for
commercial victories than for the work of justice or the
mystery of faith. The Church Entrepreneurial gets more
attention often than the church as *church* — the "little
church," the *ti-église,* as it is said in Haiti — where a man
like Lazarus and one like Francis might have prayed
together.

Pastors drawn into the world of commerce often bring
real benefits to their communities, but pay a price for these
entanglements that others do not see. Still, it's hard to
know if any person in religious life who's not a contemplative can accomplish anything of value that does not
involve some contradictions, especially in searching for

financial help; and even contemplatives and the abbots of the monasteries, as we know from Merton's journals, have been caught up in these contradictions also.

I think the presence of so many children at St. Ann's, so many daily crises, and the whole rich stew of life, emergency, activity, and hecticness compel the priest to improvise in ways that lend an almost comic pragmatism to her intermittent efforts to solicit charitable help. She doesn't have much chance to go downtown for personal solicitations; she writes some letters but they often sound as if they were done quickly, which I'm sure they generally were. The few requests for charitable grants she's let me see were rather brisk, and even somewhat amateurish, and did not have any of the customary breakdowns (like "objectives" and "evaluations") and those never-quite-convincing mathematical projections that are part of many grant proposals.

"I didn't have time for that," she told me last year in September when she had to race down to Manhattan late one night to get a letter stamped and canceled just in time to meet the deadline on an application. Her teenage secretary had just left (she was about to have her baby) and there were a number of emergencies that week. The time that might have gone into the writing of a detailed application got consumed by ordinary things like helping children with their homework, finding somebody to take her secretary's place, visiting a child's mother in the hospital, and going with Katrice to Western Beef, a local grocery, to buy necessities for the soup kitchen as the growing lines of hungry people at the church outran the limited supplies of food that came from charity.

The church gets by. Some unrepentant liberals and others acting on religious principle make generous donations to the children's programs and do not expect her to waste time with the formalities. Some of them know the kids and know the nature of her life and think her time is better spent in doing more important things, like helping Elio with his arithmetic.

What is it like, in human terms, to be the one on whom so many other people in a neighborhood rely at times of fear and darkness in their lives?

Visitors arriving at St. Ann's for the first time are generally stirred by the emotional aesthetic of the atmosphere and often comment also on the nerve with which the pastor faces down the children's adversaries. They do not always see, as I did not see at the start—because I was perhaps afraid to see—the weariness and loneliness and times of deep anxiety, which even pastors who seem poised and decorous in their ecclesiastical accoutrements when standing there before the cross to celebrate the mass inevitably undergo at times when they feel overburdened and unequal to the obligations they must bear.

We know that people in despair cry to the priest. To whom does the priest cry? I suppose the proper answer ought to be "to God." But priests and ministers need human shoulders too. The pastor spends a lot of time with children in the garden to dispel their worries and her own, and also, as I often feel, because a sense of understandable enchantment with the personalities of children is an elemental part of her own personality. "Those kids will *look* for her!" Katrice said once when we were watching Mother Martha on the sidewalk with a bunch of children who were tugging at her clothes to capture her attention. "If she's not here, they'll keep on coming back all day and asking me, 'Katrice? Did you see Mother Martha?'"

Still, the priest cannot permit the little ones to know her deepest fears. She has a son, a teenage boy whom she took in when he was twelve in answer to his mother's final prayer before she died of cancer. His father is an alcoholic. His brother and sister have been intermittently in various drug programs and in prison for the past ten years. The pastor often finds his brother lying on the sidewalk near Alí's when she goes there to get a cup of coffee in the afternoon. She waits until an ambulance arrives to take him to the hospital, where he remains only a day or two before he wanders off into whatever places offer him the medication of despair—cocaine or heroin or alcohol—and ultimately reappears outside Alí's.

A store not far from where he frequently collapses is believed to be a front for sale of drugs. Across the street, but farther up the block, there is another store in which Katrice suspects that drugs are sold as well. I've been in that store a few times with Isaiah. There's little for sale, and there are never many customers during the day; so it seems probable Katrice is right. The priest knows all of this but cannot fight on six or seven fronts at once. She has to make the surgical decision to address one crisis now, the other one tomorrow. By tomorrow, there are always several more.

One day when she and I were walking with Katrice on St. Ann's Avenue to buy some minor items needed at the church, a woman who was standing not quite on the street and not quite on the curb, but poised in what appeared to be a temporary indecision or confusion in between, gestured to the priest as we drew near. There was a child with her, maybe eight or nine years old. The woman and the pastor hugged each other and the woman kissed the priest, but looked disturbed, as if she'd just received upsetting news, so Mother Martha asked her whether there was something wrong. The woman lifted one hand in the air in front of her and held it level with the street and tilted it just slightly up and down.

"Not so good now, Mother," she said in a worried voice.

The priest looked at Katrice. Her quick reaction was to take my arm and nudge me off in the direction we were heading so that Mother Martha and the woman and her son could be alone to talk. Something of that nature happens almost every time we go out for a walk.

What does she say—what counsel is she giving, if that's even the right word—when troubled-looking people stop her in the street, then show up later for a conversation with her at the church?

"She never gives me bullshit answers, 'priestly' answers," says one of the toughest guys I know in the South Bronx, who's had a lot of problems in the courts and has been in and out of jail. He talks to her, he says, "exactly the same way I'd talk to any man. No difference. No sweet 'nicey' stuff about atonement and forgiveness. I go to see her when my ass is scared. She's tough with me. She can be very hard. I don't mind toughness. When I need her, when I'm in real trouble, I know one thing: She'll be there."

I happened to run into him one night when six or seven officers had slammed him up against the wall. When I asked him what was wrong, one of the officers slammed me against the wall as well and told me to move on. "Call Mother Martha! Please!" he yelled as he was being shoved into the back of one of the patrol cars at the curb. Did she get him out? I never learned. By the next day there were new emergencies she had to deal with. So I never even had a chance to ask.

I have the impression that most priests and ministers in neighborhoods like this one spend a large part of their lives engaged in doing things for which they couldn't possibly have been prepared by any part of their religious education. (Do seminaries teach a pastor what she'll need to know to start a literacy class or choose computer software for a mathematics class, or how to get a judge to put a child's parent into a drug-treatment program rather than in prison?) I also know that many pastors have to make a lot of difficult decisions that will change the lives of other people without ever having time to contemplate a wide array of options. Deferred decision-making is the privilege of those who look at social struggle with a relative degree of distance. At places like St. Ann's, there is no distance. Everything is present. Almost everything is urgent. The risks of making wrong decisions are one burden that the priest must constantly incur; but the luxury of making no decision, or deferring a decision, is not often hers.

There are all kinds of heroines and heroes in the ordinary world. The ones I like to spend my time with are the preachers and the teachers who take on the hardest, messiest, and most exhausting work and still come out of it somehow with souls intact and particles of merriment still percolating in their personalities. I don't know how they do it. I don't have an idea in the world of where they find the sources of their energy and joy. I used to ask the pastor questions like this; I don't ask these questions anymore. I stand there in the church on certain days and watch her at her work and simply feel a sense of awe and admiration that she ever dared to take a job like this, and doesn't plan to give it up, but muddles through the worst of times, and keeps right on.

"The people I love the best," writes poet and longtime activist Marge Piercy, "jump into work head first." Instead of "dallying in the shallows," they "swim off with sure strokes almost out of sight." When it's time to plow, they "harness themselves" and "strain in the mud and muck to move things forward" and to "do what has to be done, again and again." When emergencies come, they "work in a row and pass the bags along." They "stand in the line and . . . haul in their places." They "are not parlor generals and field deserters." The work of the world, she says, "is common as mud." When it's botched, it "smears the hands" and "crumbles to dust." Beautiful vases, after centuries go by, are "put in museums," she writes, "but you know they were made to be used. . . .

> The pitcher cries for water to carry
> and a person for work that is real.

I've thought of that final line when I was with a teacher in one of those very poorly funded schools like Morris High that get the students other schools reject and have the worst statistics in the city, but the teacher still was standing there with a big stack of papers in her hand and a real rush of energy within her voice as she spurred on the kids to finish Act Three of Macbeth, or do their book report on Toni Morrison, and did it with the same enthusiasm she would feel if she were teaching far more skillful and responsive kids at Exeter.

I've thought of it also at St. Ann's on one of those heartbreaking days when several of the children or the older people had to deal with devastating news or make decisions in which either choice was going to be fraught with danger to themselves or someone else, and I could see the empathy and anguish—and the deep-down weariness as well—within the pastor's eyes, and had to wonder if I was about to see her cry.

I've seen the priest cry only twice at St. Ann's Church. Once was when a teenage boy who had been close to her for years said something cutting and sarcastic at a time of adolescent anguish, testing out his strength perhaps to see if he could injure somebody who loved him and discovering, to his regret, that he could do it with great ease.

The other time was when she came into the crowded afterschool one day holding a cup of hot tea she had brought back from Alí's. She'd buried a parishioner that morning and then had to go to the cathedral for some reason, and her face was flushed, because she had been working with a fever for the past three days. Her hands were shaking slightly as she tried to pull the plastic cover from the cup. Then the lid went flying and the cup turned upside down and spilled its scalding contents on her hand and arm.

Katrice ran to the kitchen to get ice to press against the skin. Some of the children were nearby. They stood and stared. Mother Martha bit her lip. Then she began to cry.

What I remember is the look within the children's eyes: immediate compassion, but also unspeakable alarm to see tears in the pastor's eyes.

"She's crying," said Briana.

"Mother Martha's crying," said one of the older girls.

I know it frightened them.

CHAPTER 20

A Turbulent Intelligence

"Elio went to see his father on the weekend," says Katrice on Tuesday afternoon. "I don't think they went by bus this time. I think they took the Metro North."

I never ask the children where their fathers are if they don't volunteer this on their own. Even when they do, I hesitate to ask exactly where it is or whether they go there to visit, or how frequently. But Katrice is close to Elio and he confides in her. She tells me only what she feels I ought to know, and nothing more. I asked her once if Elio's father was far from the city. She answered, simply, "Not as far now as before—maybe two hours on the train."

Her special feelings about Elio aren't easy to disguise, although I know she tries to be fair-minded with the children and not give unusual attention to one child at the cost of any other. "He has a sweet heart and a loving smile," she says as she watches him return a basketball to the toy closet near the kitchen. "Even when he's being bad I look at him and wonder, 'Who's to know? He might become a senator!'"

He doesn't look too senatorial right now. It's easier to see him as a snappy little shortstop on his favorite baseball team. He stands there looking at Katrice and me, guessing, I think, that he's the subject of our conversation. He has a look of mild puzzlement, as if he's briefly lost in pleasing contemplation. Then the mild moment ends. A group of kids are heading to the garden with the priest and Nancy to dig up some of the hardened ground beside the fence to start the planting of spring flowers. He's off and running, out the door and up the steps next to the afterschool, to catch up with the others.

Katrice takes off the apron that she wears while working in the kitchen and smoothes down her skirt. Briana comes out of the bathroom at the far end of the afterschool and whizzes past us on her way out to the garden too.

"My feet are giving me a problem," says Katrice. "Right one's very painful. Twice they gave me steroids at the hospital last week. . . ." She tilts a bit from foot to foot, testing how the right one feels as she comes down on it. When I ask her if the steroids helped, she says, "Not really. It's still swollen. Heel is painful if I come down hard. . . ."

Some of the girls who were upstairs with a new tutor come into the afterschool and ask Katrice where everybody went. "Up in back," she says, and makes a gesture towards the door. Pineapple waves as she goes by. She has a pair of snazzy-looking wrap-around sunglasses tilted up across her forehead like a movie star.

We follow the kids outside but not into the garden. Katrice expects the truck that brings the food from City Harvest, which was scheduled to arrive an hour and a half ago. "Late . . . ," she grumbles, leaning on the metal railing just beside the door.

Since welfare cutbacks went into effect here in New York, she says, the lines at the food pantry are much longer than before. "We used to throw away the rolls when they were stale. Now we don't. Even in the morning sometimes when a child ought to be at school, a little one comes in and asks if we have bread."

"Are these the little ones," I ask, "who wait for Mother Martha?"

"Some of them are," she says, "but some I've never seen before. Some are from the homeless shelters. Some are from Brook Avenue or Willis Avenue. Some come from further off. They say, 'My mother's sick and we don't have no food.'" A few of them, she says, she'll see here once and then they never come again. Others keep on coming back, "and then on Sunday morning they'll appear here with their mother." The ones she never sees again, she says, are always in her mind.

While we're standing here, a man she doesn't like comes past the church and says hello to her. She says, "Okay." After he's gone she says, "He has this way of talking I could never stand. He says 'Hi' but that 'Hi' has something in back of it. When I pass him in the street I say, 'Hello,' 'Good-bye,' and just keep headin' on my way. . . ."

It's glorious weather, cool and bright. Warmer weather is predicted for the week ahead. Katrice is wearing only a light sweater. Vigilance and hopefulness are intermingled in her conversation as we stand here in the walkway, looking out into the street. A few days earlier, she tells me, she was walking Mariposa home to her apartment, which is up the hill from here on Cypress Avenue. "Her mother's sick. I said I'd bring her home. We were right there"— pointing to the corner of St. Ann's — "and starting to go up the hill, when shooting started breaking out across the street from us."

No one was hurt, she says, but the explosion of gunfire terrified the child. Katrice pushed Mariposa down and covered her with her own body. "By the time the cops arrived," she says, "the ones that did the shooting ran into a building, so nobody was arrested."

She looks with irritation towards the street. The food is now more than two hours late. The truck has been delayed, as it turns out, because there was a party at the UN building. The driver had been waiting, she believes, to see what was left over. It's also possible that he was simply stuck in traffic, which gets bad in midtown at this hour.

Briana reappears, with Raven, on the top step of the stairs. Briana's holding up her jersey so her belly button is exposed. She looks down at her stomach, then looks up and smiles at Katrice; then the two first-graders come downstairs and go inside to wash their hands. One by one, the other children reappear. Katrice stands guard and watches from the bottom of the stairs in order to be sure that they don't skip some steps or slide down on the flat cement wall on the side. After the last child has come down the stairs, she goes inside to get their supper ready and to count out milk containers.

Sometimes on a tranquil afternoon when there are no emergencies and all the kids are relatively well-behaved, Katrice looks at a group of them at work or play and makes a comment that comes straight from her religious faith. "To me, those are the angels," she said once last fall when we were watching Raven and Briana sitting at a table in an animated conversation with a boy I didn't know in early evening after all the other children had gone home. But each and every boy and girl who comes here to the afterschool, as Nelly and her staff, I think, would willingly agree, is *not* a sheer delight to be with every single day.

There are always three or four, and sometimes more, whose insecurities spill over into momentary episodes of meanness. A few, while sensitive to other kids on other days, will now and then appropriate the verbal put-downs and the unkind uses of sarcasm they may learn from television shows. Some may hurt without intending to be hurtful; others do it with less innocence.

A couple of the children here who have been labeled "hyperactive" in their schools—a diagnosis that's been overused but now and then describes a child's restlessness as well as any other label—can be maddening in their behavior on some afternoons. Then, on another day, they might surprise you by their perfectly responsible demeanor.

Otto, for example, who is Elio's best friend, can drive the grown-ups here into a state of frenzy. I wish I could exclude myself from this, but can't, because he sometimes drives me crazy too. He wanders around the afterschool observing what the other kids are doing and providing running commentaries on the errors that they're making in their math or writing lessons but is seldom willing to sit still for long enough to finish his own lessons. He routinely pesters me to help him with his math. As soon as we sit down, however, he removes some object like a metal padlock from his pocket and keeps opening and closing it and clanking it against the table top. At last I reach out for his hand and press it to the table.

"Do you know it's irritating when you do that?"

"Yep," he says.

"Why do you do it, then?"

"My teacher asks me that."

"That isn't a good answer."

"I know," he says.

"Would you put it away for now?"

"Okay."

He puts it back in his pocket; but, when I am forced to interrupt things briefly to reply to something Nelly asks, the padlock reappears. He keeps on clamping and unclamping it until he sees me looking at his hands again.

"Do me a favor, Otto? Please?"

Even then, he takes his time before he puts the thing away.

On other afternoons he asks if he can use one of my pens. When I give him one, he takes the cap off, tests it once to check the color of the ink, puts the cap back on, and then removes it, and then puts it on again, but never does make use of it to do his work.

He's a deeply inquisitive boy who seems to get a grasp on new ideas and concepts right away and then grows bored and makes it hard for other children to get to the point of understanding that he's reached so easily. He also has the tendency to leave his sentences unfinished. It seems to give him power when he does this since it forces other children into asking him to finish uncompleted thoughts that he leaves floating in the air. It feels at times as if he's purposely preparing traps with these unfinished statements. He'll begin to say something to Elio, then let his words trail off just as he's started to ensnare his friend's attention.

"Then what happened?" Elio might ask.

"I could tell you sometime . . . ," Otto might reply, but then he wanders off across the room while Elio remains behind and slowly recognizes he's been tricked but doesn't know exactly how this was accomplished.

I think the children understand that Otto's diffidence is not entirely innocent. There are these suspended moments when it seems he wins his victories by governing the silence he creates by calculated use of uncompletedness. Elio looks befuddled when this happens. He looks at Otto and can't seem to figure out why anyone would want to do this but perceives that it's intended to upset him.

As I've noted, Elio is not particularly skilled at using words to strike back at a child who gets on his nerves or teases him. The only big-time insult I have heard him throw at Otto when he was annoyed with him was "Dumbo," which was based upon a general impression among children here that Otto's ears are somewhat over-sized, although in fact they're absolutely normal. Elio's insults, frankly, are not terribly injurious. Still, I know it bothers Otto when the children call him "Dumbo," because he has told me that it does.

I once asked Otto's mother if there were some things I didn't know about his situation or the background of his family or his life at home that might explain his puzzling behavior. She stunned me then by telling me that Otto's older brother had been killed some years before while rid-ing on the outside of a subway train. He did it on a dare, she said, during a time when riding on the tops of trains, which was called "surfing" by teenagers, had become one of those crazy rages that are taken up by reckless kids in different cities simultaneously. "He lowered his head be-neath a bridge," she said, "but didn't see the next one, which was lower." The boy died instantly upon the impact of his skull against an overhanging piece of steel. He was only fourteen at the time, his mother said.

Otto has another brother, she has told me, who is now on Rikers Island in pretrial on a drug-related charge. On her living room door she keeps a schedule of the hours and days when she and Otto are allowed to visit him.

The eight-year-old takes Ritalin to govern his mercur-ial behavior. Perhaps this is one reason for his intermittent vagueness and perplexing diffidence, although I'm sure there could be countless other reasons for the way he seems to cultivate evasiveness and unaccomplished word-ing. I sometimes wonder if he thinks of facts as "enemies" that can be handled best by indirection; but, as I've said, it's also obvious that he gets bored more quickly with a new idea than other children do and moves beyond his own first thoughts before he has a chance to finish them.

"He gives his mother a *hard* time to go!" Katrice ob-serves. His teacher tells me he's a lot to handle in the class-room too. The medicine he takes may make it easier for him to concentrate. His mother worries, though, because she fears that it may dull his curiosity and possibly sup-press some of his intellectual intensity.

Large amounts of psychotropic medicine are given to young children in the public schools of New York City, as in public schools all over the United States; and, in some cases, medical professionals have little supervision over how these medications are dispensed. At P.S. 30, thank-fully, where every form of medication is dispensed to chil-dren by a nurse, and only in her office, children who take Ritalin and other drugs are closely supervised and also have the benefit of privacy, so other children will not stig-matize them. But there are inner-city schools where secre-taries simply walk from room to room with trays of pills and pass them out to children listed on a dosage schedule they've been handed by somebody else.

Katrice tells me that several children she and I both know are now dependent upon drugs like Ritalin. In many instances, it's difficult to know what else is to be done. If I were a teacher here and had a class of thirty children and if three or four of them were constantly in motion and dis-turbing other kids, as Otto does, I suppose I mightn't raise objections to these drugs. It does seem at times, however, that these drugs are being used in overcrowded urban schools to cope with situations that might not be so disrup-tive in a class of eighteen students where the teacher has more time to listen to the sometimes turbulent intelligence of children. That part of the pattern does seem troubling.

Otto's mother tries to stimulate, and satisfy, his curiosity by taking him to bookstores and by purchasing The New York Times at 86th Street in Manhattan, parts of which she says she reads to him at home. Sometimes on the weekend she and Otto get dressed up and go to Bloomingdale's, where brunch is served on Saturdays and Sundays. "He orders interesting dishes — like eggs Benedict!" she says. She works full-time for $16,000 yearly, which, she tells me, "makes me almost middle class in this community." She goes without food until evening on the weekdays so she can afford to cook good meals at night for Otto and can pay for all the extra things that he enjoys, like special trips into Manhattan. She also fills their home with educational materials and learning games to keep him occupied with something other than TV.

An attractive and sophisticated woman who grew up here in Mott Haven, she has had a huge amount of bad luck in her life. Homeless for a time during the 1980s, she was forced to bring her children to a dismal shelter that I used to visit in Manhattan, an atrocious place run by a man who wore a pistol on his ankle and was working for South African investors. Her older boys may have been damaged in that period of time, as were too many kids I knew. Several boys I met during those years who lived in midtown shelters were exposed to drugs and prostitution in those buildings and have since grown up into a life of crime. One of them writes to me from prison in upstate New York. I knew that boy when he was eight years old and used to spend his nights in Herald Square panhandling at traffic lights to get the money to buy food. He's spent the past six years in Comstock, at a prison called Great Meadows, one of New York's 73 state prisons.

Otto's mother hopes his older brother will be spared a lengthy sentence. She's hoping he'll be sentenced to a short-term period in bootcamp so that he will not be spending his entire youth in prison; but she says the likelihood is that he'll get at least three years. She blames herself for some of the calamities that overtook her children. It's so commonly assumed that women in her situation are to blame for their own disappointments that a mother who works hard, as she does, and who sacrifices greatly to provide well for her child, can be easily conditioned nonetheless to castigate herself when things go wrong. For some of the troubles that befell her sons, she may be right to feel she's partially to blame. For many, she is not.

Katrice is fond of Otto and she's close to Otto's mother, who is one of the most loyal members of the vestry of St. Ann's and finds the time, despite her job, to volunteer and help with programs for the children here. She hadn't been a member of St. Ann's when Otto started coming to the afterschool. As in many cases in the neighborhood, the child was the only link at first between the parent and the church.

"When I used to go to pick him up," she tells me, "I'd be feeling very 'down' some days. I get 'down' like that some afternoons and find it hard to walk into a crowded room. Mother Martha asked me once, 'Are you okay?' I was feeling terrible that day. I told her, 'No. Right now I'm not.' She just reached out for me. I realized that I had too much inside of me to carry all this on my own. I *needed* that, you know. . . ."

Otto takes an asthma pump to school. He also has a unit in his bedroom that supplies a substance known as epinephrine, which can open up his bronchioles in an emergency. She wishes she could use her Section Eight certificate — a federal housing subsidy — to move to Scarsdale or White Plains; but this is not allowed. If she ever could afford to move, she says she'd miss St. Ann's, but she believes that Otto's asthma would be better in a neighborhood with cleaner air. He might experience less tension in the suburbs too, she feels; but many of his problems, as she knows, would not evaporate so easily. Memories of certain things, she says, don't simply disappear; and Otto has a good deal to remember.

There's a funny pose he frequently assumes. He shoves his hands way down into his pockets, jingles coins or other objects, sticks his stomach out, and hums a little as he looks around the room. It makes him look like a small businessman who's just pulled off an advantageous deal but wants the world to think it's bigger than it is. There's something likable and droll about him when he does this.

On days when he's relaxed and happy he can be a lot of fun to be with. There are also days when he gives up his posturings and seems intensely serious and, suddenly, quite vulnerable.

One day when he and I and Elio were looking at the stained-glass windows in the sanctuary, Otto pointed to the image of an angel. "I know someone up there," he said in a voice almost inaudible.

"Who?" said Elio.

"My brother," Otto said.

It's the only time I can recall when he did not force Elio to ask a second question. He simply gave that two-word answer and then swallowed and looked down, because his eyes were filling up with tears. Elio knew, of course, about his brother. Without a hesitation in the world he reached his hand across the space between them.

Otto wept. Softly, Elio dispensed his standard medication. Three pats on the hand in ordinary situations. Four perhaps for truly deep unhappiness. Five or six for the unbearable. "If you stay here long enough you'll see a lot of miracles," Katrice had told me once during the first year that I visited St. Ann's.

Otto had tormented Elio so many times! Once Elio had been so mad at Otto's verbal sparring with him that he reached his fist right back over his head and punched him in the nose. He got punished for that too, so he had two good reasons to be angry with his sometimes supercilious friend. But here was Otto losing all the armor of his cleverness, exposed for once without his stratagems, and here was Elio unable to look on at someone else's sorrow without wanting to appease it.

The two boys stood together there another moment under the didactic-looking angel. I didn't say a word. Neither did they. Their two hands, clenched together tight, said everything.

CHAPTER 21

Imaginary Music

W arm weather. It's not yet the end of May, but it's been warm like this for several days. A dozen of the younger children in the garden of St. Ann's are running back and forth under the sprinkler.

Some of them are getting soaked. Others just cool off and come back to the church with water in their hair and on their shirts. The quickness and the slightness of it all may be a part of what makes it enjoyable. It seems they get almost more fun from this than from more organized exertions that take place at public pools where chlorine and perhaps a hint of adolescent danger fill the air. When they're older, some will be attracted to those public places. For now, they seem content to play under the sprinkler.

There are squirrels on the lawn, and many chirping birds. A mother stands nearby in very casual supervision, chatting meanwhile with the pastor and Katrice. Homeless people drift into the garden from the street and sit there at the bottom of the stairs and watch the children at their play.

It smells good in the garden at this hour in late afternoon. The children run and shout and cry each other's names. Otto is in a boisterous mood. He puts his hand over the nozzle of the sprinkler and directs the spray right into his own face. Elio's pants are nearly falling off. Pineapple points at Elio's rear end and tells him to pull up his pants. Otto turns the spray in her direction. She gets soaked. So does the priest. Pineapple gets up and jumps into the shallow pool made by the spray and screams at Otto. Several of the littlest ones are dancing in the water. They remind me of intoxicated elves.

Children do things like this all over the country on hot afternoons in spring and summer. They shout and play. They do not know the satisfaction that we take in watching them. Their only work right now is play. Our only work is taking pleasure at the sight of them.

Grown-ups sometimes find the children's playfulness contagious. Suddenly a grown-up woman supervising children on the swings will sit down on a swing herself and let the children push her high into the air. A group of girls swinging a rope for double Dutch might ask her if she still knows how to do it too. "Why not?" she says. The children speed the rope to double-time to see how fast the grown-up moves her feet.

Teachers who permit themselves these normal self-indulgences too often can run into problems when it's time to ask the kids to do something that *isn't* fun. If they cross the line repeatedly between the adult world and child world, the children start to think that they can cross it too and won't obey the teacher when she says it's time to put away the jumprope and go back to class to do the spelling lesson that she's written on the board. But the susceptibility

of grown-ups to the jubilant infectiousness of play in situations where it's natural can bring a pleasant chemistry into
the routine occupations of the day—and, now and then, an
interesting role reversal too.

One day that year I visited a talented young teacher
with a name that seemed ideally suited to a teacher starting
out on her career: April Gamble. Her third-grade class at
P.S. 28 in the South Bronx, not far from the Grand Con-
course and East Tremont Avenue, had sent me a big enve-
lope of letters asking if I'd visit them someday when I was
in their neighborhood. They were some of the most lively
and inviting letters anyone has ever sent me. "Dear Jonathan," a letter from one boy began. "My name is Pedro.
I am 7 years old. . . . Would you come and visit us for
6 hours so we could tell you about our life?" He signed
his letter, "From my heart to my eyes, Pedro." If I would
agree to come, another child promised, we could talk
about all the problems in "the whole why world." I waited
a few weeks until I saw a day when I would be nearby.
Then I called the principal and went to meet the children.

The teacher had 31 students and the classroom wasn't
large and the entire school was badly overcrowded and in
shameful disrepair; but Mrs. Gamble didn't seem to let this
get her down. Young as she was, she had a beautiful com-
mand of classroom practices, some of which she'd learned
from older teachers at the school and some of which she
said she learned at Bank Street, which is one of New York's
most respected schools of education. She also had her own
intriguing innovations.

At one point in my visit, the discussion I was having
with the class got out of hand. I can't remember what I
asked to set this off, but for a moment all the children
seemed to speak to me at once and many little hands and
bodies seemed to be in motion. I felt as if I'd stirred some
chemicals and inadvertently set off a small explosion.

Mrs. Gamble must have realized that I wasn't sure how I should handle things. She seemed to know exactly what to do. She rose to her feet and put one hand, with fingers curled up slightly, just beneath her mouth, and curled her other hand in the same way but held it out about twelve inches, maybe eighteen inches, to the right. I watched with fascination as the class subsided from the chaos I'd created and the children stood and did the same thing Mrs. Gamble did: all these children with one hand before their mouth, one to the side, and with their eyes directed to the teacher. What was this about?

Then the teacher started humming softly—then she briefly trilled a melody in her soprano voice—and some of the children started trilling their own voices too, and suddenly I understood: It was an orchestra, and they were the flute section! In their hands were the imaginary flutes. Their little fingers played the notes and when the teacher bent her head as if she were so deeply stirred by the enchanted music she was hearing that she had to tilt her body in response, the children bent their bodies too.

The principal, who was standing in the doorway, seemed to be as fascinated by this as the children were. You could see that she admired Mrs. Gamble as a teacher but was obviously taken also by the sweetness of her manner—the precision of her fingers on the keys! And then the teacher danced a bit from foot to foot before the children and I thought of Papageno; and the children danced from foot to foot as well. And then the music ended and the teacher put away her flute with an efficient and conclusive motion of her hands and all the children did the same and we began our class discussion once again.

What I remembered later wasn't only an effective trick for bringing third-grade children who had grown a trifle wild back into a calm and quiet state of mind. It was also the impromptu dance the teacher did, only a step or two, but just enough to spice the moment with gratuitous amusement so that, even in regaining grown-up governance over those joyful little protons and electrons that I'd inadvertently set into motion, she also showed herself to be a woman who was not too overly "mature," or too "professional," to show the happiness she felt at making magic music for the children with a magic, and imaginary, flute.

Wonderful teachers, and especially the teachers of young children, have much more, I think, than what technicians might refer to as "proficiency." Their calling, when it's filled with merriment and beauty, makes me think of joyful priests in Sunday robes when they prepare to give communion. Their gestures — even mundane classroom operations like the passing out of textbooks or the rapid, energetic "tap-tap" of the chalk against the board — become infused with mystery, authority, and elegance, like secular epiphanies. Teaching children of this age, when it's done right, is more than craft; it's also partly ministry and partly poetry.

When Mrs. Gamble trilled her voice and ran her fingers through the air, she didn't simply "play the flute." She also played the playfulness within herself and seemed to play the spirits of the children too. She later told me that one third of all the children in her class, and in the school, suffered from asthma. You wouldn't have guessed it on that morning. For a minute there, we might have been a thousand miles from the city in a magic forest where the evening air smells fresh and green and not one of the spirits of the woods has any trouble breathing.

Back at P.S. 30, a retired music teacher, Clifford Hudson, who once ran the music program in an affluent Long

Island suburb and now teaches choral music in Mott Haven twice a week, is taking a break between rehearsals for a concert that is scheduled to take place here a week later. Sitting on the edge of the stage, a black man of about my age, he says he also teaches part-time at a college that enrolls large numbers of black and Hispanic men and women from the inner city and that he encourages the college students in his class to work as volunteers with younger children.

"I refuse to let them talk in 'street talk,' 'jive,' or 'dialect,'" he says, "in working with these children"—which, he notes, some volunteers are prone to do "in order to 'communicate' with urban children"—"because these children do know mainstream English and they don't regard it simply as 'white people's language.' It's the normal way of speech for many. When they speak in street talk it's a choice they're making and I happen not to think that it's a *good* choice, and I don't permit it."

An organist and pianist and composer steeped in classical traditions, he tells me that his mother graduated from a normal school, had studied "Latin and calculus," and "had a set of Harvard Classics in the bookcase in our living room." He says she couldn't gain employment as a teacher in that era and was forced to earn a living as a household maid. At night, she read him poetry and played him operatic music on the phonograph. "She kept an upright piano in our house and gave me piano lessons—made me practice every day. . . ."

He talks to children about social ethics and politeness—"What counts most," he tells the kids, "is how you treat a lady, how you treat the sick and elderly"—and, if a child misbehaves or calls another member of the class out of her name, his voice becomes the slightest bit severe. Unlike a few exceedingly severe black educators that I've visited in public schools, however, some of whom don't ever seem relaxed and seldom smile when they're with their students, Mr. Hudson has a warm, informal style and he seems to revel in the time he spends with children here. "This is nourishment for me. I'm 62 years old, but I'm still able to be young. . . ."

He reaches out for one of the fourth-graders who's been lying on her stomach looking at her spelling book during the break between rehearsals and just barely grazes her barrettes, then looks down at his hand. The smile in his eyes somehow conveys nostalgia.

The other children come back from their break and the rehearsal starts again. There's a piano below the stage, an upright, like the one he says his mother had when he was a young boy; and while the children line up on the stage, he starts to play a quiet piece that might be Mendelssohn or Brahms, until the children seem composed.

"This is a love song that I wrote," he says in introducing the first number. While he nods his head above the piano keys, the 25 or 30 third- and fourth- and fifth-grade children start to sing. Next they do a lively finger-snapping song, called "Old Man Tucker," that I've never heard before, then a show tune called "High Hopes," and then an old Al Jolson song "Hello My Baby," and then "Summertime," in which the children smile at each other when they sing "your Mama's good-lookin'." He gets up from the piano then and leads them in a song I used to sing on picket lines with children and their parents in the 1960s when I was a teacher, "This Little Light of Mine." Standing just beneath the stage, he swings his arms like Seiji Ozawa swinging his baton before the orchestra at Tanglewood. The children lift their voices high and sing the final song, which Mr. Hudson says they plan to sing for fifth-grade graduation.

This song I sing
The world didn't give it to me
And the world can't take it away.

"Yes, that's good—that's right," says Mr. Hudson in approval as they sing. The principal, Miss Rosa, who has come down to the front part of the auditorium in time to hear the final song, joins the children in the final verse and then claps loudly.

New York City once had comprehensive art and music programs for the children in the elementary schools. Most of this was terminated years ago as a cost-saving measure at a time of what was called "the fiscal crisis" in New York, around the same time that the city also took school doctors from the elementary schools and more or less dismantled what had once been very good school libraries in order to save money on librarians and books. Since that time there have been several long-extended periods of great prosperity in New York City, and the city's revenues, of course, have soared in recent years during the escalations of stock values, which have brought unprecedented profits to the banking and investment principalities of Wall Street; but the savage cutbacks in the personnel and services available to children in the city's public schools, who now are overwhelmingly black and Hispanic, have not been restored.

So third-grade kids at P.S. 28 learn to make do, and make music, with imaginary flutes; and the children here at P.S. 30 get a couple of hours of good choral practice once or twice a week with a retired black instructor who received his love of music from a mother born to segregation in the South and does his best to pass these treasures on to children born into another kind of segregation, nearly as absolute but possibly a good deal less genteel and less protective than the somewhat milder kind of rural isolation that his mother knew some sixty years before.

The detail that stuck with me was the way he reached his hand out to the child who was lying on her stomach next to him and lightly touched her on her hair. I've seen Mr. Bedrock do exactly the same thing: reaching out one of his hands to graze one of the children on the shoulder, or an elbow, or her hair, not even looking up but knowing somehow that the child's there. The children in his class like to pretend that they're eavesdropping on his conversations, peering up at him obliquely like small espionage agents, with stage smiles. He'll just reach out while he and I are talking and locate the child's hand or arm and maybe draw the child in to him and hold her head beneath his arm like a good-natured soccer ball, and then look down and act surprised, as if to say, "What have we here?"

Mr. Bedrock used to teach at Temple University. He was a war resister in the 1960s and served time in prison. He's a deeply serious man, and he's politically tough-minded. His observations about life among the children, his belief in their intelligence and moral goodness, and his recognition of the obstacles that many face, as well as his intense, unsparing condemnation of New York for its apparently eternal acquiescence in the racial isolation of these children, had a powerful effect in focusing my own perceptions of the neighborhood and reinforcing my beliefs about the structural inequities that narrowed opportunity for many of these girls and boys.

Political loyalties, however, as some of us learn belatedly, do not automatically equate to qualities that make a teacher likable, exciting, or successful in the classroom. I think that Mr. Bedrock's pedagogic victories have less to do with his political beliefs than with his willingness to let the children know him as the somewhat undefended, open-hearted, earnestly affectionate good person that he really is.

"She misbehaves," he told me once about a child who was making faces at him while we spoke, "because she knows I love her."

Sometimes his students do get out of hand. When they do, he seems to know the way to get them back under control. Mrs. Gamble has imaginary music for this purpose. Mr. Bedrock has his own approaches, which do not exclude raising his voice from time to time, although his far more usual approach to moments of disorder is to show a truly pained expression on his face and to convey his disappointment in a voice of mournful sorrow. "I don't understand why there is *any* need for table six to talk about the definition of a simile," he said one day this fall when I was in his class. "I admit it isn't a terrific lesson but you're *not* making things easier by talking." When the children saw him smiling after those distressing words, they looked relieved and actually did quiet down to keep their teacher happy.

Both Mr. Bedrock and Mrs. Gamble are politically sophisticated people. Yet both respect, and keep alive, another part of the imagination that does not belong especially to politics or even, really, intellection; they both retain their playfulness and, even more than that, they *learn* some of that playfulness from being in the company of children.

I was with Mr. Bedrock once in April when he took a group of older boys for mathematics. The subject of the lesson was "improper fractions." Isaiah was in the class that day and the idea of "proper" or "improper" fractions struck him as amusing. Mr. Bedrock asked him what he found so funny and Isaiah simply said the words with an exaggerated English accent, in the phrasing you might hear in films about the British upper class. Mr. Bedrock picked up on Isaiah's humor and continued with the lesson on improper fractions in a very funny, very "proper-sounding" imitation of an English gentleman. It was only a brief moment in a long day of instruction, but it helped to lighten up the lesson and perhaps to animate a subject that the students here apparently had had a hard time learning.

In the cafeteria one day, a child in his fourth-grade class came up to him with several very tiny cakes with decorations in the frosting, which she'd brought from home. She held them on her hand and told him, "Look!" and asked him if he wanted one for his dessert. They were the size of postage stamps. There was something so mysterious about the way she seemed to speculate upon those little cakes!

"I don't know . . . ," he said. "They look too good to eat."

He peered into the child's hand as if the cakes were tiny works of medieval sculpture. "Did your mother make them?"

"No," the child said, "they're from the store."

"I don't know . . . ," he said again, making it seem a difficult decision. Then he chose one of the cakes and popped it in his mouth and ate it in one swallow.

"Is it good?"

"I'm full!" he said.

The child laughed and went back to her table.

Why does this remind me of the moment in the garden of the church when Mother Martha and Katrice were watching Otto and the other children playing in the sprinkler? It is, perhaps, only the pleasing insignificance of a spontaneous connection between adult sensibilities and juvenile amusement. Elio's pants are falling off. The priest, who went to court this afternoon to get a teenage boy released from the Manhattan lockup called "The Tombs" and who returned with the frustration that she almost always feels when coping with the overloaded courts, is suddenly relaxed and carefree, and gets soaked!

Grown-ups need these moments just as much as children do. The water refreshes the bodies of the children and renews the torpid air of afternoon. The laughter of the children is refreshing too. Carried away by unimportant bellicose preoccupations, some of them call out from time to time to make sure that the grown-ups are not missing anything that's going on.

"Look, Katrice!"

"What is it, child?"

"Look, Katrice!"

"I'm looking!" says Katrice.

"Look! Look, Katrice!" another child cries.

"Lord's sake, child!" says Katrice. "What more do you want of me? I'm *looking!*"

She sounds slightly put upon. It's part of her manner, though. Her Caribbean lilt, as always, is quite beautiful and full of tenderness. I am reminded of imaginary music.

CHAPTER 22

A Rich and
Varied Life

Education writing, as John Holt observed when he and I were teaching high school English in the summer at the Urban School in 1966, is frequently a way of speaking indirectly of our own biographies and of rethinking our own lives, allowing us to write disguised confessionals without being obliged to speak explicitly of our regrets or fears or disappointments.

I was relieved to hear him say that because I had had that thought about the writing I was doing but had wondered if it might be risky to concede this. In the present book, I think his observation is particularly apt. I think the state of mind in which I came to talk with children in the Bronx was shaped and modified to an unusual degree by several factors in my own experience, including my nostalgia for the years when I was a young teacher and the longing that I felt to be there in the classroom once again, and also, in a very different way, by my anxiety about the illness of my mother and my father.

I know that my concern about my parents had a powerful effect upon my mood on many days when I was with the children at St. Ann's—and, indirectly, on a great deal of the writing I've done since. I think it's had a quieting effect upon my tendency to write polemically. Complicated arguments with angry intellectuals lost much of the attraction they had held for me in previous years. I no longer felt much appetite for winning victories in that particular domain. The gloominess and letdown of late afternoon were what I looked on as my enemies. I wanted to see the sun stay up there in the sky a little longer.

I wasn't so close to my mother and father in the years when I was more politically engaged, which were also years in which I wrote with a determined productivity that left me little time (or gave me an excuse to think that I had little time) to give them the attention they deserved. As my mother was confined increasingly to her apartment and my father had to move into a nursing home after he was diagnosed with Alzheimer's disease, I felt a lot of anger at myself for all the opportunities I'd missed to spend unhurried time with them. As my father slowly lost his wonderful proficiency with words I wanted most to talk with him. As his memory began to fail—although this was selective at the start—I wanted most to draw him out about the details of the things he did remember.

My father had led a fascinating life that had involved dramatic changes in direction and, at one important moment, in the choice of his career. He grew up in South Boston, but his parents moved, when he was eight or nine, to Roxbury, which by the 1920s was the Jewish neighborhood of Boston. He went to Boston English High School, and he worked his way through Harvard College, where he majored in psychology and spent his summers working at a psychiatric hospital. He went directly into Harvard Law School after college, pressured by his mother, who had wanted him to emulate his older brother, who had finished law school a year earlier. Only after traveling to Europe on a fellowship one summer to investigate the work of specialists in schizophrenia and meeting the man who coined the term, the great physician Eugene Bleuler, at his home in Switzerland, and later talking with the elderly physician and psychologist Pierre Janet at the Salpêtrière in Paris, did he make up his mind to give up law school and go back to Harvard College for two difficult semesters of organic chemistry, biology, and German. By the end of that year, he entered Harvard Medical School, which was the start of yet another long and sometimes convoluted journey.

For many years he worked in the development of medications to control grand mal and petit mal, the seizures undergone by epileptics. He then became more interested in the diagnosis of brain tumors and the study of brain injury. Still later, he devoted himself solely to psychiatry. His memories of the psychiatric work he did were fading quickly by this time; but his memory of what he did during the 1930s and the 1940s in the area of neurological impairment remained crystal-clear until about three years ago.

One of the most moving conversations that I had with him in 1996 involved his effort to explain to me, and to the people who took care of him, the reasons for the cerebral malfunction that afflicted him. With great precision he explained why certain recent memories were inaccessible while others, such as memories of boys he knew and played with in first grade in 1912 and of the teachers he admired most at Harvard in the 1920s — Alfred North Whitehead, in particular, and Charles Townsend Copeland — were not only easy to recall but fresh and

287

vivid, as if these were people he'd just seen or things he had just done. He spoke of the brain chemistry, and of the size and texture of a "neuron," and he indicated where exactly in the cerebellum various brain functions — certain names of which he could no longer summon up — were likely to be centered.

When he could not find a word he needed, he did not appear to be especially annoyed but seemed to be amused — and *interested,* like a scientist — to recognize a symptom of the very chemistry he was describing. He smiled at these moments. "You see?" he'd say. "That illustrates my point." I could imagine him in 1939 or 1940 leading young physicians on grand rounds at Boston City Hospital, stopping at one bed, and then another, to discuss each case, and then arriving at a patient who presented the most perfect case of all to illustrate a point that he was making, even though the patient in this instance was himself. One of the nurses was upset by this; but most of the staff members were profoundly moved by his display of scholarship and by the charming and old-fashioned elegance with which he told them what was wrong with him.

Experiences like these had two effects on me. They heightened my respect for his capacity to reach beyond immediate predicament and find delight and dignity where others might have settled for self-pity. But they also were, of course, reminders of the toll of time, as well as of the probable prognosis for the future. My father delivered these lectures from his bed or from a chair; he couldn't get up without assistance any longer and he needed help with dressing, urinating, shaving. The lectures on brain function, as I knew, could not go on forever. Soon he would cease to be the doctor and remain only a case for other doctors to describe.

I came from evenings with my father with a stronger sense than ever of the foolishness of thinking that we know the journey we are meant to take or can predict the consequence of almost any set of choices we may ever make. The pedagogic mania associated with predictive phrases such as "outcome-based instruction," and the whole idea of leading kids in middle school to settle on careers and then make "choices" on the basis of decisions of this sort, seemed even more unsettling and dangerous to me than ever after these discussions with my father. I was glad no teacher tried to predicate his future when he was a boy of seventeen and being pressured by his mother and his brother to become a corporate attorney. It would have robbed the world of a good doctor and it would have robbed his patients of a sensitive and understanding friend.

My father's life gives me renewed respect for people who do not insist on too much certitude about the maps they're using and do not insist on knowing in advance what destination they'll arrive at in the ends of days. I wanted the children that I knew to have this opportunity as well. I wanted them to have the richness and the thoroughness of education that my father had received, but I also wished that they could know some of the freedom and the intellectual capaciousness that he had known but which he had to struggle to achieve: the courage he had found to turn his back on expectations and adult determinations and the restlessness of mind that could permit him to risk everything by giving up the law because his longings drew him all at once in an entirely new direction.

It had been hard for him to strike out on his own. Harvard Law School wasn't easy to get into. A Jewish kid who came from a poor neighborhood in 1927 and got into "The Law School," as the Harvard Law School was referred to here in Boston in those days, was on the way to a respectable career that promised affluence and intellectual prestige and an established role in the community. To give that up because he had been stirred by his acquaintance with two elderly and brilliant European doctors and was fascinated by the theories they discussed with him about brain chemistry seemed very risky to his teachers and his mother. He did it anyway. Somehow the sheer bravado of this choice, the very knowledge that he was engaged in an adventure of unusual defiance, helped to fire up his energies and intellect enough so that he did it, not just with success but, as I realized later, with nobility and honor.

It will seem incomprehensible to many people, I am sure, that I would look at Elio and other children of his age in the South Bronx and then project upon them lessons I imagined I had learned from my own father. Reasonable people might observe that scarcely more than 10 percent of children from Mott Haven even graduate from many of the local high schools with degrees that could enable them to enter any four-year college and that very, very few of these survivors could conceivably get into colleges like Harvard, let alone go on to Harvard Law School. Hypothesizing aspirations for these children from my father's life, or from my own, therefore, seems utterly romantic to some people. Even some black and Hispanic educators whom I've known for years just smile at me when I say things of this sort. They put their hand quite firmly on my elbow, as if they're affectionately checking on my mental health, and look me in the eyes and tell me that I'm dreaming.

"These children are not *going* to be lawyers and psychiatrists," I'm told. "They'll be very lucky to get jobs as medical assistants or as sanitation workers with a union and some good health benefits." (Yes: Black and Hispanic educators do say things like this to me, and not only political conservatives, but lifelong activists and intellectuals who have the deepest loyalties to inner-city kids but also know the outer limits of the possible or what they view, at least, as outer limits.) Several of the inner-city school officials who are close to me politically, and personally, have told me nonetheless that they regard it as unrealistic, even overreaching, when they see me juxtaposing aspirations and ideals from regions of experience that seem to come out of two different worlds.

"It would be nice," they'll say, "if *all* these kids could go to Europe someday, as your father did, and study with the great professors and attend distinguished universities and someday lead exciting, richly cultivated lives. Some of them might do it, four or five out of a hundred. The majority will not." To hold up dreams like that, they tell me, more or less in words like these, is "just not doing anyone a favor."

It's at this point that the conversation often turns to more pragmatic matters like "delivery of skills" and "productivity" and "readiness for work." The inner-city schools that can deliver quickly marketable skills are not perceived by school officials as impoverished places that betray the children of the poor but *praised* as places that position them for more successful lives. "That's the way it is," some realistic educators say, although not always without sadness in their voices. I recognize that there's some truth in what they say. The question, for me, isn't whether this is so but why this needs to be.

My father was not simply an effective medical "technician." He also read philosophy and memorized the verses of John Milton, Robert Browning, and John Donne. He once spoke French and German beautifully, and knew Italian too. Even now, bits of these languages will reemerge in conversation, often with no relevance or cogency but with precise and elegant pronunciation: brief, wonderful reminders of the fullness and diversity of inner life achieved by someone who was never trained to be a "useful" or "productive" number in America's economy but educated to inherit treasures.

What I'm asking is a relatively simple question: Why shouldn't Ariel and Pineapple inherit treasures too? My father's mother was ambitious for her sons. *Their* mothers are ambitious for *their* children. They may not know which program or which school or which curriculum will lead to European languages or schools of medicine or other destinies beyond the few that they can dream of. (My grandmother didn't know about things like that either. She could barely read a word of English when my father won his medical degree.) But they *want* the best things for their children, even if they cannot name those things and even if they do not know the steps by which they are to be achieved.

We owe it to these children not to let the doors be closed before they're even old enough to know how many rooms there are, how many other doors there are beyond the one or two that they can see. Eleanor understood this. She knew more about those "other doors" than many mothers in Mott Haven do. She set her longings on Brown University. It was an embodiment of dreams. Her daughter didn't get into the mansion she had hoped for. She got partway at least. Most children in the poorest places do not get even partway.

I don't think that we can silence these realities by "reinventing" structural contrivances or making "lists"— of books, or standards, or exams. Separate schools, divided racially and segregated economically, are fearful mechanisms for apportionment of destinies. Apartheid education always was, and it remains, an instrument of class assignment. New slogans are invented every decade to convince us that this really isn't so. A few book titles (two more plays of Shakespeare, one more book by Maya Angelou, or one by Alice Walker) may be added to the reading list to make it sound more "cultural," less "basic," more "advanced." New "expectations" are announced: new acronyms invented. "All children *will* succeed!" we're told. It's usually not so. Things generally continue as they were.

I don't like it when my language is too absolute. We all know there are dozens of exceptions. We cling to the exceptions, like theologies; and yet our hearts are never utterly convinced by this kind of theology. What will actually *happen* to these children that we know? How many will find the kinds of opportunities my father found, the doors that were, if not wide open, at least partly open for a poor kid of his color then, and which he later also opened up for me?

I think of the way that seasoned urban school officials speak to me at times when they can see me drifting into these scenarios of naive protestation. They can't afford these luxuries. Their obligation is to mediate injustices within the status quo and give sufficient evidence of incremental gains to justify a trifle more investment. Most of the school officials I have known are deeply moral and sophisticated men and women who are well aware of the impossible position in which they are being placed. In public they sound confident. In private they do not. They open up. They voice their heartache and frustration. They speak a lot about conflicting dreams.

Pineapple has changed her mind about career objectives six or seven times since we first met when she was in the autumn of her kindergarten year. At one point about three years ago she was convinced she wanted to become a supermodel. She used to show the other girls the way a supermodel is supposed to walk across a room and pose and hold her arms and twirl around. Some of the children teased her because she did not have the proportions of a fashion model. She also teased herself about this, once, as I remember, in a very funny way when we were standing by the fence that runs along the garden of St. Ann's. It's one of the most vivid memories I have of her amusing way of speaking of her plumpness.

In order to describe this, I should first explain that there are two gates to the garden at St. Ann's: a wide gate, through which almost everybody enters, right next to the room in which the afterschool takes place, and a narrow one that isn't actually a "gate" but really just an opening between two railings of the fence that someone widened many years ago so that a child could get in at night, for instance, if the pastor was away and if the other gate was closed. Mother Martha gave a beautiful sermon once about the two gates to the garden. She told the Bible story of the wide gate and the narrow gate (the "strait gate" in the gospel) and explained the meaning that the two gates have in Scripture. She said that when the grown-ups feel so low in spirit that they're worried about losing faith in God they ought to find a way to spend some quiet time with two or three of the young children and should ask them to describe their vision of God's kingdom, "which they know a lot about," she said, only half-playfully, "because they enter at the narrow gate. . . ."

The trouble is that Pineapple could not get through the narrow gate! She took me out there when I asked about this story and she showed me where the bars were bent. I asked if that was how she got into the garden but she shook her head. "Un-uh! If I ever tried to do that, I'd get stuck halfway!" She stood in profile by the railings so that I could see the reasoning behind this. She patted her stomach, pointed to the railings, and said, "Look!" to make it obvious that she could not fit through.

Pineapple gave up her plans to be a supermodel well over a year ago. Right now, she says she plans to be a doctor. There she is at P.S. 65 on Cypress Avenue in the South Bronx, one of the lowest-scoring schools in New York City and, despite the efforts that the chancellor has made, perhaps the most deficient elementary school that I've routinely visited since I was teaching in a school nearly as bad some thirty years before; but that's her dream, at least for now. She wants to be a pediatrician or a surgeon.

Is it sensible to ask if this is realistic? Is it proper to alert her to the many doors she'll have to batter open if she really plans to do this? Is it fair to warn her that some of those doors may turn out to be closed for good within a few more years if she goes on from here into the middle school that serves this neighborhood, then to the high schools to which children from that school are more or less inevitably tracked? Is it dangerous to recognize that, in her case, it may already be too late? Is it better not to think of this too closely but to pray that she may be one of the glorious exceptions? Could Mother Martha intervene on her behalf? Should I get on the phone and call some of my friends downtown? Could someone that we know manipulate the odds enough for her to get into a somewhat better secondary school, a private school perhaps, from which the kids routinely go to college? Then where does that leave Ariel and Elio and Stephanie? Why shouldn't all these children have that opportunity as well?

Triage solutions are in fashion now. Hence, the popularity of vouchers among well-connected people, even some in very poor black and Hispanic neighborhoods. That opens up a gate of sorts for a small fraction of the children of poor people. What of the rest, who wouldn't likely be invited to pass through those very special kinds of gates and wouldn't likely even know of their existence?

"Strait is the gate and narrow is the way which leadeth unto life," said Jesus, "and few there be that find it." That sounds appropriate for life eternal, but it doesn't need to be that way on earth; and certainly it shouldn't be like that in this abundant land in which we live. There should not be two gates to the riches of *this* kingdom. There should not be a narrow gate for children of the poor, a wide and open gate for children of the fortunate and favored. There should be one gate. It should be known to everyone. It should be wide enough so even Pineapple can get in without squeezing.

We are told that it was like that once for many children of poor people in this nation. Will it ever be that way for children of Pineapple's race? Some of my optimistic friends in New York City think it will; some of the school officials lead us to believe we don't have long to wait. I pray that they are right. I hope that some of us will live to see it.

CHAPTER 23

Saying Goodbye

Hot weather returns to New York City in the final week of June. Pineapple wants to talk with me alone, so we go out into the garden and she picks a grassy spot above the sprinkler and slides. It's a sunny afternoon. A few of the children from the neighborhood are playing on the swings. Some of the older girls are showing off their expertise with yo-yos far above us on the flat part of the hill.

"Yo-yos have come back!" Isaiah's mother told me several weeks ago. "My God, Jonathan! Do you *remember?* How old does that make you feel?"

The truth is that I'm happy to see yo-yos coming back because it means that Giga Pets are going out of fashion at long last. Unlike those irritating electronic creatures, yo-yos don't make noises, and a yo-yo can't distract a child from a conversation once it's tucked away within her pocket.

A year ago you might have seen two or three yo-yos at the afterschool. Now almost all the children, Pineapple included, seem to have them. Her yo-yo is a plain one, made of wood, the kind we had when I was in third grade in 1945. She isn't fooling with it, though. She's got it in her hand and simply looks at it from time to time during our conversation.

She begins by asking me if I remember when I met her when she was in kindergarten.

"Yes," I say.

"What was my teacher's name?"

"I don't remember."

"I used to write my numbers in reverse."

"That I *do* remember."

"Want to see me do it?"

"Okay," I say.

She reaches for my paperpad and shows me how she used to write a "5" or "7" in exact reverse, as if in a mirror.

"Can you do an '8' like that?" I ask.

She seriously tries it, then says, "Hey!" when she discovers I was fooling her, then shows me how she used to write her name in mirror-letters also.

When I put my pen back in the pocket of my jacket she looks at my hand and asks me why I have a Band-Aid on my thumb.

"I have a cut," I say.

She studies the Band-Aid. "Can I see it?"

"No."

"Why not?"

"Because you can't."

She asks me how I cut myself and I reply, "I can't remember."

"I know how. . . ."

"I bet you don't."

"Your dog?"

"What do you mean?"

"She bit you?"

"No. She doesn't bite."

She presses me to find out how I cut my thumb but drops the subject soon and looks down at her knees. At last she looks up with a lot of feeling on her face and tells me that she was upset last night because her older sister, Lara, found out yesterday that she has to repeat fifth grade.

The news comes as a real surprise to me because her sister studies hard and when I visited her class this year, her teacher told me she was doing well. New tests, however, have been instituted in the New York City schools and strict promotion policies have suddenly been put in place. Children who were getting good grades all year long but scored beneath specific levels on the new exams are being told they cannot be promoted. Several of the mothers have been at the church today to talk with Mother Martha.

The nonpromotion news has cast a cloud over the afterschool the past few days. Some of the children who were not promoted didn't even show up for the afterschool today. Pineapple says her sister cried last night. Her mother and father went to school to see the principal this morning, but it seems from what they later tell me that they still don't understand exactly why she has to be held back.

Pineapple's class was given an examination too. She's going to be promoted but seems troubled, and confused, because she's not as good a student as her sister, who has always been one of the avid readers at St. Ann's and helps Pineapple with her homework. Several of the other kids in the fifth grade, moreover, who don't read as well as Lara seem to have done better on the new exam.

Pineapple gets up and throws her hands out with a kind of shrug and looks around her on the grass. A few feet above us on the hillside there's a wooden arch that's painted like a rainbow. It's been here as long as I've been visiting St. Ann's. At some point in the past I think it held a swing. There are two rusted screws extending near the midpoint of the arch where chains may once have been attached. Pineapple looks up at the arch, then walks beneath it, reaching up to see if she can touch the screws, looks at me and makes another shruglike gesture with her hands, walks around the arch a single time, looks up and smiles vaguely, and then walks around it three or four more times.

I make the mistake of taking out a cigarette. She doesn't notice this at first, but when I take a book of matches out and light a match she stops dead in her tracks and points right at the match.

"Un-uh," she says.

I quickly put away the cigarette and match.

"You have asthma."

"Yes. I know."

"Why do you smoke?"

"I don't know why."

She puts her two hands on her hips. "Why don't you stop right now?"

"I *will* stop, soon," I say.

She tries her yo-yo, lets it sleep there at the bottom of the string, then pulls it up.

"Okay," she says. "That's it."

It's not clear to me whether she means that we've resolved the issue about P.S. 65 and the examination and her sister's nonpromotion or if she believes that she's just settled something with me about smoking. She says, "That's it!" sometimes as if it were a way of bringing something slightly messy, or confusing, or aesthetically displeasing, to a satisfactory conclusion. I've heard her say it also when she's finished an assignment for her teacher or has had a quarrel with another child and was contradicted and came back with a reply that struck her as conclusive. Last summer, on her mother's birthday, she showed me a card that she had bought for her. Under the printed message on the inside of the card, she'd signed her name and written this:

"I love you — and that's it!"

Later in the afterschool I see her playing with her yo-yo in the open area beside the stairs. She does it well but has a pouty look. The worries we'd discussed are obviously not resolved. When her mother comes to pick her up at six o'clock, she gives me one last wave, halfhearted, though, as she goes out the door.

I spend the next two days at P.S. 30. The news is generally better for the children here than for the kids at P.S. 65, but the mood in Miss Reistetter's class is not as happy as on other days because she's told the children that she won't be teaching here next year. She's just been offered a position in the suburbs of New Jersey, where she lives; and, while she says that she was torn about accepting it, she tells me candidly that she'll be paid $4,000 more. Adding to this the money she will save on transportation costs (about $2,000) and the cost of buying school supplies for her first-graders here in the South Bronx — which runs up to $1,000 yearly — she'll end up with nearly $7,000 more. She has 28 children in her class here in the Bronx. Next year she'll have only 22.

These salary and class-size differentials are well-known to teachers in New York. The salaries paid to a beginning teacher in the city at the time when Miss Reistetter had to make this choice, in spring of 1998, were less than $30,000. In the richest suburbs of New York, the starting salaries were over $40,000. At the other extreme, for veteran teachers with advanced degrees, the highest salary they could expect to earn in New York City was a little less than $60,000. The highest salaries for veteran teachers in the wealthiest suburban towns were over $90,000 and would rise by 1999 to just about $100,000 — $30,000 more than what Miss Rosa, principal of an entire school, receives.

School inequality, for people who do not have children in the schools, may often sound like something vaguely incorrect in a democracy but still remain rather abstract. Many people, in addition, are not sure what money "buys" in public schools; so the actual effects of inequality remain obscure to them, and indeterminate. This morning in Mott Haven the abstractions fall away: The children of the South Bronx are about to lose a talented young teacher who has graced their lives with real instructional effectiveness and a great deal of disciplined delight over the past two years. The children of a middle class community — not one of the wealthy suburbs, she informs me, but a comfortable neighborhood whose student population includes very few black or Hispanic kids — will be the winners.

There's no complexity about the reason. Miss Reistetter's family has no money to assist in underwriting her career. Her mother is a classroom teacher also. Her father is deceased. She has a student loan of more than $20,000 to repay. Her car was hit and damaged on the bridge into New York two weeks ago and, because of problems in insurance coverage, she will have to pay most of the cost to get it fixed. She needs her car to get to school because she isn't paid enough to live in New York City and have extra money left to lead a normal private life. She loves the children here at P.S. 30, but she's not a saint and took no vow of indigence when she became a teacher.

She's only one of dozens of good teachers I have met in urban districts like Chicago and New York who come to love the children that they teach for two or three brief years in inner-city schools, then pack their lesson plans and learning games and poster boards and all the good experience they've gained and all the useful classroom methods they have mastered after the initial period of trial-and-mistake, and head off to suburban systems where their talents are rewarded with not only better pay but often far more dignified conditions and they are not asked to dig into their pockets to buy storybooks and crayons and construction paper for their pupils.

Miss Reistetter introduces me to an amusing boy whose uncle, she believes, was a drug dealer whom I wrote about some years before. The child's uncle and his mother, who were feared in this community for many years, were murdered by competing dealers in two highly publicized assassinations. The boy, who's short and stout and brings to mind a fireplug with thick and bushy hair, is sitting at a table opposite two other boys — "named Horace and Virgil!" Miss Reistetter tells me with her usual enthusiasm for coincidence. Sitting with the three boys is a girl who talks nonstop — "a motor-mouth!" the teacher says, "but very bright" — who tells me, when I ask her, that she's named Christina.

Christina, at the teacher's invitation, takes a stapled folio of writing from a folder on her desk — the title, which is written on the cover, is "My First Grade Memories" — and shows me all the book reports she's written in the past ten months. "This one was my favorite," she has written in neat printed letters, "becase I like The Auter."

Under the title ("Three Little Pigs") she's summarized the plot in three short sentences. Under this, she's drawn a picture of three small pink pigs next to a fuzzy creature with four feet who stands beside a green-and-purple house beneath a yellow sun and two blue clouds. The pigs look more like laundry bags with curly tails than animals. She runs her finger over their pink bellies and says, "That's how I draw pigs."

"What's this?" I ask her, pointing to the fuzzy figure by the house.

"The woof!" she says, pronouncing it without the "l," as do most of the younger children in the neighborhood, so that the "woof" does not sound big and bad at all.

When I ask how old she is, she looks at her fingers, but not long enough to count with them. It's just a glance, as if she's checking to remind herself that, if she needs to, she could use her fingers; but she doesn't need to, and she quickly says, "I'm seven."

"How old will you be a year from now?"

"Next year?" she says, not looking at her hands this time. "Next year, I'll be eight."

"How old will you be the *next* year after that?"

"The next year, I'll be nine."

"The year after that?"

"Then I'll be ten."

"How old do you think the teacher is?"

She looks up at the teacher. "Sort of a teenager."

Instead of going down to lunch today, which is the next-to-final day of school, the class remains here in the room to have a party. Two of the mothers have come in with paper plates and pizzas and "fudge sundaes" (brownies topped with whipped cream) for dessert. To quiet the children after lunch, the teacher turns the lights off and invites them to lie down for a few minutes on a carpet, where she sits beside them on a stool and sings a song about noses and ears and other places on the body, and she touches different places on her body as she sings.

Once they're calm she gives out various awards to children who "improved the most" in different subjects such as "penmanship" and "math." But she makes sure that nobody's left out by giving every child inexpensive paper-covered books she's bought for them.

"You know I'm proud of everyone," she says, looking especially at Virgil and his desk-mate Horace, who are whispering to one another, "even when you misbehave."

Then the children go back to their chairs and start to clean the papers from their desks and choose the stories and the colored drawings that they want to bring home to their mothers. One of the bigger boys is dragging a waste-paper basket from one table to the next, while other children help the teacher clean the boards and others put some of the books and plants in cardboard cartons for the teacher to take home.

"He can dance," Christina tells me, pointing to the boy the teacher had identified to me before, whose mother and uncle were gunned down six years ago.

"Want to see?" he asks.

He falls into a rapid dance-step without waiting for my answer.

At two o'clock the graduating fifth-grade students have a party in the gym. Some of the girls, including Stephanie and Ariel, are wearing grown-up dresses. They walk around the edges of the gym, lifting their hands before their mouths and making comments on the boys, who mostly stand together looking awkward and uncertain how to entertain themselves.

In a courtyard of the building just behind the first-floor hallway, five or six of Mr. Bedrock's fourth-grade students who have stayed behind to help him clean his room are trying to keep cool by sitting in the shade beneath a high brick wall, beyond which is the garden of St. Ann's. Mr. Bedrock's shirt is soaked from the humidity and heat.

"This was my tenth year of teaching," he remarks as I sit down beside him near the wall. "I hate the kids to see me when I'm tired like this, but I'm feeling it right now. I'm 53 years old.

"I didn't start 'til I was in my forties because I taught college first. In a way, I feel a little cheated that I started late, because I know I can't put in the energy young teachers can. . . ."

He watches the children sitting near us on a low ledge made of several beams of wood. "Well, that's not always so. I do it for long periods of time, but then, on days like this one, I can feel my stamina collapsing, and I hate it when that happens, because I *enjoy* the time I spend with children and I know they think of me as someone they can talk to when they need to without being careful of their words. But when my energy runs down I get short-tempered, and it's not their fault, it's mine, and I feel bad about it when I'm driving home."

He runs his hand over his brow, which is perspiring, and through his short-cut greying hair.

"Yo-yos are back. . . ."

"I know."

He calls one of the children to his side and asks if he can try her yo-yo.

"First say 'please.'"

"Please," he says.

She offers him her yo-yo and he slips the loop around his finger and allows it to drop once but doesn't pull it soon enough, so that it wobbles at the bottom of the string and he has to rewind it.

"I used to be good at this," he tells the child, or himself, as he attempts to do it more methodically.

The children watch to see if Mr. Bedrock still knows how to make the yo-yo sleep before he gives the tug that makes it climb back to his hand.

In front of the school the children from St. Ann's are waiting in a line to file up the street. Elio and Tabitha are standing next to Nancy, who looks cool in summer shorts and sneakers. Mothers are standing on the sidewalk, waiting to collect their children as they file from the door.

Saying goodbye to children in the final days of school is hard for teachers everywhere. In September when you meet them they are simply 25 or 30 little mysteries, some well-behaved, some frightened, some precocious, some of them more problematic, some of them unmanageable squirmers, some of them eternal "motor-mouths," as Miss Reistetter said about Christina, but all of them still packages with unknown contents and still-unknown possibilities. By June there may be fewer mysteries, but a new chemistry has taken place. They're all *your* children now and you don't usually like to let them go.

Bittersweet days of bashful parting fill the final weeks of class for little kids in happy elementary schools like P.S. 30. For children who have strict and loving teachers with the good old-fashioned tenderness of Frances Dukes, those days are filled with rituals that many of us remember from our own best days in public schools.

Wednesday is the final day. It's even hotter and more humid than the one before. My light-blue shirt has turned dark blue against my skin by twelve o'clock. Miss Dukes, however, doesn't look as if she's bothered by the heat. Wearing a polka-dot silk suit and sitting calmly at her desk, she has a quietly commanding style.

Like many of the older female teachers whom I've met in inner-city elementary schools, she speaks to students in the firm entitled way grandmothers speak to their grandchildren. She doesn't use much of the innovative lingo and does not appear to know the newest and most fashionable phrases that have filtered into school-reform discussion. She does know children, though, and she's lived long enough to speak to them with a degree of earned authority and, for these reasons, represents a source of strength and moral reassurance for the younger teachers in the school.

She's not as strict today as she would usually be, but still insists the children do their lessons right up to the hour after lunch. When I come in, the students are presenting recitations of a story from a big anthology that they have open on their desks. She calls a name. The child comes up to the front, holding the book. One by one, the children read their passages aloud and then sit down.

Elio reads his passage in a good clear voice. Some of the other children read almost inaudibly, however. The teacher has to interrupt a child who cannot be heard.

"A little louder, sweetheart. We want everyone to hear."

Tabitha reads a full page of the story, which is a retelling of the fable of the boy who cried "wolf, wolf." Her voice is soft, but she pronounces every word (except for "woof!") correctly and the teacher praises her profusely. "She couldn't understand a single word she read last fall, but she's worked hard," she says. "I tutored her during my prep times and I got a lot of good cooperation from her mother. . . ."

Tabitha sits down and other children take their turns and then the teacher leans back in her chair and asks them to describe the story, using their own words. "Okay then," she asks them, "what is this about?"

A child named Violeta lifts her hand. The teacher recognizes her, and Violeta gives her answer. Then Miss Dukes restates the story's theme by reading the last line: "A liar will not be believed even when he speaks the truth." She uses the opportunity to lecture them a bit about the need "to tell the truth at all times," but particularly to their mothers, and goes even further then by urging them to tell their mothers everything that troubles them and never hold back secrets. "Mothers have broad shoulders! Mothers are strong people! You can tell them *everything!*

"Also, children," she says, looking at the faces of the ones who sit the closest to the front, "don't *ever* miss an opportunity to tell your mother that you love her, even if you're angry."

The children pay her close attention. Something in her voice conveys a depth of feeling that has no connection really with the story they've been reading. "I want the boys here to remember this: When we come into the world our mother cares for us. But when our mother's very old and she is getting ready to depart the world we have to care for *her*. So I want every boy here to grow up into a good strong grown-up man, so you will always be there for your mother. . . .

"You know what? I don't have a brother, so I had to grow up strong so I could take care of *my* mother. . . ."

Her voice trails off. She looks down at her hands.

"Don't *ever* miss an opportunity to tell her that you love her," she repeats.

Elio looks solemn while she's speaking. The other children nod respectfully. A moment of silence. Then the teacher stands and tells them, "Well . . . , we have some birthdays."

Elio, as it turns out, is nine years old today. Another child, named Marissa, will be eight tomorrow. Miss Dukes asks both of them to stand before the blackboard while the class sings "Happy Birthday." At the end of the song, the children sing, "How old are you?" Elio sings back, "I'm nine years old." Marissa sings, "I'm eight years old." The class sings back a blessing in reply and then the two sit down. Miss Dukes gives everybody birthday cake, then lets them have a fifteen-minute period to chatter and relax.

I sit at a table next to Tabitha, who's cleaning out her desk and also working on a letter to her teacher.

> Dear Miss Dukes
> I am going away
> I am going to see my grandmother
> I hope Im going to have fun
> Your my best friend
> Forever think you!
> Tabitha

The punctuation's mostly missing and there's no apostrophe in "I'm." Except for "your" and "think," however, every word has been correctly spelled.

Across the table is an interesting boy who's talked with me before. He usually wears glasses, very thick ones, with pink plastic frames. His glasses are broken, though, he tells me, and he's waiting for a new pair; so, for now, he squints at me as he displays a folder of the book reports he's done. He pulls one out and offers it to me and says that I can keep it, then proposes I might want to color in the illustration that he's drawn. The book is called The Lazy Spider and, beneath his book report, he's drawn a spider hanging headfirst from a slender thread.

"You could color it in," he says.

I ask what colors I should use.

"You could make this black," he says, tapping the body of the spider, "this part red," tapping the legs. "And this is white," he says, touching the head.

"This in here is a lot of eyes," he says.

"What color are the eyes?"

"They *could* be red . . . ," he says, and squints again as he looks up from where he's leaning very low across the page.

Some of the girls and boys are clustered at the teacher's desk. "Thank you, dear," she's saying to one and another of the children who are giving her the gifts or messages they have prepared for her. Tabitha looks hesitant, then walks around the teacher's desk and offers her the letter that she's written. She watches as the teacher reads it and looks terribly embarrassed when the teacher tells her, "Thank you, sweetheart," but she overcomes her shyness to reach out and give her teacher one last hug and one last kiss.

"She couldn't understand a word she read ten months ago," Miss Dukes repeats as Tabitha goes back across the room and settles in her chair and looks down at the surface of her desk.

"All but two of my children will be going to third grade," she says, which might not mean so much to teachers in suburban schools but is unusual — a triumph really — for a teacher this year in this district of New York.

Elio has a brand-new tennis racquet on his desk: a birthday present from Miss Rosa. When he brings it up to show Miss Dukes she asks him, "Did you know that I play tennis too?"

"You do?" he says.

"I do!"

The idea of their teacher playing tennis seems to be surprising to the children. She's such a dignified lady that it's hard to picture her in shorts and jersey running back and forth across a court chasing a ball. She surprises them more, and me as well, by telling them that she knows how to Rollerblade! — which she reveals as if it were a scandalous confession for a lady who is so respectable and proper. The children smile at the idea of Miss Dukes on Rollerblades. Miss Dukes is smiling also, with that almost wicked look that older women who are teachers sometimes have when they reveal something about themselves that nobody who sees them only in the classroom would find easy to imagine.

A little after two o'clock, a group of girls who have just graduated from the fifth grade come to say goodbye. They wouldn't have dared to interrupt this class on any other day; but there they are, in summer dresses, ready to go on to middle school and gaily chatting with Miss Dukes as if they were no longer subject to the rules of strict behavior that she's famous for enforcing but have earned the right at last to come into her room the way a teacher might and go up to her desk and talk to her as if they were — almost — her grown-up peers. She permits them this, but doesn't look entirely happy to see Ariel's bare shoulders and to see another girl wearing high heels.

This too, the final visit from the graduating students, is another bit of ritual that some of us remember from our days in elementary school. The older kids look so grown-up to second-graders. Three months later, when they go into sixth grade, they'll be the youngest children in their schools and may not have the same self-confidence again for many years and, in some cases in this neighborhood, as teachers like Miss Dukes know all too well, they'll never have this kind of easy confidence and springtime inno-cence again.

Two-fifteen in second grade, and Elio is in his chair, and Tabitha in hers. Across the table from Tabitha is the boy who broke his glasses and who told me how to color in the picture of the spider. It was rowdy in the room the past few minutes, but the party's over now and every-body's seated where they're supposed to be, the children at their desks, Miss Dukes at hers.

"This year we had 29 children in our class," she tells them in that pleasant Southern-sounding voice she some-how never needs to raise too loud in order to be heard, "and I think that everybody knows that was too many. Next year, I'm afraid you may have even more. The way that things are going now, it could be 31, or 34. . . . So you need to respect your teacher, and each other, and be good in every way, and if you are, if you're polite, you'll save your teacher's voice—because you know how many troubles I had with my throat this year. . . .

"I'd like to see some of you children go to college and work hard so you can study to be teachers. So all of the mistakes your teachers made when you were growing up, you can be sure you'll never make. So you can be much better teachers to your students than I was to you.

"And this summer, above all, children, please be safe! And never talk to strangers who approach you in the street. And, every night, please put a book beneath your pillow.

"And be good to your mothers. And listen to your mothers. And be respectful to your mothers. And those of you who will be going to your grandma's for the summer, please don't let her give you too much candy.

"All right then. . . ."

"Goodbye, Miss Dukes!"

"Goodbye, children."

"All right then . . . ," she says again.

"Goodbye!"

"Goodbye!"

"All right then . . . ," the teacher says. "I love you."

EPILOGUE:

EASTER 1999

"The World Serious is about to start," said Elio one day while he was working on arithmetic with Mother Martha. It was October 1998. The Yankees had won the pennant three days earlier by defeating Cleveland. I looked at my calendar that night and marked the day when San Diego would arrive at Yankee Stadium for the first game of the series: "World Serious begins today, says Elio."

As in the past, his errors and misstatements often are more interesting than the literal precision in the words of children who are less spontaneous. Are they actually "misstatements"? Usually I think they are. I don't think he listens and pronounces carefully. When he used to say The Lord's Prayer before supper he would say, "The King will come!" instead of "kingdom come"—just like that, as if it were a news announcement. Instead of saying "hallowed be thy name," he'd pose it as a question. "*How* will be thy name?" he'd ask with gentle emphasis upon the first word of the question. The syllables of "trespasses," the sibilance of which entangles many little tongues, would frequently be given an unusual revision too. "Give us a day of daily bread," he'd ask, and so he would continue in a cheerful rush of partly right and partly mispronounced or mis-remembered words that like a little river in the forest disappeared into an underbrush of tangled words at one point or another, only to reappear at last in one big double-shout of celebration, like a football cheer: "The power forever! Amen!"

He's learned the errors of his ways since then and now says almost all the words correctly. He still elides the whole last portion of the prayer, however. "The power" and "the glory" and "the kingdom" and "forever" and "Amen" get piled up into a kind of snowbank that he slides right into before tearing into dinner.

I asked him recently if he remembers the first time we met. He said he doesn't. I don't either. At some point in February or the early part of March in 1996 his friendly presence simply jumped into my life. I'm naturally glad it did; and saying it this way, of course, is an intentionally offhand way of saying something I'm afraid to say in any other way, because I know that Elio will read this someday when he's old enough and I don't want to overdo the stuff about my gratefulness because I know it will embarrass him.

I hope the world does not become too serious too soon for Elio or any of the other children at St. Ann's. I hope he has a while yet to look out of his bedroom window at the moon on quiet nights and speculate about its state of mind. I hope he still has time to listen to God's tears but doesn't have to shed too many of his own. I hope his father can come home from prison soon. I hope his teachers and his mother never lose their patience with his questions.

Seven years have passed since I first visited the neighborhood around St. Ann's; nearly a year has passed since the intensive period of dialogue and interaction with the children that has been recorded in this book. Some things have changed since then; and some remain the same. The faculty at P.S. 30 has been relatively stable. A few of the teachers I was fond of there have since retired or moved on to teach in other schools in other neighborhoods; but Mr. Bedrock and Miss Suarez are still there. So too is Miss Dukes, although she's told me that next year will be her last.

Miss Rosa, still a forceful and inspiring presence at the age of 64, remains in charge. She's threatened to retire every year since I first met her there in 1994. ("I'm no spring chicken anymore," she said to me that spring, although she still was younger, by some 40 years, than the impressive age that Elio initially assigned her.) I hope that she remains there with the children for a few years more. P.S. 30 would not be the place it is without her.

One of her most able colleagues, Stefan Zucker, runs an innovative subdivision of the school known as Mott Haven Village, which includes a sixth grade and a seventh grade in which some of the children in this writing are enrolled. He hopes to add another grade next fall, so that the children in Mott Haven Village will be able to remain here right up to the time they enter high school. He wishes he could keep them here for four years after that until it's time to go to college, but the funding for those added years is not available in New York at the present time.

The staff at St. Ann's, although it changes and expands from year to year, retains a good deal of stability as well. Given the pressures of the work and the perennially insufficient budget of a church that must rely entirely for its income on outside support, there has been a reassuring continuity of personnel within the programs serving children.

There are more people working with the children now. Eleven grown-ups, three of whom are men, four of whom are mothers or grandmothers, one a university instructor who is something of a wizard with computers, and several college students who have roots in the South Bronx tend to the needs of children from the age of five or six to twelve, with always four or five teenagers who come back for help and reassurance and to offer help as counselors and tutors. The college students come and go at intervals, as do some of the unpaid volunteers and the professional staff members. The grandmothers remain.

Some of the children in this book will soon be adolescents. Tabitha's only nine, and Elio is not quite ten, but Pineapple will be eleven soon, and Ariel is twelve, almost thirteen. Taller now, a bit more cautious in their humor and subdued in silliness, they're children still in all respects. The elemental innocence and sweetness of their personalities endure.

I measured the children one day in the fall by asking them to stand against the trunk of the big maple tree beside the fence next to the swings. Tabitha was nearly four feet tall. Elio was four feet two. Pineapple was four feet six. Mariposa, the littlest one, was barely forty inches high. She seemed to think that forty inches was a lot. "Oh my Gawd!" she said, pretending to be stunned at hearing this and falling over backwards on the lawn. Her legs, in bright-red tights, stuck straight out in the air in front of her.

I had a tape measure with me when the afternoon began, but I misplaced it somewhere, so I used a ruler.

I placed the ruler on each child's head and made an ink-mark on the tree. Everyone seemed eager to be measured. Some of them stood on tiptoes. If they stood on tiptoes I subtracted a few inches. Pineapple's sneakers elevated her an extra inch. My measurements were anything but scientific. I subtracted an inch for sneakers. She behaved as if she saw this as a genuine injustice.

I was back at St. Ann's in December.

Tabitha showed me an essay she had written for a science class at school. She was supposed to read it aloud on the next morning, so she asked my help in sounding out two words she didn't know: "paramecium" and "amoeba." She learned to pronounce "amoeba" without trouble but, as often as she tried, could not say "paramecium."

I ran into Isaiah's mother in the street on Monday. We went for pizza to a place across the corner from Alí's. "Leave it in!" she told the man behind the counter. "I like it hot and crispy." She crossed herself before she grabbed the pepper can to sprinkle pepper on the pizza.

Mr. Geiger, who has taught Isaiah now in several different grades, said that Isaiah had been having a good year in academic terms — "a *wonderful* year, in fact," he said — but that he had a bad time still with asthma. I asked Isaiah about this later when I met him in the lunchroom. He was surrounded at the table by three girls who like him; he insisted he was feeling fine.

The boy in Tabitha's class who gave me a picture of a spider last spring ran right up to me on Tuesday when he saw me heading for the stairs. I'd given him a copy of The Little Prince the day before. His glasses were broken again, however, so he said he hadn't started reading it.

Briana was sitting in the afterschool on Wednesday looking at a big book about "Mr. Frog" and "Mr. Toad."

One of the girls showed me a novel called Felita. Another girl was reading Harriet The Spy. Elio was looking at a book called Sounder, one of my favorites, but he hadn't yet decided if it was too hard for him. Pineapple's older sister, Lara, handed me a science-fiction novel, called The Giver, and said that I could borrow it. She said she was about to start The Secret Garden. Mariposa was examining the pictures in a story about ladybugs with personalities.

Otto told me something wonderfully mysterious that afternoon. I'd been giving him an update on my dog. Out of the blue, and with an interesting smile, he announced, "My dog has dreams."

"I think almost all dogs have dreams," I said.

"But I know what he dreams," Otto replied.

"How do you know?" I asked.

"Because . . . ," he said, "I think I go there with him when we sleep."

"Go *where?*" I asked.

"Go where you go when you're asleep," he said.

I asked him if he could describe this feeling, because I have had this intimation too.

"Well . . . ," he said. "It's sort of like, when we wake up we look at one another, and we both know that we've been somewhere — *together.*"

Pineapple isolated me on Thursday afternoon and asked me, rather slyly, what I'd like to get for Christmas.

"Anything I want?" I asked.

"Anything," she said.

"A horse," I said.

"That costs too much."

"How much money do you have?"

"Seven dollars is the most that I can spend."

"A necktie," I suggested.

"I don't know how much that costs."

"A yo-yo?"

"Okay," she agreed.

She left a reasonable pause and said "Okay. . . ." a second time and then she left a second pause in which I knew what I was supposed to say but, knowing her strategic purposes, decided not to say it. She looked as if I had outwitted her for once.

"How about *me?*" she finally had to say.

"You?" I said.

"Me," she replied.

"What would you like?" I asked.

She obviously had thought this through, because she had a list prepared and pulled it from her pocket right away and read it to me on the spot and watched to make sure that I copied down the three specific things she and her sisters had decided on.

Pineapple and her sisters are not greedy children. Even when they worry that they're overreaching they do not reach very far. The toys she listed for her younger sister weren't the kinds of things you see at very costly stores. One was a plastic doll that comes with diapers and a baby bottle and which pees into a potty when you feed it. Another was a light-brown doll that walks and crawls in answer to your voice. The present she had chosen for her older sister and herself was something they had evidently seen on television. It was called The Clueless Headphones and, as I would learn when I went out to Toys "R" Us, was this year's latest rage, eclipsing Giga Pets and lighted yo-yos and the other gadgets that had been the rage a year or two before. I found the headphones and the walking-talking doll near where I live. The doll that pees into its potty was, however, out of stock at all the stores I tried in Massachusetts and I had to go to several shopping malls before I finally found one in New Hampshire.

Pineapple's such a skilled manipulator! If she hadn't cornered me the way she did I would have talked myself into imagining that three attractive children's books with illustrations would have been the ideal Christmas gifts: a willful misconception foisted upon children by their grown-up friends and relatives for generations. I still try to foist my favorite books on children at St. Ann's at every opportunity throughout the year, but not at Christmas time. Christmas wishes for most children that I know run in less onerous directions.

I had to mail my Christmas presents for the children to Katrice this year because I had to stay close to my mother and my father. It was the first Christmas season I had not been able to be at the church since 1993. It didn't seem like Christmas. There was one light snowstorm on December 22, but the days were mild and the snow had melted by the morning.

One of my favorite cousins died that week. He'd had leukemia and succumbed to an infection and died painfully. His youngest son, a man of 25 who still looks like a college undergraduate, was teaching second grade in Harlem. His students sent him messages on handmade cards they'd colored in with crayons. He kept them close at hand and kept rereading them as he was sitting there beside the bed in which his father died by labored exhalations, each breath painfully recorded on a bedside monitor in greenish moving lines that wavered fitfully but had been sloping downward steadily all afternoon.

"God can save your father," wrote one child who, not knowing of religious differences, had drawn a cross and, knowing but perhaps not thinking of my cousin's race, had drawn two big and little pictures of my cousin and his son, both colored brown, and holding hands. Some of the cards were written to my cousin. "God is locking out for you," one of the children said to him. "I love you."

After my cousin's funeral I visited my father at the nursing home. He was in stable health but thought that it was 1912. He spoke about "the Gate of Heaven," an impressive-looking Roman Catholic church whose priest had been a good friend to his parents when they were, he told me once, the only Jewish family in South Boston.

He didn't seem to recognize me when I first came in that night, but then surprised me when a doctor came into the room. "I don't think I've introduced you to my son," he said. His voice had a congenial sound, as if the two of us were at the Harvard Club for lunch ten years before and one of his physician friends had stopped by at our table.

Later that night, he spoke about a boy named Danny Sullivan who was his playmate when he was in first or second grade. At one point he asked, "Have you seen Ma?" He always called my mother by her name but called his mother "Ma." I knew that, at that moment, he believed I was his brother.

It wasn't sad to be with him, because he didn't seem to be unhappy. His confusions obviously puzzled him but didn't seem to frighten him; and now and then there was a moment that appeared to be lucidity. One night, a woman who was visiting a patient suddenly collapsed and seemed to have gone into shock. My father somehow got down on the floor and took her hand and pressed his fingers to her wrist to find her pulse, then moved his fingers slightly in the practiced way that doctors do until he'd found exactly the right spot. Appearing to be reassured, he stayed there at her side until one of the nurses had arrived. These residues of competence, infrequent as they were, resurfaced on occasion and would catch the notice of the nurses and attendants, who have never failed to treat him with the same respect they show to other doctors.

Another night, as I was just about to leave, he took my arm and said something in Yiddish, which his mother spoke but which I hadn't heard him speak in 45 or 50 years. I asked him, "Daddy, can you say your name in Yiddish still?" He thought for a moment, then said, "Hershel Leben"—Harry Leo—and then put his arms around me and began to cry.

"It's been a good trip, hasn't it?" he asked.

"Yes, Daddy," I told my father. "It's been a beautiful trip. You made it good for all of us."

My mother was 95 years old that week. My father wasn't strong enough to leave the nursing home and come in town with me to celebrate my mother's birthday, so I went alone but brought my dog, because her presence makes my mother smile and makes both of us relaxed. She isn't permitted in my mother's building, so I have to sneak her in from the garage. One of my mother's neighbors, whom my mother doesn't like and whom she calls, depending on how spirited she feels, either "a witch" or "a psychotic," ratted on my dog, so we got thrown out of the building early; but we had enough time for our dinner and the birthday cake and I had brandy with my mother and she gave cake to my dog and, all in all, it was a happy visit and the stupid business with my mother's neighbor offered some relief from thoughts about my father's absence from our celebration.

The weather remained snowless in New York and Boston during January. Martin Luther King Day fell, as always, on a Monday, even though his birthday was a day or two before. A teenage boy named Gabriel was stabbed in the heart three times that day outside of Otto's house, which is across the street from St. Ann's Church. He died in the operating room later that night. A friend of the murderer was murdered in retaliation in the same encounter.

"There are two large stains of blood on the cement where Gabriel was stabbed," said Mother Martha. "Gabriel was Jefferson's cousin, so this is another loss he has to bear and try to understand. He made a point of bringing me to see the shrine where people had left notes and photographs and flowers and a number of small candles on the sidewalk at the spot where Gabriel collapsed. He left a package of Rice Krispies treats for Gabriel because he said they were his favorite snack.

"Then it began to rain, so everything was moved inside the building so the notes and pictures wouldn't get all wet and so the candles wouldn't be extinguished by the rain."

The news from Mother Martha and Katrice became more hopeful at the start of February. A well-known dancer, Jacques D'Amboise, who'd heard about the children's program at the church, had come to talk with Mother Martha and decided to begin a series of dance classes. "He did a trial class to see how it would go," she said. "Elio was in the group. He was the star!"

"Was Pineapple there?" I asked.

"Yes," she replied. "Most of them were. Otto too. He's doing so much better now, no longer taking Ritalin. His mother's so relieved. I think he has more reason to be happy. The other kids accept him so I think he's learned he doesn't need to drive them up the wall. Score one for our children!"

Pineapple, Mother Martha said, had gotten thinner in the past two months, but, according to Katrice, she still did not look too much like the skinny fashion models she once viewed as her professional role models. "She dances *good!*"

Katrice insisted when I asked. Thinking of Pineapple doing pirouettes, her arms above her head, her feet in sweat socks pointed high up on her toes, I felt a twinge of envy and regret that I had not been there.

The light-hearted messages were interrupted by disturbing ones during the weeks that followed. An innocent man who was an immigrant from Africa was shot to death one night by the police in the South Bronx. His death before a fusillade of more than forty bullets from the guns of four policemen who had fired, almost point-blank, as he stood before the doorway of his home set off more than a month of protests leading to a civil disobedience campaign. A wide array of ordinary citizens and advocates and members of the clergy of diverse religious faiths, including Mother Martha, were arrested.

More painful to the children were some other deaths that took place in the streets and neighborhoods around St. Ann's, which Mother Martha called "the ordinary dyings," most of which get little notice from outside the area. Two boys were gunned down in a late-night killing just outside a store on St. Ann's Avenue a few steps from Alí's, where I'd been getting coffee for so many years. One of the boys died instantly. The other would survive, I later learned.

Miss Rosa had to speak about this killing to the children on the intercom at P.S. 30 prior to dismissing them because there was a rumor of a payback killing in the playground opposite the school. "This is Mama Rosa speaking," she began her message to the children, as she told me in her office when I got back to New York to visit her late in the afternoon a few days after the event. At times like these, she said, a principal has to attempt to draw on every bit of credibility she may have earned in children's eyes, speaking not as an official of the school but as a parent—

or, in this case, a grandparent—which is not a way all principals can speak, because the children do not view them always with the confidence that they invest in her.

Later in the spring she had to speak to children in that role again when one of her first-graders was incinerated in a fire that swept through his home. The six-year-old, according to a child who was close to him, had gotten out but then ran back into the building in an effort to retrieve his teddy bear and was unable to escape a second time. Mother Martha wasn't sure the part about the teddy bear was right but seemed reluctant to discuss it when I asked. The story of the teddy bear, however, was repeated by some other children who had known the boy who died. The notion that he'd tried to save his bear and that the two of them, the boy and bear, had been consumed together, may have softened the effects of grief and given the illusion of a purpose to the purposeless.

There were other tragedies in weeks to come. Three girls, all twelve-year-olds, were raped in a short period of time in the South Bronx, one on a roof, one in a hallway, and one underneath the stairs of an apartment building. A fourteen-year-old hanged herself at school and was discovered by a classmate in the toilet stall in which she somehow had attached the rope. A sixteen-year-old boy was shot and badly wounded by an officer near Morris Park. Another young man was shot in the face on St. Ann's Avenue, again on the same corner as Alí's. But the story of the boy who died to save his bear, as children in the neighborhood insisted that he did, retained a special meaning for the children, and a sense of closeness—even, possibly, an element of moral glory—that the other tragedies did not.

"This was his chair," the child's teacher told me on my next trip to New York. It was during recess. She was sitting at one of the children's tables, grading papers in the quiet of the room before the kids came back. "For days after he died they wouldn't let another child sit here," she recalled. "If another child tried to take his place they'd say, 'This was *his* chair.'"

I've had conversations like this with schoolteachers in the past after a child in their class had died of illness, in an accident, or, as in this case, in a household fire. The recent presence of the child in the class, the place he sat, the things he used to say and do, the way he looked the last time he was there, are always recollected vividly and painfully by teachers, who may often suffer longer with these memories than children do.

"He was a sweet boy and was terribly attached to me," the teacher said. "He used to bring me pictures he had drawn for me."

From a folio of children's work she took a picture of a boy painted in blue and chalky white: a large round head, a round heart for a nose, two round blue eyes with long blue lashes, and two rudimentary arms. The background was a blue-black sky dotted by stars.

"Friday he was here. We had a party in the corridor that day. The children broke piñatas. He was excited, happy! with that happy face of his! 'Look!' he said. 'Look, teacher! I have candies!' He was absent Monday and he died on Monday night.

"He did go back into the building—to get *something*," she believed, but she did not know what it was. "One of the papers said they found his body in a closet. Another said that he was found behind a sofa. His sister said he thought his father was inside. He went 'to save his daddy.' Others say it was the bear. . . ."

She pulled another picture from the folio. "He did this for me just two weeks ago." It was a picture of a parrot with the red and green and yellow colors of the tropics.

There was a note to her beneath the parrot's feet. "I love you, Mrs. Caraballo."

The children came upstairs from recess. The teacher stood behind the chair in which the child used to sit and watched the other children take their chairs. I went downstairs to visit with Miss Suarez in her kindergarten, then to talk with Mr. Bedrock, then to see Miss Rosa for a while. Throughout the afternoon I couldn't get those long blue lashes from my mind.

"He was alive and now he's dead," said Tabitha, who told me that she knew the boy. She's in the third grade now. She knows the story of the teddy bear and does not like it when I seem to question whether it is accurate or not. Miss Rosa later spoke with me about the way the children build these small mythologies, and why they do, and why a grown-up shouldn't look too hard into these pieces of belief. Like Mother Martha, she resisted my attempts to clarify the "truth" about the boy and bear. I'm glad the children have these women to defend and honor the epiphanies they weave around the unacceptability of grief.

"Is it because there are no graves in Egypt that you have taken us out to die here in the wilderness?"

The words of Exodus 14 come early in the liturgy for Easter; but images of death and wilderness were hard to hold in mind on Easter Sunday at St. Ann's amidst the cheerful-looking children and adults who gathered in the sanctuary of the church at ten o'clock. Even the reproaches of a boy who wondered why I hadn't been here for so long gave me a feeling of belonging, not of exile.

Pineapple and her sisters were supposed to serve as acolytes but showed up thirty minutes late, so Mother Martha had to scramble to find other children to assist her in the mass. Pineapple's mother had forgotten that it was the start of daylight savings time the night before and had neglected to advance the clock. It wasn't until the pianist had begun the "Alleluia" and the congregation rose to sing the words—a moment of intended sacredness and celebration—that the three girls entered from the back door of the church and slipped into the pew beside me.

"We overslept," Pineapple said, then crossed herself, sneezed twice, and rubbed her eyes, then rearranged the way that we were seated in the pew, insisting that Briana climb across my knees and sit beside me to the left while she remained beside me on the right where she could whisper in my ear and offer commentaries on the sermon, which had already begun before she and her sisters finally settled down.

I started making notes about the sermon but soon lost my concentration with the children next to me. Pineapple's older sister, Lara, and the little one, Briana, had on matching hats of starched white linen with the brims tucked back. Under the brim that held the tuck their mother had inserted fresh white daisies. Pineapple wore no hat and had no daisy. Her hair was decorated with translucent butterflies, however.

The butterflies appeared to be the new "thing" in the neighborhood this spring. I'd noticed one of them three days before when I was walking with the children in St. Mary's Park and saw something that seemed to shimmer in Briana's hair. I asked her where she got it and she answered matter-of-factly, "At the Chinese store," and took it off and placed it on my hand. It lost its fascination for me once I held it. On my hand it was a plastic curiosity but in Briana's hair it looked like gossamer.

At the end of the sermon, Mother Martha read the "creed," which states the basic tenets of belief in the divinity of Jesus, and his crucifixion, and ascent to heaven—

information which, like many Jewish people who participate without discomfort in the other portions of a Christian service, I tend to pretend that I don't hear, although of course I do. Then the pastor lifted both her hands and asked the people in the church to join her in confession of the things they had done wrong.

Pineapple looked at me when I did not kneel down. When I whispered to her that I do not say confession, she gave me another look and then requested my knee-cushion and knelt down and closed her eyes and pressed her hands together flat and moved her lips and stayed there longer than her sisters did. I studied the top of her head and had to wonder what tremendous sins she had committed to require such a lengthy recitation.

A moment later, everyone was on their feet. "Stand up," Pineapple said. The pastor and her acolytes had stepped down from the altar and were coming up the aisle to say "peace" to people in the congregation. People turned to wish each other a good Easter. Many stepped into the aisles to give hugs to one another.

"Peace, Jonathan."

Briana offered me one of her carefully placed kisses and then scrambled to the aisle to give kisses to as many other people as she could before decorum was restored.

After the pastor and the acolytes had circulated through the congregation and the people who had stepped into the aisles had been seated in their pews again, the pianist started playing something that was meant, I think, to reestablish a more solemn mood before communion would begin. The windows of the church were closed because the weather, although bright and sunny, still was cool. A mild fragrance from the incense that was rising from the censer drifted through the air.

I wrote a memo on my pad to ask the priest someday the purpose of the incense. I wrote it in capital letters:

"WHAT'S IT FOR?" Pineapple was looking at my pad. "It brings our prayers to heaven—with the smoke," she said, and lifted both her hands to indicate the way the incense rises in the air.

"See the way the smoke goes up?"

"Yes," I said.

"That's how our prayers go up," she said, then let her two hands flutter down.

Soon after that, the preparations for communion started. Mother Martha held a big white wafer high up in one hand. In her other hand she held a cup of wine. Pineapple was whispering the pastor's words into my ear, as if perhaps she thought I couldn't hear.

"The body of Christ," she said. "The bread of heaven."

When the wine and wafer had been consecrated people in the front began to leave their pews and file to the altar. I stood up so that Briana could get past me but remained there in the pew until the children had come back. Pineapple studied me again when she returned. It wasn't a reproachful look. She knows what my religion is. Possibly, however, she's not clear on what this actually implies or whether it's a good excuse for staying in the pew when everybody else in church is up in front there kneeling on the floor.

She didn't try "conversion tactics" on me in the way that Leonardo did when he assured me that the bread is "good" and told me I should "try it." She simply gave me one more look, then shrugged, and let the matter rest and straightened up to listen to the priest. Mother Martha made a number of announcements now and named the people who had been bereaved in recent weeks, which was a long list on this Easter at St. Ann's, and people who were sick and those in prison, which was not a short list either, and invited us to pray for them and said a final prayer and then began the last procession, with the line of acolytes behind her, up one aisle and around the back by the baptismal font, then down the other aisle to the front and then, the acolytes behind her still, right out the door.

"That's it," Pineapple said.

So in this way the Easter service ended and the children went outside into the sun where people gathered after church to chat with one another before some went home and others went downstairs to the soup kitchen, where Katrice and Elsie by this time were spooning out the mashed potato on the plates already piled with roast beef and greens, and adding lots of gravy to the top of the potato, which I know is not, officially at least, the bread of heaven but for many people like Katrice is part of the communion too, and is good also.

I stayed behind a while in the sanctuary when the others went outside. I had no reason to remain, but it was cool and peaceful there and possibly I wanted time to organize my thoughts before I went downstairs to see Katrice. I was looking at the ceiling, where I noticed that there still were several lights that didn't work. Above me to the right side of the church was the didactic-looking angel that had captured Otto's interest on the day he opened up to me and Elio about his brother. It didn't look the way I thought an angel ought to look. A century old, or even older, it was rather stiff and prim and looked like a New England debutante. It lacked Pineapple's buoyant credibility.

I couldn't seem to get my mind to focus on religion much this morning at St. Ann's. Some of my thoughts were far away in Boston with my mother, who had had a bad week with arthritis. Some were with the boy named Jefferson whose cousin had been murdered three months earlier, because he had been sitting close to me in church but didn't say hello or wish me "peace" and walked right by me without recognition, and he seemed detached from other people at the church as well. The rest of my thoughts, I know, were with Pineapple.

Her whispered words about "the bread of heaven," which I had already heard in Mother Martha's voice, may have been meant to be instructional. Perhaps she was attempting to slip in a bit of pastoral encouragement under the guise of repetition. I know it bothers children when a grown-up doesn't seem to know the liturgy and prayers. I try to pretend. I study the pages of the prayer book if I have one. I say some of the words. I sing the songs or hum generically and vaguely when I'm not sure of the tune. These ruses and pretenses do not work. Pineapple's elbow nudgings and the looks she gave me when I failed to stand up at the proper time, or turned to the wrong page, or followed the wrong prayer, made her appreciation of the situation all too clear.

My parents' illnesses and, in my mother's case, anxieties keep me at home more often now. Every time I leave her bedside she gives me three kisses, one on my forehead, one on my right cheek, and one on the left, and says, "God bless you," and I say, "God bless you," in return. We never know which night will be the last one.

My mother has seen this world for nearly an entire century. She was a fourteen-year-old student at Girls' Latin School in Boston on the day the Red Sox won their last World Series. She follows them faithfully. She loves Pedro Martinez. She will not forgive the pitcher Roger Clemens for his treachery in leaving us and, even worse, now pitching for New York, a team, of course, which she dislikes. She's unhappy also with Bill Clinton for his personal behavior and what she believes to be his "sell-out" of the poor. She likes his wife. She likes Ted Kennedy and Reverend Jesse Jackson. My mother's an old-fashioned liberal. You don't find too many people like her anymore. I wish that she could live forever. I know she can't, but when I pray I always ask for one more year.

I go back to Mott Haven when I can, and when I know I need to. Every time I do, I feel renewed in spirit by the generosity and understanding of the children and the love and courage of the grown-ups at the church.

Katrice's swollen feet still seem to give her a good deal of pain, and now she has another worry on her mind because her doctor told her last week that he saw "something he didn't like" in looking at an X-ray of her breast. She has a cancer history, so a referral is in order. Miss Elsie has some problems with blood sugar — she's a diabetic — and she suffers from high blood pressure as well. Mrs. Winkle, who will soon be 85 years old, is in good health but moves more slowly now. Others in the older generation who come in to supervise the children at the afterschool are suffering the usual infirmities of age.

Still, life abundant fills the church on weekday afternoons when children crash into the room at three o'clock with all the pent-up energy that children have when they're released from school. The younger ones still race into the older women's arms to bring them up-to-date on all the interesting news.

"Guess what, Katrice?"

"What is it, child?" she replies as she looks down upon a package of excitement that will not let go of her.

"Katrice?" the child says again.

"Words to tell, and ears to hear," Katrice says rhythmically, not really to the child, more to me or to herself.

Her fingers go to work at helping to unbutton buttons and unwrap the child from her winter coat, which is too heavy for this season. The child squirms beneath Katrice's hands. At last, her arms released from padded sleeves, she brings the coat across the room and reaches up to hang it on a hook.

Elio doesn't end up on the overturned blue milk box in the corner of the kitchen anymore. Other children take the space he used to occupy. Katrice still stands there by the child who's in isolation, with her disapproving looks and knowledgeable nods. She tells me that she still does not like leaving here at night. She always feels a sense of letdown when the final child has gone home, she says.

"Okay, that's it, I guess. . . ."

It sounds a little like Pineapple in her "mop-up" mode. The difference, though, is that there isn't the same feeling of finality. When Pineapple says, "That's it!" she doesn't say, "I guess. . . ." She wraps it up and leaves no room for anyone to open it again. Katrice, like almost anyone who's lived for more than fifty years, knows more about the unpredictables in life. The uncompletedness of most experience is part of what permits her, and compels her, to be tentative.

She stands there in the kitchen doorway as the last one leaves, her arms folded so firmly.

"You leaving now?"

"Not yet," I say.

"Okay," she says.

I step outside with her to say goodbye and watch her as she goes out to the street and heads up St. Ann's Avenue in the direction of her home. "No one runs from good," she told me once. Yet people do. Night comes, and we have other obligations.

At home, reminders of the children are on every side of me. The walls are covered with their writings and their pictures. In the place of honor is a present that Pineapple gave me several years ago, an imitation stained-glass window that she made from tissue paper, brightly colored with green paint and with a wash of light-blue ink. It's a landscape: grass and sky and one tremendous puffy-looking cloud that looks like an amoeba or a fish or a distended blimp that's losing air, and also, partly hidden by a hill, a jolly-looking thing with orange rays that look like dragons' teeth and is supposed to be the sun.

It's right here in my window so I get a chance to see it every morning when I come downstairs. It's a slight thing. I would guess she did it quickly. When I asked her recently if it was supposed to be a rising sun or setting sun, she seemed at first not to remember what I meant. "That old thing?" she finally said. "I gave that to you *years* ago!" She thought about it for a time, then said she wasn't sure what she intended. "You decide," she told me uselessly.

Friends who see it here cannot decide if it's supposed to be the end of day or the beginning. Either way, I think that orange thing with dragons' teeth is beautiful; and, at the risk of being sentimental about somebody whose sunny disposition brings a lot of joy into a world that has too many cloudy afternoons, I like to think it's rising.

St. Ann's Scholars

A discretionary fund has been established for the pastor of St. Ann's to use in ways that benefit the children in this book, with special emphasis on education and the opportunities for college. Readers who would like to add their own support may write to St. Ann's Scholars, St. Ann's Church of Morrisania, 295 St. Ann's Avenue, Bronx, NY 10454. Those who would like to know of other organizations advocating on behalf of children in New York and elsewhere in the nation may write to the author at HarperCollins Publishers, 10 East 53rd Street, New York, New York 10022.

Notes

1   THOMAS MERTON: *Conjectures of a Guilty Bystander* (New York: Doubleday, 1968).

2   ASHLEY AND MARY-KATE: These are the names of twin girls who starred in a television program, called "Full House," that was popular with children.

DESTRUCTIVE CONSCIENTIOUSNESS: See citation from Erik Erikson, note for page 119.

3   PEDIATRIC AND MATERNAL AIDS IN NEIGHBORHOOD IN PREVIOUS YEARS AND TODAY: For previous years, see data in my book *Amazing Grace* (New York: Crown, 1995). Infantile HIV is far lower in the South Bronx now because of perinatal treatment, according to Dr. Irwin Redlener and other physicians at the South Bronx Health Center (see note for page 33). Maternal AIDS and HIV, however, remain high. The neighborhoods served by Lincoln Hospital and Bronx-Lebanon Hospital, which include the St. Ann's area, have the highest rate of new HIV infection in young adult and older adolescent females in the nation, according to Redlener and his staff.

PEDIATRIC ASTHMA: See note for page 87.

4   AREA IMMEDIATELY SURROUNDING ST. ANN'S CHURCH POOREST IN NEW YORK CITY: *Newsday,* May 31, 1993.

RACIAL SEGREGATION OF MOTT HAVEN: See notes for pages 31 and 32.

UNEMPLOYMENT OVER 45 PERCENT IN SOUTH BRONX: *New York Times,* November 2, 1997. This may be a conservative estimate. A survey by the Citizens Housing and Planning Council published in 1998 concludes that "only half the working-age men and one third of working-age women held jobs" in the South Bronx neighborhoods the survey sampled, according to *City Limits,* April 1998. For the Bronx as a whole, which includes the affluent enclave known as Riverdale, official unemployment has ranged between 8 and 11 percent between 1997 and 1999 (*New York Times,* April 16 and October 20, 1999); but this figure does not include sectors of the population called "discouraged workers" and those who have never been consistently employed.

UNEMPLOYMENT OVER 75 PERCENT IN ST. ANN'S NEIGHBORHOOD: Estimates by Reverend Martha Overall, priest of St. Ann's Church, and parents and teachers in the neighborhood. For families of children attending P.S. 30, which draws on a somewhat wider demographic spread, Aida Rosa, the principal of P.S. 30, estimates an unemployment rate of 65 to 70 percent. Neither estimate includes people on workfare, few of whom have been able to obtain permanent jobs.

5   MY FIRST ACQUAINTANCE WITH CHILDREN IN THE SOUTH BRONX: See *Savage Inequalities* (New York: Crown, 1991) and *Amazing Grace,* cited above. My first visits to a child's home in the South Bronx were in the fall of 1989. My first visit to a school in the South Bronx was to Morris High in February 1990. My first visit to St. Ann's was in 1993.

Chapter One

19   ST. ANN'S CHURCH: Historical information on the church is given in *Amazing Grace,* cited above.

Chapter Two

28   CHILDREN IN LOCAL PUBLIC SCHOOLS HAVE LOWEST CHANCE OF ADMISSIONS TO THE CITY'S COLLEGE-ENTRANCE SCHOOLS: Of the 32 elementary districts of the New York City public schools, District 7, in which all these children are enrolled, has the fewest number of students who obtain admission to elite schools such as Stuyvesant High School. (See *Amazing Grace,* cited above.)

STATISTICS FOR MORRIS HIGH SCHOOL: See note for page 217.

31   PRISON STATISTICS: See note for page 155.

A SEGREGATION RATE OF 99.8 PERCENT IN ELEMENTARY SCHOOLS SERVING THIS NEIGHBORHOOD: According to a report published in 1997 by the Citizens' Committee for Children of New York, there were 10,989 children in the public elementary schools of District 7, of whom 26 were white. (*Keeping Track of New York City's Children, A Citizens' Committee for Children Status Report,* 1997.) Two years later, in 1999, the Citizens' Committee found only 21 white children in the district (*Keeping Track of New York City's Children,* 1999).

31, 32   RACIAL SEGREGATION OF PINEAPPLE'S SCHOOL IN 1993 AND 1994: *Amazing Grace,* cited above. (See, especially, pages 123 and 150.)

RACIAL SEGREGATION OF THE NEW YORK CITY PUBLIC SCHOOLS: *New York Newsday,* May 20, 1994. Harvard Professor Gary Orfield, who has written widely on this issue, notes that *Newsday's* statement is derived from statistics that apply, more broadly, to all of New York State, which has the nation's most segregated public schools; but he adds that this distinction is primarily because of the segregation of the New York City schools. (Correspondence of Professor Orfield with the author, December 1999.) See also Gary Orfield and Susan Eaton, *Dismantling Desegregation: The Quiet Reversal of Brown v. Board of Education* (New York: The New Press, 1996) and Gary Orfield and John T. Jun, "Resegregation in America's Schools," a report released by The Civil Rights Project, Harvard University, June 1999. "New York is a 'tale of two cities,' and it should come as no surprise that each of these cities has its own school system," wrote David Dinkins prior to the time he was elected to be mayor. "Thirty-two years after Brown v. Board of Education . . . , the New York City Board of Education continues to operate two separate and inherently unequal school systems." (*New York Times,* letters column, July 9, 1986.)

SEGREGATION ACCELERATED BY POLICIES OF CITY PLANNERS SINCE THE 1950S: See, for example, Robert Caro, *The Power Broker: Robert Moses and the Fall of New York* (New York: Knopf, 1974).

FEDERAL HOUSING SUBSIDIES USED TO DEEPEN PRE-EXISTING RACIAL SEGREGATION: A mother in the neighborhood gives me this example. The building in which she lives near St. Ann's Church charges $1,400 for rent each month. She can afford to pay only $250. The rest is paid by Section Eight, a federal subsidy. The subsidy, however, is attached to this specific building in the Bronx and can't be carried with her to another neighborhood, in a racially mixed suburb, for example. "I'm not allowed to transfer this," she says. "It locks me in." If these subsidies were separated from specific buildings, so they could be used to underwrite suburban rentals, racially integrated housing would be possible in many more suburban areas around New York.

INTENTIONALITY IN THE WAYS RACIAL AND ECONOMIC ISOLATION HAS BEEN REINFORCED: In an interview in Albany in 1997, former New York governor Mario Cuomo spoke with candor of the way this has been done. "We took a lot of poor people and jammed them into parts of the city where . . . there were not enough school seats, there were not enough hospital beds, there certainly were not enough job opportunities. . . . We created entire enclaves of poor people. We doomed them because there was no way they could get work. . . . We did that and we did it deliberately." Interview with Chris Mercogliano and Mary Leue, *Journal of Family Life,* Vol. 3, No. 2, 1997.

33   PETER EDELMAN CITED: The former Assistant Secretary of Health and Human Services, who resigned from the Clinton administra-

tion when President Clinton signed the welfare bill of 1996, is cited here from correspondence with the author, October 1999.

UNDIAGNOSED OR UNTREATED ILLNESSES: Dr. Irwin Redlener, a professor at Montefiore Medical Center in the Bronx and president of The Children's Health Fund of New York, who is described in chapter 13, discussed with me a number of positive developments in health care in the Mott Haven area, but was careful not to understate persisting medical inequities. "There is every bit as much untreated illness in these neighborhoods as in the early 1990s," he observes; but he also notes that diagnosis is less frequently the obstacle than follow-up. "Primary care, including diagnosis, has substantially improved," he says, because of the proliferation of neighborhood clinics. The problems, he says, lie in "access to the care that diagnosis ought to *lead* to"— the specialized services, including surgery, for instance, that cannot be offered in a local clinic and require hospital referrals. At this point, he says, several roadblocks stand before a person in the neighborhood in need of care: lack of medical insurance; Medicaid denial, which is often automatic (even though illegal) under New York's stringent workfare policies; "ill-defined provider attitudes," by which he means, for instance, the reluctance of some intake personnel to guide a person properly through application stages; inhibition; fear; and lack of information on the patient's part—"a cluster of inhibitory factors," as he words it. During a visit to the South Bronx Health Center on Prospect Avenue, which Dr. Redlener and his wife and colleague Karen Redlener founded six years earlier, a community-based clinic that provides the kind of on-site primary care we had discussed, I spoke also with Dr. Alan Shapiro, medical director of the center, and his colleague Dr. José Del Pilar. Dr. Del Pilar, a psychologist who worked previously at Rikers Island and now, as he puts it, works "with the other half of the family" here in the South Bronx, spoke movingly of the depression, often chronic, among older women in the neighborhood who are, he said, not only burdened with their own health problems, but also obliged to function "like case managers for all the problems of their children and grandchildren." (Conversations at South Bronx Health Center, September 1999.)

Chapter Three

38   "CONFINE YOUR LIGHTS": The lines are cited from the opening section of "The Womanhood," part of a longer work called "Annie Allen," for which Gwendolyn Brooks received the Pulitzer Prize for poetry in 1949, now included in Brooks's *Selected Poems* (New York: HarperPerennial, 1999).

42   "THERE ARE SOME CHILDREN WHO ARE LIKE WINDOWS": The words of the unnamed Massachusetts teacher, identified only as

an "experienced" educator, are cited in the August 1994 edition of "Approaching Thunder," a small quarterly newsletter for New England teachers, published in Boston.

43 "I SHALL CREATE": Gwendolyn Brooks is cited from her poem "Boy Breaking Glass," which is included in a collection of her work, titled *Blacks* (Chicago: Third World Press, 1987).

44 $10,000 TYPICAL YEARLY INCOME OF FAMILIES I KNOW IN NEIGHBORHOOD: This is based on conversations with families in 1998 and 1999. In 1991, median household income in Mott Haven was $7,600 (*New York Times,* November 5, 1991), with families in the St. Ann's neighborhood generally poorer than the median. According to *The New York Daily News* (February 24, 1998), nearly half the families in Mott Haven and three nearby communities—Port Morris, Melrose, and Hunts Point—have incomes below $15,000.

45 PER-PUPIL SPENDING IN NEW YORK CITY PUBLIC SCHOOLS AND SOME OF THE WEALTHIEST SURROUNDING SUBURBS: In the 1997–1998 academic year, New York City spent about $8,200 per pupil (an average figure which includes special education). In the same year, Great Neck and White Plains spent approximately $18,000, Jericho nearly $19,000, and Manhassett nearly $20,000. (New York State Education Department Fiscal Analysis and Research Unit, memo from Darlene Tegza, Principal Education Planner, September 16, 1999; and "School-Based Expenditure Reports, Fiscal Year 1997–1998," Board of Education, City of New York, January 1999.) Actual spending on a child in an ordinary ("mainstream") elementary-level classroom in New York, as in other districts, is lower than the average figure because special education classes are far more costly than are mainstream classes. See also note for pages 215, 216.

$5,200 SPENT ON ORDINARY CLASSROOMS OF THE PUBLIC SCHOOLS IN THE SOUTH BRONX: Chancellor Rudy Crew told me this in conversation during a dinner hosted by Time-Warner on November 13, 1996. New York City is one of very few communities in the United States in which less money, in inflation-adjusted dollars, was invested in a child's public education in the late years of the 1990s than in the beginning of the decade. (See, for example, *New York Times,* February 7, 1997 and *Savage Inequalities,* especially page 237, cited above.)

DIFFERENCES IN TEACHERS' SALARIES: See note for pages 301–302.
UNDERSTATEMENT OF THESE INEQUALITIES: See, for example, *The New York Times* (May 27, 1999), which states that average per-pupil spending in the city is "nearly $4,000 less than in the most affluent suburbs." In reality (see note for pages 215–216), New York City spent nearly $10,000 less than suburban Great Neck and nearly $12,000 less than suburban Manhassett in the preceding school year, which is the latest year for which numbers were available at the time.

Chapter Four

52 CHILDREN'S PRISON CONSTRUCTED OPPOSITE A JUNIOR HIGH ON ST. ANN'S AVENUE: The Horizon Juvenile Center, as the juvenile prison is called, was built to replace an antiquated detention center known as Spofford in Hunts Point, although the city now intends to reopen Spofford, after renovation, in the winter of 1999–2000. The new facility occupies about two thirds of a large block bordered on the south and north by 149th Street and Westchester Avenue, and on the west and east by Brook Avenue and St. Ann's Avenue. Opposite the children's prison on St. Ann's Avenue is a middle school, I.S. 162. One block to the south is an elementary school, P.S. 27. One block to the north is South Bronx High School. See also note for page 154.

Chapter Six

78 IN HEAVEN YOU "PAY FOR THINGS YOU NEED WITH SMILES": The child's ideas about heaven are related in *Amazing Grace,* cited above. I had previously told her and some of the other children of the death of a dog I had had for many years.
"THE SUBSTANCE OF THINGS HOPED FOR, THE EVIDENCE OF THINGS NOT SEEN": Hebrews 11:1, King James Bible.

79 "A FLASH OF EASTER": The words are those of Deborah Smith Douglas, an ordained elder in the Presbyterian Church who is now active in the Episcopalian denomination. These words, as well as a discussion of the notion of "prevenient grace," appear in an essay, "To See with the Eyes of the Heart," *Weavings,* January/ February 1997.

81 "DO NOT BE CONFORMED TO THIS WORLD": Romans 12:2, New Revised Standard Version of the Bible.

Chapter Seven

86 MEDICAL INCINERATOR IN MOTT HAVEN: See *New York Newsday,* October 16, 1991; *New York Times,* November 2, 1991, and September 8, 1992; *Riverdale Press,* May 13, 1993; *New York Newsday,* September 8, 1993; *New York Times,* September 5, 1995; *New York Daily News,* May 14, 1996; *City Limits,* June/July 1996; *New York Times,* May 11, 1997, and June 27, 1997; *New York Daily News,* September 18, 1998, and May 6, 1999; *New York Times,* May 6, 1999; *City Limits,* July/August 1999. A partial summary of the legal violations committed by the owners of the medical incinerator, and penalties provisionally imposed upon them, is provided in a consent order drafted by the New York State Department of Environmental Conservation on July 22, 1998. The document, which was distributed to people in the nearby neighborhoods, records 100 violations of environmental law and proposes, among other penalties, that the owner of the incinerator, Browning-Ferris Indus-

tries, Inc., contribute money for asthmatic children to go to asthma camp. *The New York Daily News* (February 24, 1998) notes that the operators of the waste facility had violated pollution laws more than 500 times. According to Raphael Sugarman, who covered the South Bronx for *The Daily News,* Browning-Ferris finally paid $250,000 in settlement of the dispute (*New York Daily News,* May 6, 1999). See also Sugarman's excellent articles on air contamination in Hunts Point (*New York Daily News,* February 4, 1996) and on a medical outreach program for asthmatics (*New York Daily News,* March 11, 1999), *Daily News* columnist E. R. Shipp's strong article on environment, race, and respiratory illness (*New York Daily News,* June 4, 1996), and a carefully researched series on the asthma epidemic in the South Bronx and in other New York City neighborhoods which appeared in *The New York Daily News* during February 1998.

87 "WASTEFUL PROTEST IN THE BRONX": The editorial condemning neighborhood activists and parents who opposed construction of the medical incinerator appeared in *The New York Times,* November 11, 1991. "Medical wastes are not only unsightly but dangerous," the paper said. "No one wants them in a residential neighborhood. Under New York's zoning laws, the only place for such a facility is in a zone in which residential construction is forbidden."

88 PROTESTS AGAINST INCINERATOR: Among the groups and individuals that led the fight to close the waste facility were the Riverdale Committee for Clean Air; the Hunts Point Awareness Committee; the New York Public Interest Research Group; Gregory Groover, former pastor of Bright Temple A.M.E. Church in Hunts Point; Reverend Earl Kooperkamp, a former pastor at St. Ann's; Carlos Padilla and Marian Feinberg of the South Bronx Clean Air Coalition; and hundreds of parents, including a number of those described within this book.

SEVERE ASTHMA CONTINUES TO TROUBLE CHILDREN IN THE AREA: According to Dr. Irwin Redlener of Montefiore Medical Center and The Children's Health Fund in New York (see note for page 33), asthma "remains unabated" in the area and, indeed, "seems to be worsening." Hospitalizations for asthma in Mott Haven and contiguous neighborhoods in 1995 were 14 times as high as on the affluent East Side of Manhattan, according to *City Limits* (April 1998), and hospitalization rates in poor minority communities appear to have continued rising since. According to specialists at Mt. Sinai Medical Center (*New York Times,* July 27, 1999), hospitalization rates for asthma among children are "as much as 21 times higher in poor minority areas" of New York than in even "the hardest-hit areas of the more affluent communities."

JOHN ROSEN CITED: Dr. Rosen, a renowned specialist in the medical effects of environmental factors at Montefiore Medical Center, discussed toxic factors in the Port Morris, Mott Haven, and

Hunts Point areas in conversation with me in October 1996 and with my researcher Marilyn Weller in a follow-up discussion in November 1999.

CONCENTRATION OF WASTE INDUSTRIES IN HUNTS POINT: *City Limits,* June/July 1996. Also see *City Limits,* September/October 1999, and note for page 86.

Chapter Eight

98 PARENTAL ACTIVISM: One group of politically active women in the South Bronx is Mothers on the Move, who have shaken up many assumptions about parental "resignation" in the past five years. Mothers were also active in the protests that shut down the medical incinerator in the South Bronx (see chapter 7), have vigorously protested conditions in the Diego-Beekman buildings in which many of the St. Ann's children live, and are active in the education work begun in recent years in the South Bronx by ACORN (see note for page 217).

PEDIATRIC AND MATERNAL AIDS: Conversations with Dr. Irwin Redlener and his staff at the South Bronx Health Center, September 1999. (See note for page 3.)

99 OPTIMISTIC PRESS REPORTS ON SOUTH BRONX: See, for example, "Slouching Toward Utopia in the South Bronx," *New York Times,* December 5, 1993, and "A South Bronx Very Different from the Cliché," *New York Times,* February 14, 1999. By 1997, the recently built townhouses were selling for prices as high as $185,000 (*New York Times,* November 2, 1997), far beyond the means of the families in this book, whose typical yearly income is $10,000.

IMPROVEMENTS IN PEDIATRIC HEALTH AND PRIMARY CARE: See note for page 33.

IMPROVEMENTS IN PRIVATE COMMERCE: According to Bronx Borough President Fernando Ferrer, 32,000 new jobs have been created in the Bronx since 1994 (*New York Amsterdam News,* March 23/ March 31, 1999). During the same period, however, many previously existing jobs were lost as major employers left the area. Kitchenware manufacturer Farberware, for example, closed its plant in Mott Haven in 1996 (*New York Times,* April 10, 1997), taking away some 700 jobs in what had been the borough's largest factory. Farberware's departure was followed shortly after by that of another major manufacturer (*New York Times,* April 4, 1997), leaving an additional 200 workers without jobs. On balance, there have been net gains, according to Ferrer, who believes there will be more gains in the years ahead, especially in industries that process and recycle trash, which he expects to be one answer to the loss of jobs in manufacturing; and his intention, as he expressed it in a speech in March of 1999, is to "spin garbage into gold," according to *The New York Daily News,* March 11, 1999. The Bronx, however, according to the same story in *The Daily News,* is already "particularly hard-hit in handling the flow of the city's garbage."

108   "ORDINARY RESURRECTIONS": The words are those of Reverend Robert C. Morris, an Episcopal priest in the diocese of Newark and director of an interfaith education center, known as Interweave, which is based in Summit, New Jersey, where I met with Reverend Morris in October 1998. He is quoted in part from our conversation and in part from an essay, "The Advent of Resurrection," which appeared in *Weavings,* November/December 1997.

Chapter Nine

113   96 YOUNG MEN AND WOMEN ARRESTED IN THE EARLY MORNING: The mass arrests, long in preparation by the federal Drug Enforcement Agency, took place on December 17, 1996. See New York City Police Department press release, " 'Operation Triple Play' Dismantles Twelve Drug Gangs," December 17, 1996. Also see *The New York Times,* December 18, 1996.

114   "THE MOTHER, SON, AND FOSTER FATHER": This was spoken by a child in the kindergarten of St. Augustine's School on Franklin Avenue in the Bronx.

116   TEACHING FIFTH GRADE IN THE PUBLIC SCHOOLS OF NEWTON, MASSACHUSETTS, AFTER AN INITIAL STINT IN BOSTON: I first taught fourth grade in Boston in 1964–1965, then ran a freedom school, based in a church in the same neighborhood of Dorchester, which also served children in the bordering neighborhood of Roxbury, in 1965 and 1966. From 1966 to 1968, I taught fifth grade in the Davis School in Newton, Massachusetts, which was one of the first districts to participate in a suburban busing program, known as METCO, which continues to this day. From 1968 to 1973, I was one of the teachers and directors of The Storefront Learning Center in Boston's South End, where my initial co-directors were Bessie Washington and Thelma Burns.

119   "DESTRUCTIVE FORMS OF CONSCIENTIOUSNESS": In writing of "the general problem of man's exploitability in childhood," including not only the "overt cruelty" to which a child may be subjected but also other forms of injury such as "sly righteousness" in adults, Erik Erikson speaks of "the life principle of trust," without which, he says, "every human act, may it feel ever so good and seem ever so right, is prone to perversion by destructive forms of conscientiousness." Erik Erikson, *Young Man Luther* (New York: Norton, 1958).

    MR. ROGERS'S OBSERVATIONS ABOUT SILENCE: These comments were made in June of 1998, in Washington, D.C., first at a luncheon hosted by the Annenberg Public Policy Center, then at greater length while we were waiting in National Airport for our planes, a noisy place in which to have a talk with a soft-spoken man about the possibilities of silence.

Chapter Ten

122   HOW MY CONVERSATIONS WITH THE CHILDREN BEGIN: On some occasions, children ask in advance if we can focus on a subject of immediate concern or one we've talked about before. On other occasions, I introduce a subject we've discussed before because I'm eager to pursue a point one of the children may have made to which I know I hadn't been attentive or responsive. Almost all these conversations overlap with earlier or later conversations; many were condensed, and some combined, in editing these passages.

125   "DO YOU KNOW YOUR FATHER'S NAME?": This question, or one much like it, comes up often among children in the neighborhood, as I've noted elsewhere in this book and in *Amazing Grace*. Discussions of "knowing the face" of a parent (or the face of God) come up often, as well, and are worded often in phrasing that suggests the children's immersion in Biblical language.

Chapter Eleven

137   INVESTMENT LANGUAGE IN SPEAKING OF CHILDREN: O. Bradford Butler, former board chairman of Procter & Gamble, is cited from "Securing Our Futures: A Report of the National Forum for Youth at Risk," Education Commission of the States, September 1988.
"INVESTING IN FUTURES": *The Boston Globe,* March 1, 1989.

138   DEMOGRAPHICS OF STUYVESANT HIGH SCHOOL IN NEW YORK: See *Amazing Grace,* cited above, pages 152 to 154, and "Secret Apartheid II," New York ACORN Schools Office, May 5, 1997.

139   INNER-CITY CHILDREN PERCEIVED AS ENTRY-LEVEL WORKERS: See also notes for pages 238 and 239.

141   NO LEVEL PLAYING FIELD IN EDUCATIONAL COMPETITION: For a brief, firsthand perspective on the two systems, racially and economically distinct, within a single New York City neighborhood, see Katha Pollitt in *The Nation,* June 8, 1998. The growing tendency of wealthy parents in New York to hire private tutors or examination coaches to prepare their elementary-level children for the newly instituted state exams creates another level of inequality. Private agencies also provide expensive programs to give applicants to schools like Stuyvesant High an extra edge on their exams and to coach college applicants for SATs, in some cases at costs as high as $300 an hour (*New York Times,* January 9 and April 9, 1999).

Chapter Twelve

145, 146   MEDICAID AND FOOD STAMPS CUT OFF WITHOUT WOMAN BEING GIVEN REASON: By federal law, Medicaid and food stamp eligibility is determined on the basis of income and is unrelated to a person's status in the welfare system. In New York City, however, starting, it seems, in 1997, welfare workers began a practice of removing people from all benefits when cutting their subsistence income and failed to advise them that they could continue to receive food stamps and Medicaid by filing separate applications. Several cases were filed to reverse this policy, which was applied also to people applying for benefits for the first time. For case summaries: Welfare Law Center, 275 Seventh Avenue, New York, NY 10001.

146, 147   TREATMENT OF HOMELESS FAMILIES AT EMERGENCY SHELTER: The Emergency Assistance Unit, run by the city of New York, is not legally permitted to leave homeless families on the floor at night, according to Dr. Irwin Redlener (see note for page 33); but this has been its practice for many years. For background on the way homeless families have been treated at the city's emergency units for more than a decade, see my book *Rachel and Her Children* (New York: Crown, 1988).

147, 148   FOOD PANTRY AND SOUP KITCHEN AT ST. ANN'S: There are three primary sources for the food provided by the church: 1) Food for Survival, a food bank that provides imperishables contributed by supermarket chains and large food corporations; 2) City Harvest, an organization that receives perishable foods, which are leftovers from downtown parties and conventions and overstock from specialty shops; 3) suburban churches, which now and then deliver baked goods such as bread and other foods.

152   SHENTASHA'S SERIOUS PROBLEMS: The child's identity is heavily disguised. Time factors and other details have been changed, as in some other situations in this narrative. Shentasha is no longer living in the neighborhood.

154   PRISON BARGE FOR JUVENILES IN SOUTH BRONX: The Vernon C. Bain prison barge in Hunts Point, purchased by the city for $150 million in 1992 (see *Amazing Grace*, cited above) and previously used exclusively for adult inmates, was put into use for children a few years ago after Spofford juvenile detention center in Hunts Point was closed (see note for page 52). In 1998, the city held a total of 6,497 children between the ages of seven and fifteen in detention at one point or other in the course of the year. Of these, 5,173, all thirteen years old or older, were held in secure detention. All male detainees in secure detention were held on the barge for the first ten days — about 100 at a time. The annual cost of keeping a child in secure detention in New York in 1998 (see subsequent note) was $93,000. Average city-wide expenditure per pupil in the New York City public schools in 1998 was $8,213; and the actual expenditure per pupil in a mainstream third-grade classroom was $5,200 (see notes for page 45). After the Spofford facility is reopened in January 2000, the prison barge, according to city officials, will no longer be used for children. ("Juvenile Detention in New York City," a fact summary

released by The Correctional Association of New York, September 30, 1999.)

155 PRISON STATISTICS AND EXPENDITURES: There are 70,000 inmates in the New York State prison system, over 10 percent of whom are HIV-infected (*New York Times,* February 18, 1999) and 83 percent of whom are black or Hispanic (Elizabeth Gaynes, The Osborne Association, see below). The present number of inmates represents a nearly six-fold increase in the prison population over 1973, when there were 12,500 inmates in state prisons in New York. There are, at any given time, some 20,000 inmates in the New York City jails, most of them on Rikers Island. The city's cost per adult inmate is $64,000 yearly. For juvenile detention, costs run from $78,000 yearly for nonsecure detention to $93,000 for secure detention (three fourths of juvenile detainees are in secure detention). Blacks and Hispanics make up 92 percent of inmates in the city's jails and 95 percent of children in detention, according to Gaynes (correspondence with the author, October 1999). Only 10 percent of city inmates have received high school diplomas or a GED, again according to Gaynes, who is director of The Osborne Association in New York City, which operates in conjunction with The Correctional Association of New York and represents the most reliable source of data on the inmate population of the state and city. According to The Correctional Association, there are now more black and Hispanic people in state prisons in New York than in state universities (*New York Amsterdam News,* February 4/February 10, 1999). *The Washington Post* (December 4, 1998) reports, as well, that New York State now spends more money on its prison system than on its universities. See also "The Casualties of War," by Ellis Cose, in *Newsweek,* September 6, 1999.

Chapter Thirteen

160 TRIP TO WASHINGTON WITH SOUTH BRONX CHILDREN: May 31, 1996. The march on June 1, 1996, was organized by The Children's Defense Fund. A follow-up program, known as Stand for Children, coordinates the work of advocates in several states and is organized by Jonah Edelman. (Stand for Children may be reached at 1834 Connecticut Avenue, NW, Washington, D.C. 20009; phone: 1-800-663-4032; Web site: www.stand.org.)

164 DR. REDLENER'S INITIATIVES FOR CHILDREN IN NEW YORK: *New York Times,* February 27, 1998; *New York Daily News,* June 1, 1998; *New York Times,* July 24, 1999. (See also notes for pages 33 and 87.)

165ff. QUESTIONS OF DANGER IN EAST TREMONT AND MOTT HAVEN NEIGHBORHOODS: The 48th Precinct, which includes most of East Tremont, is one of the few in New York City in which homicide was on the increase in this period from 1997 to 1998 (*New York Times,* September 26, 1998). The 40th Precinct, which includes the St. Ann's neighborhood, seemed to have become safer in these years.

166 TEACHER AT TAFT HIGH SCHOOL MURDERED: The death of this highly admired teacher, Jonathan Levin, is reported in *The New York Times,* June 8, 1997.

Chapter Fourteen

172 THE WOLF WHO LIKED TO EAT: The story, which Miss Dukes tells partly in her own words, is "The Wolf's Chicken Stew," by Keiko Kaszà, included in a literature anthology entitled *Silly Things Happen* (Boston: Houghton Mifflin, 1991).

173 SCARCITY OF BOOKS: This is a less serious problem at P.S. 30 than at a number of other schools in low-income neighborhoods of New York City, because the principal, Miss Rosa, reallocates funds, whenever possible, to meet the most important needs. Still, teachers here, as elsewhere in the poorest sections of the city, spend their own funds often to provide their students with essentials. Many also buy books simply to infuse their classrooms with the richness of resources found in affluent communities.

174 PARENTS IN WEALTHIER NEIGHBORHOODS RAISE MONEY INDEPENDENTLY TO SUPPLEMENT SCHOOL BUDGETS: *New York Times,* July 23, 1995; June 17, 1996; September 20, 24, 25, 28, and October 8, 1997.

RACIAL DEMOGRAPHICS OF P.S. 30 AT THE TIME I WAS VISITING MISS DUKES'S SECOND GRADE: Approximately 30 percent of the children were black and 70 percent Hispanic, with some children having parents who are both black and Hispanic.

175 "BORROW," "CARRY OVER," "EXCHANGE," "REGROUP": Isaiah's teacher, Mr. Geiger, who is a talented math teacher, notes that the latter two terms provide more accurate descriptions of what's really going on in these transactions and that one of his goals is to be sure the children understand the processes involved in reaching a result. Sound mathematical instruction, however, isn't the only reason why the classroom terminology has changed in New York City. Another reason, teachers tell me, is that children are obliged to recognize the new terms on their state examinations.

176 "P.S. 30 HOLDS 900 CHILDREN": In September 1999, enrollment rose to nearly 1,100 when another school nearby was closed and many of its students were reassigned to P.S. 30.

183ff. BILINGUAL KINDERGARTEN TAUGHT BY CARMEN SUAREZ: My description of the back-and-forth between English and Spanish may not make clear the careful way this conscientious teacher separates the languages in presentation of a lesson. The lesson on the English vowels, for example, was part of one unit of instruction. The subsequent lesson in which children write words on the board beginning with various letters was part of a separate unit, taught primarily in Spanish. Miss Suarez speaks conversationally to children in both languages; but the lessons are taught separately.

184, 185   THE LAMB WHO IS LOOKING FOR HIS MOTHER: The children read this book in two editions, one in English, *Who Will Be My Mother,* written by Joy Cowley and illustrated by Rita Parkinson (Auckland: Shorthand Publications, 1983), and one in a Spanish adaptation by Patricia Almada (Auckland: Shorthand Publications, 1987). I've translated parts of the Spanish into English as the lesson was proceeding, but Miss Suarez reads the story in one language, then the other.

186   SCHOOL PHYSICIANS TAKEN FROM THE ELEMENTARY SCHOOLS: In 1970, 400 doctors tended to the health of children in the New York City public schools. By 1993, the number had been cut to 23, most of them part-time. (*New York Daily News,* June 22, 1993.) Since that time, some clinics have been reestablished in the high schools and, by 1999, about one tenth of New York City's public schools, almost all of them secondary schools, had clinics staffed by nurse practitioners, most of them affiliated with hospitals such as Montefiore Medical Center in the Bronx. Dr. Irwin Redlener and his colleague Dr. Alan Shapiro (see note for page 33) believe that school-based clinics, staffed by nurse practitioners who work in liaison with physicians at community health centers, represent an ideal model for addressing health needs in the public schools. The state, however, has recently placed a moratorium on school-based clinics and intends to phase out funding for these programs in the spring of 2000. (*New York Times,* April 21, 1999.)

SEASONED INTUITION AMONG TEACHERS AT P.S. 30: Among the experienced teachers who have taught some of the St. Ann's children are Lorna Danvers, Sandra Hernandez, Rita Zarensky, Laurie Berger, Luis Quinones, Edith Simmons, Regina Uffer, Alicia Reitmann, Barry Geiger, Maria Stratageus, Jasmin Harrinarine, and two younger but already seasoned and proficient teachers named Susan Lopez and Sylvia Gross. Miss Rosa has demonstrated a rare gift for attracting and maintaining a core group of highly committed teachers, including these and others mentioned elsewhere in this book, and many others whose classes I had not yet visited during the time this narrative takes place.

Chapter Fifteen

195   INNER-CITY SCHOOL IN WHICH I TAUGHT IN BOSTON: I described this school in *Death at an Early Age* (Boston: Houghton Mifflin, 1967).

198   THE TEACHER THE CHILDREN CALL "MISS G": Angela Gallombardo is now a teacher specializing in instructional uses of computers at a middle school in the South Bronx.

200   HIGH TURN-OVER OF TEACHERS AT P.S. 65; MATH AND READING SCORES; OTHER INFORMATION ABOUT THE SCHOOL: P.S. 65 was one of ten troubled schools in New York City taken over by

Chancellor Rudy Crew in April 1996. According to *Education Week* (March 25, 1998), the "reconstituted" school was required to emphasize test preparation, do intensive work on literacy, provide pre-kindergarten whenever possible, develop an integrated arts program, add books to its library, reduce class size, and upgrade technology. Some of these goals — the emphasis on tests, the upgrade of technology, and improvement of the library — have been fulfilled; and I am told that a number of the children now receive a half-day of pre-kindergarten. *Education Week* observes, however, that the school began the fall of 1996 with 28 first-year teachers in a staff of 50 and that half these 28 teachers left the school in June of 1997. Scores in math and reading rose in the initial aftermath of Dr. Crew's reforms, but then declined on tests administered in spring of 1999 (*New York Daily News,* June 10, 1999), although the test scores later were alleged to be inaccurate because of errors in the ways they were computed. A veteran teacher at the school confides in me that an obsessive pressure to drill students solely for examinations has been taking a high toll on the morale of faculty — "It forces me to be an automaton," this talented and highly personable teacher says — but that a number of good teachers and some excellent paraprofessionals from the community remain at P.S. 65 as this book goes to press.

200, 201   PINEAPPLE'S FOUR TEACHERS: The fourth of her four teachers, Josefina Díaz, whom I've had an opportunity to talk with and observe, stabilized the class and is remembered with gratitude by Pineapple.

201   NONWHITE NEW YORK CITY NEIGHBORHOODS ARE ASSIGNED THE LARGEST NUMBERS OF UNCERTIFIED INSTRUCTORS: "There is a direct connection between uncertified teachers, minority neighborhoods, and schools with low scores" in New York City, notes David Jones, President of the Community Service Society in New York. The lowest scoring school districts in 1999, he observes, were in Mott Haven, Morrisania, and the Tremont sections of the South Bronx, and in Central Harlem, "all black and Hispanic neighborhoods, all with 25 to 30 percent uncertified teachers." At P.S. 57 in the Bronx, he writes, "where 94 percent of fourth-graders failed to meet state standards on the reading test, 36 percent of the teachers are uncertified." At P.S. 27, where 92 percent of students failed to meet the standards, "58 percent of teachers were uncertified." There was a time, he continues, when the city's schools "provided a free education that helped to lift generations of New Yorkers out of poverty and into the middle class. That was when the system educated mostly white European immigrants. Now the student population is overwhelmingly black and Hispanic, and it is underfunded and ignored by the state." ("The Urban Agenda," column by David Jones, *The New York Amsterdam News,* November 18–November 24, 1999.)

202 CHANCELLOR OF NEW YORK CITY SCHOOLS TAKES OVER P.S. 65:
See note for page 200.

Chapter Sixteen

208 FREEDOM SCHOOL IN BOSTON: The program, which I directed
jointly with a community leader named Julia Walker and a very
close friend, Rebecca Morris, was based in a small church on
East Cottage Street in Dorchester and ran from roughly two P.M.,
when public school let out, to ten P.M. or later in the evening.
Highly committed parents in the neighborhood, some of whom
I'd come to know in the preceding year when I was teaching
fourth grade in a local public school, helped us rent and paint a
few apartments on a nearby street, where classes were conducted
to relieve the overcrowding in the church itself. A mixture of
politically motivated activists from the community, some of whom
had worked in civil rights campaigns, and intellectuals from Cambridge and suburban areas, including instructors from MIT and
Harvard and a talented young writer named John Leonard who
would later become a well-known literary editor and critic, and
several older women organized by synagogues and churches, as
well as student volunteers from Milton Academy and Groton,
came in shifts to tutor children individually or in small groups.
The program, like several others in other politically committed
churches in the black community of Boston, grew out of the
protest movement that had spread to Boston from the South in
the preceding years.

212 "A LION IN A ZOO" BY LANGSTON HUGHES: Published posthu-
mously in book form in *The Sweet and Sour Animal Book* (New
York: Oxford University Press, 1994).

214 P.S. 30 CONSISTENTLY SCORES HIGH COMPARED TO OTHER
SCHOOLS IN THE SOUTH BRONX: In spring of 1999, for instance,
P.S. 30 ranked fourth highest in its reading scores among the fifteen elementary schools of District 7 (including P.S. 65, which was
temporarily under the governance of Dr. Crew). Of the three elementary schools that scored higher, two were schools for talented
and gifted children. (The city-wide scores were published in *The
New York Daily News,* June 10, 1999.)
FEW OF THE CHILDREN ARE ADMITTED TO HEAD START: Only
17,000 children in New York City, according to *City Limits* (*Fax
Weekly,* September 9, 1996), were enrolled in Head Start in the
years when the children at P.S. 30 were preschoolers. The excellent preschool run by P.S. 30, in a separate building from the
school, can accommodate only a fraction of the eligible children.
Conversations with parents and teachers indicate that less than a
third of the youngsters in the neighborhood get any kind of education prior to their kindergarten year. Even kindergarten is not
mandatory in New York.

215   LARGE CLASS SIZE IN FOURTH AND FIFTH GRADES AT P.S. 30 IN
FALL OF 1999: The chancellor's decision to close a failing public
school nearby (see note for page 176) led to the addition of more
than 150 children to the student population of P.S. 30. Miss Rosa
insisted on lowering class size in the primary grades to as close as
possible to 20 children; but this priority (a good one, given the
options) led to several upper-level classes ranging between 31 and
35 when school began.

  OVERCROWDED CLASSES IN NEW YORK: Elementary school classes
holding as many as 43 children and, in one instance in the
Bronx, a kindergarten class with 50 pupils were reported by the
press in 1996 and 1997. High school classes were reported to
be very large as well. At Evander Childs High School in the
Bronx, for instance, "dozens of classes . . . had more than 34 students," as *The Times* noted, while the teachers' union reported
classes at John F. Kennedy High School in the Bronx beginning the year with 45 and 54 students (*New York Times,* September 5, 6, and 14, 1996; January 3, 1997). New York, according
to *The Times'* Joyce Purnick (April 29, 1996), needed 93 new
schools "just to relieve the present overcrowding," but she noted
that not one high school had been built for children in the Bronx
since 1973. For further information on endemic overcrowding in
Bronx schools, see *Savage Inequalities,* cited above; *The New York
Daily News,* September 26, 1996; and *City Limits,* August/Sep-
tember 1997.

215, 216   WHAT WOULD BE POSSIBLE AT P.S. 30 WITH A PER-PUPIL BUD-
GET AT THE LEVEL OF GREAT NECK OR MANHASSET IF IT ALSO
HAD COMPARABLE PHYSICAL FACILITIES: In 1997–1998 (see note
for page 45), New York City spent about $8,200 per pupil, includ-
ing special education, and an actual sum of $5,200 per pupil in a
mainstream elementary classroom. In the same year, Great Neck
spent about $18,000 and Manhasset nearly $20,000. Even after
recognizing that figures in Great Neck and Manhasset were considerably lower, as in New York City, for mainstream classrooms
than for special education, it is still apparent that principals in
Great Neck and Manhasset had more than twice as much as principals in New York City did to spend per pupil in their mainstream classrooms. If Miss Rosa had had twice what she had in
resources in that academic year, per pupil, she would have
had nearly $4.7 million more than she, in fact, did have. Even
if increased administrative costs and overhead and indirect ex-
penses such as payroll benefits for staff consumed as much as
25 percent of this, a very large sum would remain for use in direct
services to children. Increased resources of only $3 million, for
example, would make possible the hiring of 25 already well-
experienced teachers at the current maximum salary of $60,000
each, making possible class size of 18 or fewer children in all
classrooms at the school, as well as a year of developmental

preschool for about 200 children who are presently unserved, using a very high per-pupil estimate of $8,000 for a year of preschool education. A good deal of money, clearly, would remain to meet some of the other needs I have referred to in the text. All of this lies in the realm of fantasy for South Bronx principals today; and class-size reduction would remain impossible, in any case, unless the physical facilities of P.S. 30 were enormously expanded. Twenty-five extra classrooms would require a new building. Even ten extra classrooms are impossible within the building as it stands.

216 MIDDLE SCHOOL ACROSS THE STREET FROM P.S. 30: Last year (1998–1999) was said to be an especially bad one at the school, which is called I.S. 139. Academic work appeared to be in disarray, and police cars were arriving frequently. The assignment of a new principal this year (1999–2000) has, however, reawakened guarded optimism.

A BETTER MIDDLE SCHOOL ON ST. ANN'S AVENUE: I.S. 162, at East 149th Street and St. Ann's Avenue, is also known as the Lola Rodriguez de Tió Academy of Future Technologies. The one child from St. Ann's who attended the school in September 1999 said that only a small number of kids from P.S. 30 were admitted. In a visit to this highly attractive and apparently successful school in 1998, I saw only a handful of children from the St. Ann's area. The principal confirmed my impression that few had applied or been enrolled.

217 MORRIS HIGH SCHOOL STATISTICS: According to the "Annual School Report, 1997–98," of the New York City Board of Education, Division of Assessment and Accountability, Morris High enrolled a total of 1,896 students in October 1998. Of this number, 1,196 students were in ninth grade, while only 86 students were in twelfth grade. On average, according to Michael Nemoytin, head of the English department at the school, 50 to 70 students graduate each year. Nemoytin's estimate is consistent with the Board of Education's "Four-year Longitudinal Report" (class of 1998), which indicates that 66 students in the class received diplomas. The Board of Education reports an unofficial drop-out rate of less than 25 percent for Morris High, because a large number of students are classified under the category "discharged" and therefore not included in the drop-out figures. The class of 1998 began, for example, with 465 students who were classified as "entering" ninth-graders in 1994. Of these, 66 received diplomas in 1998, 120 did not graduate but remained enrolled, 54 were listed as "drop-outs," and 225 others were listed as "discharged." The total of "discharges" and "drop-outs," according to these school board figures, was more than four times as large as the number of students who graduated. By far the largest class at the school is the ninth grade, which includes both entering ninth-graders and those repeating, sometimes for a second time. I've known very good teachers and administrators at the school, which

I have visited on several occasions between 1990 and 1999. New York City tracking patterns, however, render Morris High the school of last resort for many children who attend deficient middle schools. (See also subsequent note for page 217.)

DENIAL OF CHOICE OF HIGH SCHOOL AMONG CHILDREN IN THE NEIGHBORHOOD: A series of well-documented studies of this process have been published by an experienced advocacy group called ACORN. See especially *Secret Apartheid,* New York ACORN Schools Office, April 15, 1996, and *Secret Apartheid II,* New York ACORN Schools Office, May 5, 1997. *Secret Apartheid II* documents the account I was given by Reverend Overall concerning high school applications by the children from the St. Ann's neighborhood. "Honor roll students at Junior High School 139 in the Mott Haven section of the South Bronx . . . ," ACORN notes, "were rejected from all eight of the high schools they had listed on their application forms." The education these children had received, says ACORN, "was for the track to Morris High. . . ." (For further information from this dynamic community-based organization: New York ACORN Schools Office, 845 Flatbush Avenue, Brooklyn, NY 11226.)

217, 218   MOTHER MARTHA CAN SOMETIMES INTERVENE TO HELP THE CHILDREN GET INTO A BETTER SECONDARY SCHOOL: Teachers intervene as well. Mr. Bedrock tells me, for example, of two children he recommended to a racially integrated middle school near the United Nations building in Manhattan. Miss Rosa's special assistant, Eileen Costello, tells me of other children from P.S. 30 who have won admission to good high schools in Manhattan or to unusually good small high schools in the Bronx and later went to four-year colleges. The numbers of those who win these opportunities are very low, however.

Chapter Seventeen

220   JOHN HOLT CITED: The author of several influential books on children, including *How Children Learn* (New York: Dell, 1983), Holt taught writing and English literature, as I did also, in 1965 and 1966 in a program called the Urban School, which was, essentially, an early prototype for Upward Bound and took place in the summers at the Commonwealth School in Boston. Holt and I remained close in subsequent years during a time when Thelma Burns and I were organizing the Storefront Learning Center in Boston's South End and Holt would visit periodically for evening seminars we held for parents and teenagers.

220, 221   ROBERT COLES: See especially *The Political Life of Children* (Boston: Atlantic Monthly Press, 1986) and *The Moral Life of Children* (Boston: Atlantic Monthly Press, 1991).

Chapter Eighteen

233 PARENTS ARE MADE TO FEEL WELCOME AT P.S. 30: The school has a strong community coordinator, named Maria Acevedo, and Miss Rosa has a socially committed special assistant, named Eileen Costello; but virtually all staff members at the school, including security guards, custodians, and secretaries, who represent the front line in school offices, are welcoming to parents. Running a school, Miss Rosa told me once, "is more art than knowledge," and nowhere is this more apparent than in the receptive atmosphere she has created for the parents of the neighborhood and in her responsiveness to their concerns. Teachers who are having hard times in their lives know they can turn to her as well. An unselfish and affectionate woman, she is, like most great principals, a uniquely original person who will not be easily replaced.

234, 235 ISAIAH ASKS ME TO VISIT HIS HOME AFTER SCHOOL: The time reference here ("six months ago"), like all such references, applies to the time I wrote this, not the time of publication.

237 PINEAPPLE'S DIET: She has given me permission to divulge this.

238 MEMORIAL CARD FOR BOY FROM MORRIS HIGH SCHOOL: His name was Roberto Robles. His killing took place in March of 1994.

238, 239 TIMEKA'S MIDDLE SCHOOL: I.S. 183, The Paul Robeson Magnet School for Medical Careers and Health Professions, is not a magnet school in the commonly accepted sense of one that draws together students from a variety of racial groups, but a classically segregated school with hard-working teachers, impoverished students, and rock-bottom scores.

239 "SCHOOL-TO-WORK" IN NEW YORK CITY: The city's middle schools in low-income communities seem to be moving more and more in the direction of what is called "industry-specific" education. "Embedding these schools within industry," says Dr. Crew, "gives us the chance to restructure the way sixth through eighth graders are taught." (*Imagine, The Chancellor's Newsletter,* Spring 1999.)

Chapter Nineteen

245 VESPERS AT ST. ANN'S: "Vespers" refers here to the timing of the service, not the liturgy. The liturgy that Reverend Overall uses for vespers is actually the one prescribed for "compline" (last prayers of the night) in The Book of Common Prayer.

246 "A SPACE OF LIBERTY, OF SILENCE": Thomas Merton is cited from *The Asian Journals of Thomas Merton* (New York: New Directions, 1973).

247 SEWAGE PROCESSED IN WEST HARLEM: *New York Times,* November 30, 1989; June 22 and September 1, 1992; April 18 and May 28, 1993; February 4, 1995; and *New York Daily News,* editorial, July 5, 1994.

248   "AN UNAMBIGUOUS, PLAIN-SPOKEN WORD LIKE 'SEGREGATION'" SELDOM USED BY NEW YORK CITY PRESS IN REFERENCE TO NEW YORK: An honorable exception is *The New York Daily News,* which, with refreshing candor, uses the word straightforwardly where it applies, as, for example, in a famous front-page headline, "Segregated at Birth," describing the racial segregation of maternity wards at prestigious Mount Sinai Hospital some years ago. (*New York Daily News,* October 18, 1993.)

249   PAULO FREIRE CITED: The exiled Brazilian educator, whom I met initially in Mexico, lived in Cambridge, Massachusetts in 1969 and in Switzerland for much of the time from 1970 to 1980. He frequently returned to the United States during those years, however. The conversation cited here took place in 1979. Freire, who died in Brazil in 1998, is best known among North Americans for *The Pedagogy of the Oppressed* (New York: Continuum, 1981).

250   PAUL PARKS CITED: A former president of the Boston NAACP and, at a later time, secretary of education of the State of Massachusetts, Parks was one of the leading figures in the civil rights campaigns in Boston, beginning in the 1960s.

257, 258   MARGE PIERCY CITED: "To Be of Use," published in a collection of the work of several poets, *Cries of the Spirit,* edited by Marilyn Sewell (Boston: Beacon Press, 1991).

Chapter Twenty

267, 268   USE OF RITALIN: Arguments against the medicating of children with Ritalin and similar drugs are presented in *Ritalin Is Not the Answer,* by David Stein (San Francisco: Jossey-Bass, 1999) and *Talking Back to Ritalin,* by Peter Breggin (Monroe, Maine: Common Courage Press, 1998). Dr. Alan Shapiro, who directs the South Bronx Health Center (see note for page 33), defends the use of Ritalin with children in appropriate situations and believes that it is not overused, but probably underused, in poor minority communities. He also believes that parental anxieties in regard to drugs like Ritalin, although understandable for reasons rooted in social and medical history, can work against the interests of children who would benefit from these drugs. I nonetheless subscribe to the concerns that Otto's mother has expressed.

269   HOMELESS SHELTER IN MANHATTAN: The Prince George Hotel, its management, and its ownership by South African investors are discussed in my book *Rachel and Her Children,* cited above.

Chapter Twenty-one

275   VISIT TO APRIL GAMBLE'S CLASS AT P.S. 28: The principal of the school, Edvige Mancuso, told me at the time of a more recent visit, in June 1999, that the school remains overcrowded and that the building, which was erected in 1897, is still in need of repair. Fresh paint, however, has cheered up corridors and ceilings, and

there are now both art and music programs in the building. This year or next, she tells me, there will be a clinic in the school.

280   DISMANTLING OF ART AND MUSIC PROGRAMS IN THE NEW YORK CITY ELEMENTARY SCHOOLS: "From the city's fiscal crisis of the 1970s until the late 1990s," notes a newsletter to parents from New York Schools Chancellor Rudy Crew, "the vast majority of our schools were without arts teachers and arts programs. An entire generation of . . . students suffered through this 'Dark Age.'" Since 1997, with the help of charitable groups such as the Annenberg Foundation and the Center for Arts Education, art programs have been partially restored, while a number of other charitable groups, including a foundation created by cable channel VH1, have done their best to stitch together music programs in some schools. A patchwork, in effect, of mostly charitable or grant-supported programs in both art and music, which principals piece together as they can, substitutes today for what was once a systematic portion of curriculum. Stefan Zucker, an administrator at P.S. 30, notes that when he began to teach in New York City elementary schools in 1969, "every school had a full-time licensed art and music teacher and librarian." In the mid-1970s, he says, "I saw all of that destroyed."

DISMANTLING OF SCHOOL LIBRARIES: "Since the mid-1970s, as budget cuts have forced schools to lay off librarians . . . and overcrowding has eaten up space, elementary school libraries across New York City have disappeared," says *The New York Times* (March 11, 1996), citing the Fund for New York City Public Education. The immediate precipitating cause of these and other cutbacks in the schools was New York City's fiscal crisis in the 1970s (see preceding note); but even now, with recent municipal surpluses of $2 billion (1998) and $1.4 billion (1997), according to *The New York Times* (April 23, 1998), the city has not restored these programs. P.S. 30 is the exception to the rule in having a good-sized library which is staffed full-time by a library director, named Maria Rodriguez, who works sometimes in collaboration with story-readers from the local public libraries and is assisted by student interns from a local high school.

281ff.   MR. BEDROCK'S TEACHING STYLE: He asked me to be sure to speak here of a teacher he refers to as his mentor, named Maria Stratageus, who also teaches, or has taught, a number of the children from St. Ann's. A glowing teacher with a natural affinity for children and a strong no-nonsense style in the classroom, she, like Mrs. Harrinarine and several other teachers mentioned here, would be a stand-out on the faculty of any elementary school.

Chapter Twenty-two

285 JOHN HOLT: See note for page 220.

295 TRIAGE SOLUTIONS: See, for example, "Bad Lessons," an op/ed essay by Charles Murray, in *The New York Times,* January 8, 1993. "STRAIT IS THE GATE AND NARROW IS THE WAY": Matthew 8:14, King James Bible.

Chapter Twenty-three

301, 302 TEACHER SALARIES IN NEW YORK CITY AND SURROUNDING SUB-URBS: Salaries for teachers rose during the decade, but the gap between the city and its wealthy suburbs has remained unchanged or widened slightly. In the fall of 1993, for instance, starting salaries were $27,000 in New York, but $42,000 in Great Neck and Scarsdale. Median salaries were $43,000 in New York, but $71,000 in Great Neck and Scarsdale. Maximum salaries were $54,000 in New York, but $80,000 in Great Neck and $81,000 in Scarsdale. Even significantly less affluent suburbs paid higher salaries than New York City did. The *average* salary paid to veteran teachers with advanced degrees throughout Westchester County was $24,000 higher than the salary paid veteran teachers with advanced degrees in New York during this time. Nearly three years later, in spring of 1996, pay scales in the city still were far behind those in exclusive suburbs. By that time, the most highly qualified teachers in Scarsdale were receiving $99,000, and those in comparably wealthy White Plains and Mamaroneck $92,000, while the highest salary in New York City remained $60,000. Maximum salaries for teachers in the city now, in 1999, according to Aida Rosa, principal of P.S. 30, are $64,000 and will rise in the year 2000 to $70,000 — nearly $30,000 less than what an experienced teacher in Scarsdale was earning four years earlier. (For these statistics, and those in the text, I have relied upon data from the New York State Education Department, Information, Reporting, and Technology Services; a clarifying memo of September 16, 1999, from Ellen Zebrowski, Assistant in Educational Data Systems at the New York State Department of Education; *The New York Times,* January 18, 1995; and interviews with Angela Gallombardo, teacher at P.S. 65; Aida Rosa, principal of P.S. 30; Michael Nemoytin, English Department chair at Morris High; and other teachers.)

303 CHILD WHOSE UNCLE AND MOTHER WERE ASSASSINATED: The child's identity has been disguised, as are the identities of all children in this book.

305 GRADUATING FIFTH-GRADE STUDENTS: Some of the graduating children were able to remain at P.S. 30 in a program called Mott Haven Village, which is under the direction of Stefan Zucker and which now (autumn 1999) extends to eighth grade.

313 MISS DUKES IS WORRIED THAT CLASS SIZE WILL RISE: Class size did

rise for the upper grades, but not until the fall of 1999 (see note for page 215). Miss Dukes, however, has a second grade of 22 children in this, the 1999–2000 academic year.

Epilogue

319 MOTT HAVEN VILLAGE: See note for page 305.

320 STAFF AT ST. ANN'S CHANGES AND EXPANDS: By late autumn of 1999, there were thirteen grown-ups tending eighty children in the afterschool. The present educational coordinator is a bilingual educator of Ecuadoran origin who carries on the program in a form consistent with the one described within this narrative, but with continuing innovations.

THE CHURCH RELIES FOR ITS INCOME ON OUTSIDE SUPPORT: The primary sources are the Episcopal Diocese of New York and charitable gifts and grants from individuals and other donors.

TEENAGERS WHO COME BACK TO HELP AS TUTORS: One is the boy described in chapter 16 under the pseudonym of Benjamin. Now doing well at secondary school outside the Bronx, he has become a skillful and empathetic mentor to the younger children. Fourteen teenagers, including Benjamin, now participate also in an advanced tutorial program at the church.

325 "GOD IS LOCKING OUT FOR YOU": This is the child's spelling.

328 INNOCENT MAN SHOT BY POLICE: The death of Amadou Diallo, who was an immigrant from West Africa, the reactions of New Yorkers, and the mass arrests of advocates and ordinary citizens and members of the clergy are described in *The New York Daily News,* February 13, 1999; *The New York Times,* February 13, 14, 15, and March 29, 1999; and *The New York Amsterdam News,* February 11/February 17, 1999.

OTHER TRAGEDIES IN THE SOUTH BRONX: Some are noted in *The New York Times,* May 27, 1999, and in *The Bronx Times* (police blotter), May 27, 1999.

330 TEACHERS' REACTIONS TO THE DEATH OF CHILDREN IN THEIR CLASSES: See, for example, *Amazing Grace,* cited above.

331 "IS IT BECAUSE THERE ARE NO GRAVES IN EGYPT": Exodus 14:11, in the pastor's wording.

334 "THE BODY OF CHRIST, THE BREAD OF HEAVEN": The Episcopal liturgy for Easter is in The Book of Common Prayer (New York: Church Hymnal Corporation, 1979).

ACKNOWLEDGMENTS

In giving thanks to those, especially the children, whose stories have been told within this book, I would like to take a moment first to speak about the ones whose stories were left out or told only in fragments that cannot do justice to the qualities of voice and depth of feeling with which they were told to me. A book of episodic memoirs based on hundreds of small bits and pieces of recaptured conversation with high-spirited and energetic children cannot fail to be selective; and this isn't always by intention. There's simply an inevitable element of randomness in terms of which words spoken by a child captivate my interest, which ones I hear clearly and write down completely, which ones I partly miss, and which ones I don't hear at all — or hear but, being caught up in the conversation, do not bother to write down.

It's easier to get it right when conversations simmer slowly. When children get excited by their own ideas and are competing for my full attention with some other kids who want to speak at the same time, I have to scramble to keep up with them. In these cases, I have often asked a child to assist me by repeating something — "say that once more, slowly please" — or I've gone back to the same children later and restated what I heard in part and asked them to fill in the rest or to correct me if they thought I got it wrong.

It's easier to do this, obviously, with older children, or with someone like Pineapple whom I have a chance to talk with often and can briefly isolate at church and question carefully. Even then, there's always, inescapably, an element of the haphazard in the process since the children are no less delighted than most grown-ups are to make their statements more coherent or more lively, or more complicated, when they have a second chance. They also sometimes disagree with one another about who said what or, if it's something they can see I liked, which child said it first.

Many vivid episodes of idle banter, minor interchange, and serious discussion have, I know, been lost repeatedly as a result of the continually unexpected ways in which these conversations came about. Often there was no real opportunity to write them down. At other times, to be quite honest, I enjoyed the luxury of spending time with children with no obligation to be dutiful or disciplined. Still, I regret these losses.

But much is lost in any case. It's difficult, for instance, to avoid some losses in excision of distinctive details — not just descriptive ones, distinctive phrasings also — which is now and then required to disguise a child's actual identity. Changing names is bad enough. No substitution ever feels as right to you as does a child's real name once you know the child well. But losing bits of specificity in dialogue feels even worse. I worry often that the loss of even a few lines subtracts some of the power and uniqueness from a child's words; and, even though I try not to permit excisions to distort the meaning that I thought the child wanted to convey, I think we all know that there's no way to be sure.

Editing children's words, whether for space or for disguise, involves unsettling decisions and concerns about entitlement. Each of these decisions seems imperfect and I always ask the children to forgive me when they recognize one of the many errors I am sure I've made and which I always know I'll hear about from some of them before too long.

Several of the children who were closest to me at St. Ann's are not described within these pages, some because of privacy considerations, but most because of the constraints of space. One of these children, Lara, is Pineapple's older sister. A serious and introspective child, she is not portrayed here in much detail; nor is her older cousin, Jennifer, who is referred to only briefly but has been one of my best friends at the church. I was worried about overdoing the attention to one family at the cost of others, and Pineapple's first impression on me was so powerful that she ran off with several stretches of the narrative before I had a chance to discipline my thoughts in favor of a more egalitarian approach to conversation.

Other omissions trouble me as well. Miss Elsie, for example, fills a role no less important to the children and the priest than that of Nancy or Katrice. She suffers from diabetes, as I've noted, and had several episodes of illness in the years when I was visiting St. Ann's, but she was always there. Sheer doggedness, persistence, loyalty would bring her back day after day, month after month, when others who were less devoted would no doubt have taken medicine, or made a cup of soup, and climbed back into bed. I wish I had had time and space to speak of her, as well as other good friends at St. Ann's, at greater length.

I also wish I had a chance to speak of other churches in the Bronx and of the schools, or afterschools, affiliated with them. St. Augustine's School, affiliated with a church of the same name, is one where I've been welcomed several times. Sister Genevieve Brown, its former principal, took me beneath her tutelage some years ago and also guided me in readings that enabled me to better understand the mission and the motivation of the educators who devote their lives to children in the schools run by the Catholic Church. I'm grateful to Sister Genevieve for this and many other acts of kindness.

Another church I've visited repeatedly is St. Jerome's, on Alexander Avenue, which also operates a school and serves a mostly Mexican-American community. The priest of St. Jerome's, John Grange, who is a well-known and admired figure in the Bronx, has been a friend and counselor to me at times when I was most concerned about my father. He and I have disagreed on several matters that pertain to public policy, especially the relative degree of emphasis we place on private as opposed to public education (he is a voucher advocate and I am not). Our friendship, thankfully, has bridged these disagreements. I wish I had been able to write here at length about our conversations and our common interest in the work of Thomas Merton — and of conversations about Merton I was having at the same time with the nuns at Corpus Christi Monastery in Hunts Point, a very special place where silence is, in general, respected but occasionally broken for a visitor. I'm grateful for this also.

Selectivity imposed by narrative constraints disturbs me most of all in writing about teachers in the public schools, especially at P.S. 30. The teachers at this school whom I have known the best are those who happened to be teaching children I already knew. I wanted to follow Elio and Tabitha, for instance, through the normal hours of a day. That's how I met Miss Dukes; and I met other teachers mentioned here in the same way. There are countless other teachers at the school who have been gracious to me when I visited their classrooms, and I wish that I had had the opportunity to speak of them as well. All of these teachers, like their administrators, Mr. Zucker and Miss Rosa, have renewed my sense of what a humane place a public school can be; and I would like to thank them once again for giving me a chance to learn from them.

The people who have helped me most throughout these years are those I cannot thank by their real names. To Katrice, of course, my deepest thanks are due. I hope this narrative has made it clear why nothing I can say in gratitude will feel sufficient.

I'm indebted also to Otto's mother, who has been an understanding friend and also helped me greatly by her gift for simultaneous translation. For this, and for her hospitality in giving me a place to rest when I was running low on steam and needed a time-out from the attentiveness of children, I am grateful.

I'd also like to thank the mother of the boy I call Isaiah. She has had some difficult times during these years; many people in her situation would have yielded to despair. Even at the worst of times, she never did. I said once of Isaiah that he strikes me as a boy who never seems prepared to be defeated. His mother has tremendous courage too. We all fall down. We all rise up. She does it every day.

In efforts to expand my understanding of the pediatric challenges in the South Bronx, I was greatly helped by two well-known physicians, Irwin Redlener and John Rosen, and a young physician, Nelly Maseda, who grew up in the South Bronx and has returned to practice pediatrics there. Dr. Nelly, as the children call her, is a glowing spirit who brings more than medical savvy to her work. I have been strengthened by her friendship.

In the earliest stages of this book, I was given guidance by my oldest friend in the South Bronx, who is described in my previous book, Amazing Grace, under the pseudonym of Alice Washington. Our friendship began in 1986, when she was homeless in Manhattan. It ended eleven years later at her graveside. She used to ask me constantly about the children at St. Ann's, especially Pineapple. I know she got vitality and hope from hearing of their lives. I miss her deeply.

In the actual writing of this book, I have relied on the advice of several friends. I thank, especially, Peter Edelman, Marian Wright Edelman, Kathy Tindell, Walter Brueggemann, Charles Schultz, Paul Houston, Mike Meyer, and my patient editor, Doug Pepper. A very close friend in Texas, Robert Bonazzi, read this book in its earliest version and two subsequent revisions with his usual painstaking care. Few writers are as generous with their time as he. I look forward to the day when Robert's biography of our departed friend John Howard Griffin comes to publication.

My loyal friend and longtime colleague Tisha Graham came to her reading of this book from years of community activism and experience in education. As she has done with every book I've written in the twenty years since we first worked together, she has framed her most discerning criticisms in the gentlest of words. For this, and for the limitless unselfishness she's brought to every hour of our friendship, I am grateful.

My closest political colleague, Cassie Schwerner, helped me, time and again, by putting her good critical capacities to work on every word within this book. A tireless advocate for children who is now engaged in fighting for school equity through legal action in the courts of New York State, Cassie continues the tradition of a family that has given beyond measure to the cause of social justice in our nation. I've been fortunate to know her.

My greatest debt as a writer is to Marilyn Weller, my researcher and editorial assistant, who holds up the sky above my own particularly hectic and sometimes irrational existence. The sheer confusion of attempting to compile a book while continuing to enjoy the friendship of the children who are its central figures has at times compelled me to rely more on her gifts of flexibility and intuition than was fair. She has put in the long hours and attended to the detail-work with tenderness and patience. Without her, I could not have written this.

Again I thank the priest and children of St. Ann's for letting me come into their lives and pray that they will not find many big mistakes in what I've written here. If they do, I ask for a reprieve until I can correct these errors in a subsequent edition. I also thank my trusted friend and fellow-writer Anthony Bonilla, a former student at St. Ann's and P.S. 30, who will soon be on his way to college, and our mutual friends, Hortensia and Juan Bautista Castro, and their son John Jr. and his children, all of whom have been a part of the extended family I've relied upon repeatedly throughout these years.

Finally, I thank my mother and father, and the kindly people who take care of them. My mother helped to choose the title of this book. God willing, she'll be 96 years old when these words go to print. By then, it will be nearly spring and she'll be cheering for the Red Sox once again. I hope they will at last reward her with the victory she's been awaiting. It's been a long, long time; but she's still faithful.

Index

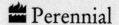 Perennial

Books by Jonathan Kozol:

ORDINARY RESURRECTIONS
Children in the Years of Hope
ISBN 0-06-095645-3

In a stirring departure from *Amazing Grace* and his preceding books, Jonathan Kozol offers his most personal and optimistic work to date. *Ordinary Resurrections* recounts the lessons he has learned—and that we all can learn— from the struggles and unlikely triumphs of children in one of America's most impoverished urban neighborhoods—New York's South Bronx.

AMAZING GRACE
The Lives of Children and the Conscience of a Nation
ISBN 0-06-097697-7

Tender, generous and often religiously devout, the children in this book speak with eloquence and honesty about the poverty and racial isolation that have wounded but not hardened them.

"Gripping, informative, deeply moral and profoundly disturbing."
—Boston Globe

SAVAGE INEQUALITIES
Children in America's Schools
ISBN 0-06-097499-0

A searing examination of the extremes of wealth and poverty, cities and suburbs and the question of equal opportunity in the American educational system.

"An impassioned book, laced with anger and indignation, about how our public education system scorns so many of our children."
—New York Times Book Review